DATE DUE

Demco No. 62-0549

**METROPOLITAN COLLEGE
OF NEW YORK LIBRARY**
75 Varick Street 12th Fl.
New York, NY 10013

The Gilded Age Construction of Modern American Homophobia

Also by Jay Hatheway

In Perfect Formation (1999)
Guilty as Charged: The True Story of a Gay Beret (2001)

THE GILDED AGE
CONSTRUCTION OF MODERN
AMERICAN HOMOPHOBIA

BY
JAY HATHEWAY

THE GILDED AGE CONSTRUCTION OF MODERN AMERICAN HOMOPHOBIA
© Jay Hatheway, 2003.

All rights reserved. No part of this book may be used or reproduced in any manner whatsoever without written permission except in the case of brief quotations embodied in critical articles or reviews.

First published 2003 by
PALGRAVE MACMILLAN™
175 Fifth Avenue, New York, N.Y. 10010 and
Houndmills, Basingstoke, Hampshire, England RG21 6XS.
Companies and representatives throughout the world.

PALGRAVE MACMILLAN is the global academic imprint of the Palgrave Macmillan division of St. Martin's Press, LLC and of Palgrave Macmillan Ltd. Macmillan® is a registered trademark in the United States, United Kingdom and other countries. Palgrave is a registered trademark in the European Union and other countries.

ISBN 0–312–23492–9 hardback

Library of Congress Cataloging-in-Publication Data

Hatheway, Jay.
    The Gilded Age construction of modern American homophobia / by Jay Hatheway. – 1st ed.
      p. cm.
    Includes bibliographical references and index.
    ISBN 0–312–23492–9
      1. Homophobia—United States—History—19th century.
  2. Sexology—United States—History—19th century.
  3. Homosexuality—United States—Public opinion. 4. United States—Public opinion. 5. United States—History—19th century.
6. United States—Social conditions—19th century. I. Title.

HQ76.45.U5H37 2003
306.76'6'0973—dc21   2003040575

A catalogue record for this book is available from the British Library.

Design by Newgen Imaging Systems (P) Ltd., Chennai, India.

First edition: June, 2003
10 9 8 7 6 5 4 3 2 1

Printed in the United States of America.

To all my students

Contents

Acknowledgments   ix

Introduction   1

1. The Origins of a National Ideology up to the Civil War   11
2. The Rise of an Urban Middle-Class in the Post–Civil War Era   33
3. Nineteenth-Century Gay America   49
4. A Period of Turmoil and Change   61
5. Nineteenth-Century American Medicine   71
6. The Debate Between Alienism and Neurology   83
7. The German Discovery of the Homosexual   101
8. American Physicians Discover the Homosexual   111
9. The Homosexual and the Physician in the 1890s   131
10. An Emerging Homosexual Identity During the Gilded Age   157
11. The Limits of Congenital Homosexuality   179
12. Conclusion   193

Notes   201
Bibliography   217
Index   225

Acknowledgments

This book has been a long time in the making, and I would like to express my thanks to St. Martin's Press/Palgrave for their steadfast support in this project. I would also like to extend a special thanks to Jim Ottney for his encouragement and editing skills, without which this book would not have been possible. Finally, I would like to thank Edgewood College, my academic home for the last dozen years.

Introduction

This is not a book about homosexuality or of homosexuals per se, nor was it written for academics who specialize in this field and whose insights are far greater than mine. My goal, instead, was to present an essay about the origins of American homophobia to the general public and students alike. Much of what follows is derived directly from questions posed to me by my students in American history, the most frequent of which has been, "But why do people hate gays and lesbians so much?" I thought I had some insight into this basic question because I had had firsthand experience. In 1975, I was a Special Forces First Lieutenant and was court-martialled for allegedly engaging in homosexual acts. The raw hate I received shook me to the core, and I sought to discover why my fellow soldiers reacted so negatively to behaviors only asserted, not even proved. The only answer I came up with was education. These men and women were literally trained throughout their lives to hate homosexuals for no other reason than that they were "faggots." That was, I thought, stupid and utterly irrational. What had any homosexual ever done to them that called forth such profound vituperation? As far as I could tell, nothing, but the fear and anger persisted despite their not even knowing a single gay or lesbian.

This had been my explanation when confronted by my students, yet it didn't seem sufficient because it was too ahistorical. Somewhere, somehow, people learned to dislike homosexuality. Homophobia, as the condition is now called, had historical roots. I realized that religion had always played a role, but my experience suggested that the homophobia I endured was much deeper than the Bible. It was an "*Ur*" emotion so profound as to almost defy explanation. I wanted to find out what was going on, so I used American history as my guide. I initially researched the Cold War period, but it soon became quite evident that I had to begin my search much earlier because so much of that literature drew upon an earlier era. I eventually worked my way back to the late nineteenth century when reports of the discovery of what we now understand as the modern homosexual made their way from Germany and

Austria to the United States. European doctors wrote of their findings in professional trade journals, and after a short while, the articles appeared in translation in the United States where they were read by American doctors. By the 1880s, same-sex attraction had been discovered in the United States, and articles about it popped up in domestic, scientific trade journals and magazines. There were only a few articles at first, but as the century came to a close, case studies were published across the country and by 1900, books and articles were commonplace. I am thankful to Jonathan Ned Katz for his exhaustive work documenting this early period, and for providing me with a fascinating insight into how the medical community perceived this relatively "new" phenomenon.[1]

My search had just begun, and now I had to make sense out of the period in order to make sense of the documents. As any student of American history will testify, we are a complex nation, and the Gilded Age was one of the more complex periods of our history's past. Yet, that is where modern American homophobia was born, thus that is where I had to focus my efforts. Was homophobia in any way related to modernization and the fear of change that this phenomenon often brings forth among those most influenced by it? What relationship, if any, did these factors have with the discovery that there were people who not only committed "vicious" acts, but were also conceptualized as having a different nature than the rest? Why was the medical community so deeply involved in their discovery and how did they relate to what Gilded Age Americans assumed about themselves and the world around them that appeared to be under attack and undermined by the discovery of the homosexual?

I do not specifically address the numerous theological arguments that condemn homosexuality. They have a long history that has been well documented and much discussed. My interest, instead, is in the new scientific theories that during the Gilded Age came to supplant the older theological positions, although Christianity still set the tone for all public and private assumptions regarding morality. Science, however, became the primary authority to which the modern American turned for insights about the natural world, a not surprising development for an industrializing nation. Within science, medicine was increasingly relied upon to supply answers to questions pertaining to the body and the mind. It became quite evident that physicians had taken ownership of what was then called contrary sexual instinct, and that they had done so according to their own admission to establish their public authority and secondarily to help those so afflicted cope in a hostile environment.

I was curious, however, to discover why, in spite of their assertions to the contrary, Gilded Age physicians caused more harm than good in their attempt to "help." In the main, it now seems quite clear that the Americans who took it upon themselves to research this condition were completely befuddled and hadn't a clue as to what made these people sexually and psychologically attracted to the same sex in the way that others were attracted to the opposite sex. Researchers speculated a lot about the etiology of what they believed was a new disease, even though they weren't sure about that either. Most of them took their cues from the Austrians and Germans, who were known to be the best-educated doctors in the world, and accepted same-sex attraction as but one characteristic of the abnormal condition of total sexual inversion.[2] That seemed logical enough because the sexual behavior of these people was obviously misdirected.[3]

This is not to say that the medical profession was "homophobic" because I don't believe it was, at least as we use the concept today to describe an irrational fear of same-sex relationships. Consider the issue from the standpoint of what was then popularly assumed about human behavior. From that perspective, the same-sex relationships crossed some well-established and sacrosanct boundaries that separated men from women, and these boundaries weren't just the product of Victorian America or the logic of capitalism. They were as old as Western civilization itself and had been ingrained as though such boundaries were inherent in what made men men and women women. Plato, Aristotle, God, St. Augustine, St. Thomas Aquinas, and just about every leading authority on human behavior since said so, including Charles Darwin himself. And it wasn't just about humans either. Each entity allegedly had essential characteristics that made it what it was, such that a square was a square by virtue of four equal sides, and a dog by virtue of its "doggieness," and so on ad infinitum. If you changed the essential characteristic of what made a dog a dog, then you didn't have a dog any more, and that was that. It was the same with people. If you changed the essential characteristics of a male then you didn't have a male any more; the same holds true for a female.

Although the definition of essential characteristics was unscientific, there was no doubt that such characteristics existed, and that was attributable less to Plato than to common sense empiricism. Everybody in their right mind knew that an essential characteristic of maleness was the sexual selection of a female and an essential characteristic of femaleness was the sexual selection of a male. Sexual dimorphism was so basic a characteristic of the species that to challenge it was absurd and ludicrous.

Sexual inverts had it wrong, and thus were not entitled to be considered either "real" men or "real" women. It was simple, really, and didn't require deep analytical thinking to understand. Yet, the question arose about how the dimorphic essence of maleness got into a female body and how the dimorphic essence of femaleness got into a male body. This question became central to all researchers in Europe and the United States because the question of essence, or more properly, essentialism, was fundamental to how most men and women in the West perceived the world even if they were scientifically unsophisticated.

Charles Darwin had clearly demonstrated in his 1859 study, *The Origin of Species*, that species were mutable. In the process, he had effectively helped sound the death knell of an essentialist point of view. Its replacement was population thinking in which the "type" was considered less important than the individual. Population thinking is based on the uniqueness of each individual within a particular species and not on some mean abstraction around which the individual may fall.[4] Indeed, variability was the core of natural selection and thus there was not one ideal "type" but rather a profusion of intraspecies variations that were inconsistent with Platonic forms and ideals, popular essentialism, evolutionary linear progress, and cosmic teleology.[5] Perhaps it should have come as no surprise that the homosexual was discovered after Darwin. It is also not surprising that homosexuality was rejected by those who were fearful of the consequences of the nonessentialist paradigm. If it were true, then what did that say about the universe, purpose, God, morality, and the alleged human immutabilities of race and gender? What did this mean for the future of the American society that presumed the validity of those characteristics? Furthermore, Darwinian natural selection suggested there was no grand design, no overall plan, no telos toward which individuals, humankind, or societies were directed. Evolution was random and included only short-term directional trends, no preplanned end goal.

Few Americans understood Darwin, and among those who did, the reception was mixed. Within the American natural science community—including medical doctors—the response varied on a continuum from full acceptance, to total rejection. If one rejected the new paradigm, then one could maintain the essentialist assertion and believe that designated intraspecies differentiations were freakish, while accepting the naturalness of other traditional differentiations, such as that associated with gender. On the other hand, one might try to combine the new paradigm with essentialism and argue that natural selection had conspired with a bad (read urban) environment to produce new types that were devolutionary in some peculiar way, like same-sex attraction. The new product had an essence to be sure, but of a sort opposite from the essentialist ideal, and thus one could juxtapose the two and try to determine what social or other ills were responsible for the degeneration. Creation by design was yet another attempt to mix the new paradigm with essentialism in that it allowed for the existence of a God as the Great Selector. Either way, humans were not completely naturalized and remained prisoners of transcendent idealism.[6] Darwin himself had muddied the waters with his theory of sexual selection in which he ascribed the existence of sexual dimorphism in humans to their different reproductive and biological functions that in turn established specific gender behaviors.[7]

American exceptionalism was another ideology with which the scientific-medical community was familiar and that influenced their understanding of the world around them. Exceptionalism was a peculiar, nationalist belief of the mostly urban, white middle-class Protestant, which initially held that the United States was exempt from the historic processes of national decline by virtue of its enlightened republican government, freedom of economic opportunity, and dependency upon divine grace. Unlike the rise and fall of European empires, the United States would rise above this cyclic tradition of growth and decay because of its unique ability to know the laws of the universe and consciously abide by them. In the aftermath of the chaos of the Civil War, rapid industrialization and urbanization created obvious social, political, economic, and cultural strains that reflected those of decadent old empire Europe. However, rather than being chucked, the exceptionalist ideology was revised to conform to the new conditions of the postwar environment by including a new emphasis upon science as the means to rationally know the cosmos and the place of humankind within it. The United States would thus continue along its path of open-ended growth by means of the liberal society guided by science. The intent was to harness the process of historical change and control it, thereby avoiding national decline, decay, and degeneration.[8]

Sexual inversion, and what we would later come to understand as homosexuality, could never be accepted within the ideological constructs of essentialism, American exceptionalism, and strict sexual dimorphism. These constructs put a premium on certainty, structure, and order— the well-known stabilizing characteristics of the Newtonian universe applied to society—without which it was believed all would be chaos and disharmony. Although Darwinism and quantum physics would eventually challenge this relatively static construct, during the Gilded

Age many people, especially the members of the middle class, assumed its legitimacy even in the face of the massive and disruptive changes brought about by war, Reconstruction, economic depression, and the processes of political, economic, and cultural nationalization. Indeed, it was precisely due to the rapidity of change that order and stability were so highly praised. Under these circumstances, it is hardly surprising that sexual inversion was rejected as normal because nothing in the development of American thought anticipated it. Here was a phenomenon that, as far as the medical community was concerned, had no predecessors and that, rather than go away, grew so rapidly as to become a national "problem." Such sentiments, of course, did not necessarily reflect how gays and lesbians saw themselves, even if they were at the margins of polite society. From Chicago to New York, gays and lesbians had been enjoying each other's company for years, if not decades, by the time they were "officially" discovered, and for the most part, they would continue to enjoy themselves regardless of what these outsiders had to say. Yet unlike Berlin, or to a lesser extent France, Italy, Holland, Belgium, Luxemburg, Bavaria, or Württenberg where homosexuality was still legal,[9] there is no record of any gay or lesbian emancipation movement in the United States until the 1920s. Except for the tiny slice of space allotted to them in the less than desirable locations of urban America in the late nineteenth century, American homosexuals were largely invisible to all but the emerging medical community that acted as the mediator between homosexuals and the American population at large. What Americans knew of homosexuals was gained from the then current medical discourse or from the popular presses, which sensationalized anecdotal homosexual behaviors and luridly drew attention to their alleged abnormalities that were themselves loosely derived from the scientific community but tailored to shock the reader.[10] After all, a good story sells, and a good story about freaks sells even better. But the fact remained that homosexuals were a threat because they represented a new perspective, one that seriously challenged the popular notions of normalcy, stability, order, and essence.

But the inverts never went away, and instead their numbers seemed to increase exponentially as researchers crawled through the backstreets and red-light districts of America's urban landscape looking for more subjects. Indeed, they were soon coming out of the dark and unabashedly presenting themselves to the public as well as to their personal physicians. It appeared to many concerned citizens and the medical community that the homosexuals were here to stay, but where did they come from and why were their numbers increasing so dramatically? No one knew, but there was a concern in the air that the rise in their numbers wasn't just some fluke or accidental by-product of modernization and urbanization. The fear was that sexual inverts were symptomatic of a trend toward moral and social decline, and that, in turn, was indicative that American exceptionalism and thus the United States was in deep trouble. What had gone wrong that inversion should exist? Was the United States so corrupted by modernization that the natural order was turned on its head, a sort of neurasthenia *in extremis*?

The conversation about homosexual sexual inversion was thus folded into a much larger national debate about the nature of change in the United States during the Gilded Age. It was a complicated debate and would pit modernists against traditionalists, science against religion, and at times, all four against each other. Fundamentally, the Gilded Age discussions about the homosexual, as opposed to homosexual acts, became metaphors for a host of concerns about order, harmony, stability, control, tradition, reason, change, gender, truth, God, morality, professional specialization, and authority. In sum, the medical discourse about homosexual inversion was about the ability of science to assert its authority, during a period of extreme social stress, to legitimately construct a national ideology of middle-class normalcy that fundamentally conformed to the traditional ideology of American liberal republicanism modified by the economic, political, and social realities of the Gilded Age.

For some individuals, mostly northern urban, white middle-class Protestant males, the future of the nation appeared to be at stake. Here was a golden opportunity for science to demonstrate its potential for respect in the national arena by offering up its expertise on homosexuality for review and acceptance. The medical community eagerly embraced the new challenge and threw its efforts into discovering what caused this terrible condition that afflicted so many, proffering therapies both personal and social. The disease of homosexuality thus became a bit player in the much larger drama of national regeneration and renewal. Yet ownership of homosexuality and of the theories that purported to explain it became hostage to the debates between neurologists and psychiatrists, or alienists as they were known then, as each vied with the public for recognition and status. Ultimate victory in this occupational power struggle would go to the specialty that could most adequately diagnose this disease and come up with a cure.

Neurology would eventually win, and the reasons are not too difficult to discern. Although alienism was older, predating the Civil War, its subject areas were the study and care of those who were insane or "alienated" from their true selves, as well as the running of mental institutions that warehoused them. Aside from the difficulty associated with a definition of insanity and the fact that patients tended to come from the so-called dangerous classes, alienism was looked upon as unscientific at worst, or at best, not as scientific as the relatively modern theories of neurology. Neurologists thus considered themselves modern in their scientific approach to the nervous system, and avoided asylum patients in favor of hospital or clinical environments where research in biology might be conducted. Unlike the alienists, the neurologists worked among, and for, the white middle-class. It was from this group that they drew their subjects and among whom they encountered their first inverts. Obviously they were not all madmen and madwomen, so something else had to account for the disease, and more often than not that something else was ultimately biological in nature and thus not subject to personal volition. In so far as this was true, sexual inversion was increasingly understood as a congenital condition of a malfunctioning nervous system and not the product of a psychologically warped mind. Yet the question remained as to what might lead to a malfunctioning nervous system. Could it be the environment or just a freak of nature? For many in the medical community, homosexuality was somehow deeply dependent upon the environment, and thus nerves rather than a person's mental capacity became the object of investigation.

For their part, many homosexuals assumed that they were freaks into whom nature had placed the wrong essence. Some disparaged their condition, and some embraced it wholeheartedly, reconciled to the fact that they were who they were in spite of the social and cultural opprobrium they felt from society at large. A few, however, embraced their homosexuality as but one of a myriad of natural manifestations of the "sex instinct" that served some as-of-yet undiscovered role in the Darwinian scheme of things. For these individuals, the natural order was a lot more complex than their opponents would concede. On a personal level, we know from diaries and medical confessions that many Gilded Age homosexuals considered themselves quite normal, and chaffed at the notion that they were somehow sick. To the doctors, these were especially baffling cases as such men—and not a few women as well—stood in direct contrast to the sensibilities of society at large, and didn't care. Society, they argued, was the problem, not same-sex attraction. This attitude worried the medical community and it gave them a great deal of anguish to know that some "perverts" relished their condition. Could this be another indication that modernization was beyond control and that the United States was not exempt from the forces of conflict and possible decline? Was it possible for an instinct as strong as the sexual instinct to be perverted from its natural end if the environment were not itself deeply out of harmony? Under these circumstances and during the period of this investigation, homophobia is perhaps a misnomer because the members of the medical community did not consider themselves irrational. Indeed, in their minds, homosexuals, congenital or otherwise, were the irrational ones who subverted the natural order. While it is true that some doctors accepted their inability to affect a cure and advised their patients to live with their disease, none of them seriously entertained the idea that homosexuality was truly natural or normal in the eternal scheme of things. If science could not prove the necessary relationship between form, function, and behavior, then all civilization was a fluke of time and space; but if this were true, then both divine and natural purpose were lies and the human species would be subject only to the wheel of fortune, a most un-American and anti-Christian notion. Clearly, such could not be the case if the United States was to survive, grow, and prosper. To think otherwise was itself a possible sign of madness or degeneracy. It was this legacy that informed much of the modern discussions about homosexuality well into the twentieth century, and it would not be until the end of the century that scholars and homosexuals themselves would seriously question the "naturalness" of gender specific behaviors, to include sex legitimated by historical, scientific, class, ethnic, or religious conventions backed by the coercive power of the state.

My interest in the Gilded Age and in the medical community of this age is by no means unique. Beginning with Jonathan Ned Katz in the 1970s, lesbian and gay historians have long recognized the importance of this period to the gay rights movement. John D'Emilio, Estelle Freedman, Bert Hanson, David Greenberg, George Chauncy, and most recently Jennifer Terry in her new book, *An American Obsession: Science, Medicine, and Homosexuality in Modern Society*, have written extensively about the discovery of the American homosexual, lesbian and gay, in the late ninteenth century.[11] This essay is intended to complement their work and to suggest additional ways to approach the issue of homophobia.

It would be easy to argue that same-sex attraction has not been well received in the West throughout the ages, but to argue that this is tantamount to homophobia is to miss a larger point. It is my contention that each historical epoch must be taken on its own terms, and if it is, then one will be in a better position to more adequately understand events and attitudes as they unfolded. There were, I believe, particular assumptions about human behavior, growth, and purpose that precluded our

American ancestors from accepting same-sex relationships on a par with heterosexual relationships, and among these assumptions were the not so insignificant beliefs in: (1) common-sense essentialism; (2) American exceptionalism; (3) rational/divine purpose; (4) the popular and scientific validity of the Newtonian cosmos; (5) the promise of Liberalism; and (6) good character consistent with essentialism. Each of these assumptions contributed to the development of a unique American ideology that came to define the middle class, and would separate the American experience relating to homosexuality from that of the English, French, or German. Perhaps the most distinguishing factor of the evolving American ideology was the emphasis it placed upon exceptionalism, character, and essentialism—three ingredients that if absent, would lead to the demise of the rest.

Late nineteenth century was certainly a time of profound change in America. It was the end of one epoch and the beginning of another, a transitional phase to a future that contemporaries hoped they could control by the use of science to assure an America that would know no bounds. The homosexual was caught up in this movement but had no real place to go, for here was a true anomaly that if legitimated spelled disaster for the exceptionalist pull as well as for the time-honored normative belief in common-sense essentialism that allowed, among other things, for a sexual differentiation between men and women. Therein was the most basic relationship of society. If civilization were to survive, this basic differentiation had to survive too. Yet, in spite of tremendous social pressures to conform to a heterosexual paradigm, the interaction between homosexuals and their doctors became a sort of tug-of-war with each side contributing to the outcome of how homosexuals would be conceptualized without giving up their demand to be accepted as normal and natural. For the medical community and society at large, much would have to give way before either was willing to accept a human nature so flexible as to include homosexuality. For homosexuals themselves, fear would have to give way to self-acceptance, and be followed by resistance to persecution and a long period of education—of the physician, the general public, and perhaps most important, of themselves. This is precisely what happened and in the process, the old paradigms found themselves in competition for public support with new ones that freed humans from the artificial constraints of human convention. Homosexuality would eventually be medically depathologized but not without its numerous critics who held on tenaciously to the pipe dreams of American exceptionalism and the rigidities of sexual essentialism.

Chapter 1
The Origins of a National Ideology up to the Civil War

The problem with homosexuality during the Gilded Age was that it was fundamentally un-American, and while this sentiment may be less strongly held at the beginning of the twenty-first century, such was not the case in the latter part of the nineteenth. Although it is true that a few individuals within the scientific community who studied the phenomenon considered it "natural" for those so "afflicted," the overwhelming majority of Americans found homosexuality thoroughly unnatural and completely abnormal, if not actually odious. Same-sex attraction, was, after all, inimical to the American national ideology, which had been evolving over the centuries since the days of the Puritans. Nowhere in that long history had anyone in his right mind ever suggested that it was good, natural, and normal for men to have sex with men or women with women. Indeed, such behavior was a profound taboo and had been condemned, as every God-fearing Christian understood, since the times of Sodom and Gomorrah, several thousand years before. On this the Bible was allegedly quite clear:

> Before they went to bed, all the townspeople of Sodom, both young and old, all the people to the last man closed in on the house. They called to Lot and said to him, "Where are the men who came to us that we may have intimacies with them." ... Then the angels said to Lot ... your sons and your daughters and all who belong to you in the city—take them away... We are about to destroy this place, for the outcry reaching the Lord against those in the city is so great that he has sent us to destroy it... The sun was just rising over the earth as Lot arrived in Zoar at the same time the Lord rained down sulfurous fire upon Sodom and Gomorrah... He overthrew those cities and the whole Plain, together with the inhabitants of the cities and the produce of the soil.[1]

On its face, the widespread popular rejection of same-sex sexual activity was a minor, albeit quite natural, aspect of seventeenth- and eighteenth-century life in America and Europe. Unlike Europe, however, some colonial British Americans of the early seventeenth century were self-consciously attempting to create a utopian society delivered from the alleged material and spiritual corruptions of the Old World. Indeed, it was the specifically Puritan experiment in justification that laid the foundation for the creation of a distinctive American ideology directed toward the free, white male in British North America. Predicated upon traditional Christian notions of mankind's fallen nature and his abject dependence on God, the evolving Puritan consensus envisioned colonial America as a place of new beginnings where the Saints, in spite of their wicked ways, might find redemption by means of their covenant with God in a modern Utopia freed from the depravity of the Old World. To be successful, however, both God and the Puritan had divinely inspired responsibilities and rules that guided behaviors, which while open to ambiguities and differing interpretations were predicated upon the fundamental assumption that humans were totally depraved creatures abjectly dependent upon God's grace for salvation. As the later Puritan minister Jonathan Edwards most eloquently stated in his now infamous 1734 sermon, "The Justice of God in the Damnation of Sinners,"[2]

> But sinful men are full of sin; principles and acts of sin; their guilt is like great mountains, heaped one upon another, till the pile is grown up to heaven. They are totally corrupt, in every part, in all their faculties; in all the principles of their nature, their understandings and wills; and in all their dispositions and affections. Their heads, their hearts, are totally deprived; all the members of their bodies are only instruments of sin, and all their senses, seeing, hearing, tasting, Etc., are only inlets and outlets of sin, channels of corruption. There is nothing but sin, no good at all.

And how was it that humans were so corrupt and wicked? They had disobeyed God's command not to eat of the Tree of Knowledge of good and evil. Punishment was swift, severe, and eternal:

> To the woman He said:
> I will intensify the pangs of your childbearing; in pain shall you bring forth children.
> Yet your urge shall be for your husband, and he shall be your master.
>
> To the man He said:
> Because you listened to your wife and ate from the tree of which I had forbidden you to eat,

> Cursed be the ground because of you!
> In toil shall you eat its yield all the days of your life.
> Thorns and thistles shall it bring forth to you, as you eat of the
> plants of the field.
> By the sweat of your face shall you get bread to eat, until you return
> to the ground from which you were taken;
> For you are dirt, and to dirt you shall return.[3]

And yet not all was lost because just as God in His infinite power could condemn mankind, He might also by His grace forgive and redeem:

> When men are fallen, and become sinful, God by his sovereignty has a right to determine about their redemption as he pleases. He has a right to determine whether he will redeem any or not. He might, if he had pleased, have left all to perish, or might have redeemed all. Or he may redeem some, and leave others; and if he doth so, he may take whom he pleases, and leave whom he pleases.[4]

Although the end of the seventeenth century saw a decline in the authority of the God-centered Puritans and the arrival of man-centered Enlightenment thought, the legacy of America as a special place exempt from the laws of history had already been established. As early as 1630, John Winthrop recognized that if the Saints were to keep up their side of the covenant, then God would provide and make New England a special place among God's creations:

> the Lord will be our God and ... will command a blessing upon us in all our ways, soe that wee shall see much more of his wisdom, power, goodness, and truth ...; wee shall finde that the God of Israel is among us, when ten of us shall be able to resist a thousand of our enemies, when hee shall make us a praise and glory, that men shall say of succeeding plantations: the lord make it like that of New England: for we must Consider that wee shall be as a Citty upon a Hill, the eyes of all people are uppon us; soe that if wee shall deale falsely with our God in this work ... wee shall open the mouths of enemies to speak evil of the ways of God and all professours for God's sake; wee shall shame the faces of many of Gods worthy servants, and cause their prayers to be turned into Curses upon us till wee be consumed out of the good land whether wee are going ... Beloved ... wee are Commanded this day to love the Lord our God, and to love one another to walk in his ways and to keepe his Commandments and his Ordinance, and his lawes, and the Articles of our Covenant with him that wee may live and be multiplied, and that the Lord our God may blesse us in the land whether we go to possess it; but if our heartes turne away ... we shall surely perish out of the good Land whither wee passe over this vast sea to possess it ..."[5]

Winthrop's profession of faith in God's providence to protect America from decay if the Articles of the Covenant are obeyed is in stark contrast with an older historical tradition with roots as far back as antiquity that expressly accepted a cyclic notion of the rise and fall of civilizations. As early as the second century BC, for example, the Greek Polybius wrote of the "law" of national growth and decline:

> Such is the cycle of political revolution, the course appointed by nature in which constitutions change, disappear, and finally return to the point from which they started. Anyone who clearly perceives this may indeed in speaking of the future of any state be wrong in his estimate of the time the process will take, but if his judgment is not tainted by animosity or jealousy, he will seldom be mistaken as to the stage of growth or decline it has reached and as to the form into which it will change. And especially in the case of the Roman state will this method enable us to arrive at a knowledge of its formation, growth, and greatest perfection, and likewise of the change for the worse which is sure to follow some day. For as I said, this state, more than any other, has been formed and has grown naturally, and will undergo a natural decline and change to its contrary.[6]

Throughout the course of Western history the legitimacy of this proposition was never seriously questioned. By the time of the Renaissance, historical growth and decline were simply assumed, for as Louis Le Roy wrote at the end of the sixteenth century when reviewing the histories of Rome, Greece, and Persia:

> For if the memory and knowledge of the past serve as instruction to the present and warning to the future, it is to be feared that since they have now arrived at such great excellence, the power, wisdom, disciplines, books, industry, works, and knowledge of the world may in the future decline as they have done in the past and be destroyed; that the order and perfection of today will be succeeded by confusion, refinement by crudity, learning by ignorance, elegance by barbarism... I foresee wars springing up in all parts, civil and foreign; factions and heresies arising which will profane all that they touch, human and divine; famine and pestilence menacing mortals; the order of nature, the regulation of the celestial movements, and the harmony of the elements breaking down with the advent of floods on the one hand, excessive heat on the other, and violent earthquakes. And I foresee the universe approaching its end through one of the other forms of dislocation, carrying with it the confusion of all things and reducing them to their former state of chaos.[7]

There were some exceptions to this rule. As J. G. A. Pocock has argued in his study, *The Machiavellian Moment*, the early sixteenth-century Florentine Republic was perhaps one such exception. The active participation of a virtuous citizenry in an era informed by Divine Grace allowed the Republic to step outside the traditional limits of history to transcend time and thus avoid change and decay.[8] In so far as this was possible, Florence could last forever as a demonstrable exception to the rule of decline and fall, but only as long as republican virtue, or moral goodness, guided the behavior of each citizen.[9] John Winthrop's New World would be another exception, but its success depended upon how well the Saints kept their side of the contract. As Samuel Willard stated in his 1688 essay, *A Compleat Body of Divinity*, Lecture IV, Question II,

> WHAT RULE hath God given to direct us how we may glorify and enjoy him?
> Answer.
> The WORD of God (which is contained in the Scriptures of the Old & New Testament) is the ONLY Rule to direct us, how we may glorify and enjoy him.[10]

By the late seventeenth century and well into the first decades of the eighteenth century, the New World was conceptualized by Christians as an exceptional place where redemption might still be realized. Although it is true that the colonies were quite fractious and independent minded, the people who lived in them, generally, differed little in their expectation that America was unique.[11] All that was required to remain so was for the colonists not to slip into depravity and wickedness, and that meant the imposition of rules to live by, either of divine or, as the eighteenth century progressed, of secular origin.

By the beginning of the eighteenth century, colonial America was teeming with numerous Protestant Christian denominations but it also began to feel the impact of the Enlightenment. Unlike the religious impetus, the Enlightenment put God aside and argued unapologetically that humankind had the mental and physiological capacity to completely know the world unaided by the Divine. God was irrelevant to this process because events took place due not to divine intervention, but to the regularity of natural laws knowable through reason. The world, as Newton had demonstrated, was a perfectly rational mechanical device in which all parts worked in a balanced, stable, harmonious whole. That man did not yet know the full extent of the laws that regulated the cosmos was not an argument that they did not exist; rather it was an argument to support the belief that humankind had not yet discovered them. That natural laws existed, that they were rational, and that they could be discovered by man was not in doubt. The consequences of their discovery were profound because once properly understood, the disharmonies and disorders of the universe would be overcome, and humankind could then progress along a trajectory of perfectibility. It was incumbent upon mankind, therefore, to find and study the laws of nature, and where practical, apply them methodologically for the betterment of society. According to Benjamin Franklin:

> The rapid Progress true Science now makes, occasions my regretting sometimes that I was born too soon. It is impossible to imagine the Height to which may be carried, in a thousand years, the Power of Man over Matter. We may perhaps learn to deprive large Masses of their Gravity and give them absolute Levity, for the sake of easy Transport. Agriculture may diminish its Labour and double its Produce; all Diseases may by sure means be prevented or cured...and our Lives lengthened...[12]

The Founding Fathers were so impressed by the "new" knowledge that they sought to apply it to human behavior, society, and government. If the natural world had laws to regulate it, as had been proven by Newton and his predecessors, then they must apply to humans as well, the latter being a part of this same world. It was thus incumbent upon educated men to know these laws so that mankind could live in accordance with nature. And what did that mean practically? Jefferson, among others of his generation, believed that the laws of nature gave humans certain inalienable rights—the rights to "life, liberty & the pursuit of happiness"—which could only be secured by the *res publica*, or by the consent of the governed. This was the legacy of Algernon Sidney and John Locke, the two English philosophers so popular among the educated elites of colonial America. The Constitution was revolutionary precisely because its republican principles acknowledged these rights. Far from being the inherently depraved dependent creatures of the Puritan imagination, humans were now reconceptualized as intrinsically rational and endowed with specific rights that when fully acknowledged and acted upon, moved mankind away from "tyranny" and toward increasing "liberty."

Indeed, as early as the 1720s, a number of British writers had taken to opposing the British Government on grounds that it was oppressive and hindered the growth and development of freedom. Known as radical Whigs, these men wanted limits to government power, and asserted that humans would never be free until their natural rights as humans were recognized. Inspired by the Enlightenment's emphasis on reason, and John Locke in particular, some of these writers, such as John Trenchard and Thomas Gordon, wrote numerous articles in support of natural rights and of the laws of nature that in turn influenced the

American Founding Fathers. Liberty, these writers argued, is a natural "God given" right specific to humans and no government had the authority to act as sovereign over the individual because,

> All men are born free; liberty is a gift which they receive from God himself; nor can they alienate the same by consent, though possibly they may forfeit it by crimes. No man has power over his own life, or to dispose of his own religion; and cannot consequently transfer the power of either to any body else. Much less can he give away the lives and liberties, religion or acquired property of his posterity, who will be born as free as he himself was born, and can never be bound by his wicked and ridiculous bargain.[13]

If Americans were to remain free and maintain their God-given liberty, they had to reject the corruptions of Old World Europe, and remain vigilant against those who, like the English Crown or Parliament, would enslave. For American patriots, this suggested overt resistance if liberty were threatened:

> But suppose my Lord, that this should be the bloody intent of the ministry, to make the Americans subject to their slavery, then let blood for blood, life for life, and death for death decide the contention. This bloody scene can never be executed but at the expense of the destruction of England, and you will find, my Lord, that the Americans will not submit to be slaves, they know the use of the gun, and the military aft, as well as any of his majesty's troops at St. James's...[14]

These radical Whig sentiments were given full expression in the American Declaration of Independence and the Constitution that followed in 1788. Central to this new nation would be the concept of liberty and what it meant to be "free." Freedom after all did not mean license, but rather the ability to live in conformity to Laws of Nature, which governed the material and immaterial cosmos. Freedom was, therefore, a fundamentally conservative principle that rested upon universally binding rules and regulations that when carefully followed, resulted in virtue. Franklin understood this, and in his *Autobiography*, he even outlined the thirteen virtues of temperance, silence, order, resolution, frugality, industry, sincerity, justice, moderation, cleanliness, tranquility, chastity, and humility that allowed for moral perfection consistent with his Presbyterian background and the Law of Nature.[15] If, however, humans acted without virtue and thus contrary to the Law, then there would be negative consequences:

> The Law of Nature (or, those Rules of Behavior, which the Nature God has given Men, the Relations they bear to one another, and the

Circumstances whey are placed in, render fit and necessary to the Welfare of Mankind) is the Law and the Will of the God of Nature, which all Men are obliged to obey. Almighty God, as Head of the System, and Supreme Governor of the Universe, will suitably animadvert upon every Violation.[16]

Thus to be virtuous implied conduct in accordance with these Laws of Nature, and that was only possible, or so the Founders believed, in a republic where mankind's natural rights had the best opportunity to be secured. But because Americans had not hitherto lived in a republic and were in general not virtuous, they put the entire enterprise of self-government in doubt. Federalist John Adams, for example, was explicitly pessimistic on this issue:

> Virtue and simplicity of manners are indispensably necessary in a republic among all orders and degrees of men. But there is so much rascality, so much venality and corruption, so much avarice and ambition, such a rage for profit and commerce among all ranks and degrees of men even in America, that I sometimes doubt there is a public virtue enough to support a republic.[17]

In spite of his doubts, Adams also argued that it was to mankind—albeit in the form of a politician—and not to God, that one must turn to correct the deficiencies in human behavior. "However, it is the part of a great politician to make the character of his people, to extinguish among them the follies and vices that he sees, and to create in them the virtues and the abilities which he sees wanting."[18]

Even Thomas Jefferson was skeptical of human nature, but his response to this concern was education, the purpose of which was, "To develop the reasoning faculties of our youth, enlarge their minds, cultivate their morals, and instill into them the precepts of virtue and order" in order that they form "habits of reflection and correct action, rendering them [selves] examples of virtue to others, and of happiness within themselves."[19] And this was possible Jefferson believed, because humans possessed an inherent understanding of right and wrong that when properly developed, guided one throughout life:

> Man was destined for society. His morality therefore was to be formed to this object. He was endowed with a sense of right & wrong merely relative to this. This sense is as much a part of his nature as the sense of hearing, seeing, feeling; it is the true foundation of morality... The moral sense, or conscience, is as much a part of man as his leg or arm. It is given to all human beings in a stronger or weaker degree, as force of members is given them in a greater or less degree. It may be strengthened by exercise as may any particular limb of the body.[20]

The defenders of the American Republic assumed virtue to be essential for its success in spite of the reality of an extremely quarrelsome citizenry. As John Adams made quite clear, corruption and venality appeared the rule rather than the exception throughout the colonies and the young nation. From Bacon's Rebellion in 1676, through the Marblehead, Massachusetts Massacre of 1677 to the innumerable acts of public violence, both slave and non-slave in the eighteenth century, through Shay's Rebellion that confronted Washington in 1787, public disorder, and overtly anti-republican activities blotted the American landscape.[21] It was precisely this type of behavior that so troubled the defenders of republicanism. Absent the ability to instill virtue by the massive imposition of force, the ultimate success of the Republic in the post-Enlightenment era of the early nineteenth century fell to education, as Jefferson had suggested. The goal, at least among the educated white male elite in the North, was the establishment of an aristocracy of virtue assisted by courses in moral philosophy. In a country that eschewed external restraints on behavior, these courses were designed to provide "internal qualities of the mind,"[22] which would imbue the individual with a moral sense that in turn would allow for virtuous behavior: "In America, it was often observed, where the coercive regulatory institutions of medieval Europe never took root, freedom rested 'upon a moral groundwork,' and morality became...the 'common law of the country.'"[23]

Colleges were enlisted to teach this subject formally, and in the early to mid-nineteenth century, moral philosophy became the bedrock of virtually all colleges in order to equip future political, social, and economic elites with insights into the "moral sciences" to help them as they went about the business of social engineering. There was little variation in the content, and textbooks covered such subjects as the nature of virtue and its application to the individual, to society, and to government. By stressing the virtuous life, educators not only hoped to facilitate the good life, but also the development of an American national ethic that would inform citizens as to how they should behave in both private and public life. Rules to live by rather than the policing ability of the state could therefore guide the model citizen throughout the course of a lifetime. These internal constraints were intended to provide proper criteria for action while simultaneously erecting "a barrier against the licentious and infidel speculations which are pouring upon us from Europe like a flood."[24]

Although these courses were decidedly nondenominational in content, they were broadly Christian in nature and drew their inspiration from the traditional Christian concern with virtue, as well as from a Scottish school of philosophy known as common-sense realism. Born in the eighteenth century during the Scottish Enlightenment, this school emphasized the ability of the mind to "know" the world as it actually appeared. This was so ubiquitous a belief that de Tocqueville referred to it in his 1835 journal, *Democracy in America*:

> Being accustomed to rely on the witness of their own eyes, they [the Americans] like to see the object before them very clearly. They therefore free it, as far as they can, from its wrappings and move anything in the way and anything that hides their view of it, so as to get the closest view they can in broad daylight. This turn of mind soon leads them to scorn forms, which they take as useless, hampering veils put between them and the truth.[25]

If the United States were to remain the one country where liberty might be truly achieved, Americans had to acknowledge a moral authority "that was at once religiously acceptable and rationally justifiable. The most suitable basis, which seemed to share alike the blessings of an ancient theological tradition and of the new philosophy [of the Enlightenment] was the moral law, a handy counterpart of natural law and an acceptable translation of the law of God."[26] No aspect of human activity was exempt, and reformers expected Americans to participate in the creation of a moral society across the board:

> These writers believed that fundamental moral truths, with both traditional and transcendental sanction, could be forever preserved and would remain everlastingly relevant to the human condition; and that these truths were especially needed in the restless, practical-minded America of the mid-nineteenth century. Not abstract principles only, but a moral spirit or sensibility—a quality of life and experience such as may be found in an agrarian community—was to remain a vital part of American life.[27]

Thus, similar to their Puritan and Enlightenment forefathers, post-Enlightenment intellectuals recognized that if America was to remain an exceptional place, rules were required, and it made no difference for the United States in terms of its special status among nations if those rules were derived from God or from nature. Liberty demanded that the individual have knowledge of what those laws required to ensure virtuous behavior, and although republicanism was received as revolutionary in Europe, the reality is that it rested upon the profoundly conservative principle of restraint. Human behaviors, similar to the behaviors of the different components of the cosmos, needed to conform to primary principles, because if they didn't, then collapse and destruction would result. Not surprisingly, antebellum educators and moralists asserted that sexual control was the critical foundation upon which all the other bourgeois virtues were built, and without which one would literally wither away and go insane, qualities obviously antithetical to a middle class. Sylvester Graham made this perfectly clear in an 1833 lecture to young men when he wrote,

> The mere fact that a man is married to one woman, and is perfectly continent with her, will by no means prevent the evils which flow from sexual excesses, if his commerce with her exceeds the bounds of that connubial chastity which is founded on the real wants of the [human] system. Beyond all question, an immeasurable amount of evil results to the human family, from sexual excess within the precincts of wedlock. Languor, lassitude, muscular relaxation, general debility and heaviness, depression of spirits, loss of appetite, indigestion, faintness and sinking at the pit of the stomach, increased susceptibilities of the skin and lungs to all the atmospheric changes, feebleness of circulation, chilliness, headache, melancholy, hypochondria, hysterics, feebleness of all the senses, impaired vision, loss of sight, weakness of the lungs, nervous cough, pulmonary consumption, disorders of the genital organs, weakness of the brain, loss of memory, epilepsy, insanity, apoplexy—and extreme feebleness and early death of offspring—are among the too common evils which are caused by sexual excesses between husband and wife.[28]

The consequences of marital sexual excess pale in comparison to the deadening effects of uncontrollable "self-pollution, or masturbation,"

> By far the worst form of venereal indulgence is self pollution...it impairs the intellectual and moral faculties, and debases the mind in the greatest degree...The heart, arteries and all the other blood-vessels, including the whole capillary system...become exceedingly debilitated and relaxed; the blood is not completely renovated...nutrition languishes, the fluids become crude and irritating...and emaciation—lassitude—general chilliness—coldness of the extremities and great debility ensue. In this state, the violent convulsive paroxysms attending the acme of venereal indulgence often cause spasms in the heart, arresting entirely its function, and sometimes producing aneurysms, or bursting its walls and suffering the blood to gush out into the pericardium, and causing sudden death, in the unclean act.[29]

The urge was considered so strong that young men practiced it not only upon threat of explosion, but also with other boys, because Graham tells us that "many of them went to the still more loathsome and criminal extent of an unnatural commerce with each other!"³⁰ The claim to have the ability to restrain one's sexual appetite thus became an increasingly important virtue for the middle-class apologists and was frequently invoked as a distinctive difference between the middle class and the lower, working classes.

Moral education was directed increasingly to those youth who were to be specially educated so that they could participate in the civil, social, and moral institutions of the Republic, and who by virtue of their future participation, required appropriate character as "there can be no other valid guarantee for the righteousness of law, and the sacredness of rights, than individual virtue and integrity."³¹ Lower-class working people were incapable of these values and indeed they were the ones who taught the unsuspecting young man the vile habit of self-pollution in the first place, since it was well known that "Servants and other laboring people of loose morals often become the secret preceptors of children in this dreadful vice."³²

So it was with people of color. The irony is that American exceptionalism was a conservative, exclusionary concept because African and Native Americans were not generally included within its perimeters, nor could they be. With respect to Black Americans, for example, no less a person then Jefferson acknowledged their innate inferiority, even if tentatively:

> To our reproach it must be said, that though for a century and a half we have had under our eyes the races of black and red men, they have never yet been viewed by us as subjects of natural history. I advance it, therefore, as a suspicion only, that the blacks, whether originally a distinct race, or made distinct by time and circumstances, are inferior to the whites in the endowments both of body and mind.³³

Furthermore, white women of northern European background, while nominally tolerated, were relegated to secondary status due to their alleged natural deficiency in the rational faculty. As Sara Evans makes clear in her study of women in America, *Born to Liberty*:

> The future of a government established on such principles [in the Declaration of Independence] clearly lay with the "virtue" of its citizens, which could only be expressed and renewed by constant participation in the life of the community. Yet the founding fathers shared a restricted vision of "the citizen." In their view, women, slaves, and the propertyless men, along with children and the mentally ill lacked the capacity for independent and rational judgment for the general good. The ringing declaration that "All men are created equal" used the word "men" quite literally.³⁴

White men, for the most part, were both the chief propagandists of the emerging national ideology as well as its chief beneficiaries. To be sure, women had important roles to play, but they were usually in support of the patriarchy, their demands for full inclusion, such as Seneca Falls in 1848 notwithstanding. But if it was true that the republican form of government rested on the virtuosity of its white citizens while simultaneously reinforcing that virtue, then on what basis might women and people of color be excluded, except on the belief that these people as a group, lacked those qualities necessary to be virtuous, and thus fully "human" as understood by the white Euro-American of his day.

This was not an oversight, however, and the exclusion of selected groups of people was based on another element of the emerging national ideology, and that was the commonly held belief in popular "essentialism." Most people of European ancestry during this time accepted the objects in the world as they appeared to them at face value. Philosophers and theologians might argue, but in general when early Americans saw a chair, they understood chair; and by analogy, a house, a cow, a dog, or a knife. Society functioned in part because there was common agreement about what objects were called and what they did or did not do. Few seriously challenged the common understanding of what objects were and what they were called. Every known thing had its own, unique and essential characteristics to which a name was attached and that could be verified by means of simple observation and then compared against other objects with different labels and dissimilar characteristics. This process was not especially novel. Indeed, an essentialist view of the universe and of the things in it is as old as the ancient Greeks. Plato was among the first in the Western philosophical tradition to fully expound upon the notion of the reality of transcendent Forms and Ideals whereby the material world is composed of objects that are copies of other worldly archetypical essences. Somewhat later, Aristotle inherited this conceptualization and argued that the essence of an object was what found "expression in the concept which the object embodies, the concept under which it must be identified if it is to be identified as what it is."[35] And what it is, it is by its very nature:

> Again, the male is by nature superior, and the female inferior; and the one rules, and the other is ruled; this principle, of necessity, extends to all mankind. Where then there is such a difference as that between soul and body, or between men and animals . . . the lower sort are by nature slaves, and it is better for them as for all inferiors that they should be under the rule of a master. For he who can be, and therefore is, another's, and he who participates in rational principle enough to apprehend, but not to

have such a principle, is a slave by nature. Whereas the lower animals cannot even apprehend a principle; they obey their instincts. And indeed the use made of slaves and of tame animals is not very different; for both with their bodies minister to the needs of life . . . And doubtless if men differed from one another in the mere forms of their bodies as much as the statues of the Gods do from men, all would acknowledge that the inferior class should be slaves of the superior. And if this is true of the body, how much more just that a similar distinction should exist in the soul? . . . It is clear, then, that some men are by nature free, and others slaves, and that for these latter slavery is both expedient and right.[36]

During the Middle Ages, Christian scholars such as St. Thomas Aquinas elaborated upon Aristotle and asserted a contrast between essence and existence such that any "substance" was an "essence" that had been given "existence" by God. Unlike the uncreated universe of the Greeks, that of the Christians was necessarily created by God. He had created "essences" and given them "life," so to speak. Here was a theological concept predicated upon a Platonic notion but reconfigured to account for Creation and the omnipotence of the Christian God.[37] Furthermore, all existence was fashioned into a hierarchy, or chain of being, with God at the apex followed by angels, humans, animals, and plants. Everything had a specific location based upon its essence that established an ordered and structured cosmos evolving toward perfection. Since humans were made in the image of God, their original essence was moral goodness, but because of the Fall, humankind was corrupted, although one could be redeemed if one voluntarily chose to live in accordance with the rules by which God ordered the cosmos. This was a real possibility, St. Thomas believed, because God had implanted reason into the soul that when applied correctly allowed humans to discover those rules and live accordingly. For those individuals who chose to apply the faculty of reason correctly, they would come to discover that each object in the sensible world had its own rightful properties contingent upon its God-given essence. For the cosmos to remain ordered, the properties of each object had to be rightful, or correct, for that object. Were this not the case, then disorder would result.

Rational inquiry demonstrated that humans were complicated because they had two natures, a physical and a spiritual, and each had rightful properties that were mutually dependent. If the cosmos were not to fall into disorder then humans had to be redeemed, and in order for this to occur, the properties of each nature (physical and spiritual) had to be correct for the essence of that particular nature. The rightful properties of the spiritual nature revolved around the ability of the soul to contemplate God, and when these properties were correctly expressed, the rightful properties of the physical nature would be too. On the other hand, if the properties of the physical nature were incorrectly expressed, then the spiritual nature suffered, and redemption was in doubt. To be successful, therefore, the properties of both natures had to be in accordance with their essence. But what were the properties of the physical nature of humans that expressed its essence rightfully? To understand this, it was necessary to know the essence of the human body. In so far as the body housed the spiritual nature or soul, its essence, at least before the Fall, was the repository of the image of God and moral perfection. As a practical matter, this meant that the body was sacred, and after the Fall, sacrilegious. To become sacred once again the body had to be cleansed of its moral imperfections, meaning it could only be used in a manner that was pleasing to God and thus be engaged in only those activities that assured moral perfection. Moral perfection was possible when the physical nature of mankind was expressed in accordance with God's commands as written in the Scripture, and among those was the command that man and woman be fruitful and multiply:

> And God said, Let the waters bring forth abundantly the moving creature that hath life, and fowl that may fly above the earth in the open firmament of heaven.
> And God created great whales, and every living creature that moveth, which the waters brought forth abundantly, after their kind, and every winged fowl after his kind; and God saw that it was good.
> And God blessed them saying, Be fruitful, and multiply, and fill the waters in the seas; and let fowl multiply in this earth.
> And the evening; and the morning were the fifth day.
> And God said, Let the earth bring forth the living creature after his kind, cattle, and creeping things, and beast of the earth after his kind; and it was so.
> And God made the beast of the earth after his kind, and cattle after their kind, and every thing that creepeth upon the earth after his kind; and God saw that it was good.
> And God said, let us make man in our image, after our likeness; and let them have dominion over the fish of the sea, and over the fowl of the air, and over the cattle, and over all the earth, and over every creeping thing that creepeth upon the earth.
> So God created man in his own image, in the image of God created he him; male and female created he them.
> And God blessed them, and God said unto them, Be fruitful, and multiply, and replenish the earth, and subdue it . . .[38]

The physical nature of mankind was resoundingly condemned, however, when the essence of male was confused with the essence of female, and incorrect properties became manifest:

> Professing themselves to be wise, they became fools.
> And changed the glory of the uncorruptible God into an image made like to corruptible man, and to birds, and fourfooted beasts, and creeping things.
> Wherefore God also gave them up to uncleanliness through the lusts of their own hearts, to dishonor their own bodies between themselves:
> Who changed the truth of God into a lie, and worshipped and served the creature more than the Creator, who is blessed forever, Amen.
> For this cause God gave them up unto vile affections; for even their women did change the natural use into that which is against nature.
> And likewise also the men, leaving the natural use of the women, burned in their lust one toward another; men with men working that which is unseemly, and receiving in themselves that recompense of their error which was met.[39]

Aquinian essentialism was particularly evident in his discussion about sex in which Aquinas elaborated upon the scriptural injunction against same-sex sexuality. His argument was straightforward, and assumed the reproductive organs of men and women were naturally complementary in accordance with God's command to be fruitful and multiply. Any other use of these organs was a form of lust, and contrary to the natural purposes for which sexual intercourse was intended:

> As stated above, where ever there occurs a special kind of deformity whereby the venereal act is rendered unbecoming, there is a determinate species of lust. This may occur in two ways: First, through being contrary to right reason, and this is common to all lustful vices; secondly, because in addition, it is contrary to the natural order of the venereal act as becoming of the human race; and this is called the unnatural vice. This may happen in several ways. First by procuring pollution, without any copulation ... Secondly, by copulation with a thing of undue species ... Thirdly, by copulation with an undue sex, male with male or female with female ... and this is called the vice of sodomy.[40]

Aquinas also argued that among the sins of lust, the worst sin was that which is "against nature" because it was a corruption of right reason, the rightful properties of human nature, and confuses the nature of the male with that of the female:

> In every genus, worst of all is the corruption of the principles on which the rest depend. Now the principles of reason are those things that are

according to nature, because reason presupposes things as determined by nature, before disposing of other things according as it is fitting. This may be observed both in speculative and in practical matters. Wherefore just as in speculative matters the most grievous and shameful error is that which is about things the knowledge of which is naturally bestowed on man, so in matters of action it is most grave and shameful to act against things as determined by nature. Therefore, since by the unnatural vices man transgresses that which had been determined by nature with regard to the use of venereal actions, it follows that in this matter this sin is gravest of all

. . .

Just as the ordering of right reason proceeds from man, so the order of nature is from God Himself: wherefore in sins contrary to nature, whereby the very order of nature is violated, an injury is done to God, the Author of nature. Hence Augustine says *(Conf. iii. 8): Those foul offenses that are against nature should be everywhere and at all times detested and punished, such as were those of the people of Sodom, which should all nations commit, they should all stand guilty of the same crime, by the law of God which hath not so made men that they should so abuse one another. For even that very intercourse which should be between God and us is violated, when that same nature, of which He is the Author, is polluted by the perversity of lust.*[41]

Aquinas' quintessential essentialist views influenced Christian, and therefore popular, essentialism profoundly. Things were not to be used contrary to the purposes for which they were made because that was against their natural end and violated the principles of reason. Not surprisingly, essentialism precluded any form of variability, and human behaviors not in conformity to the (insensible) essence were punished. The system was closed, complete, and logical from the perspective of an educated Renaissance European as well as an American colonial Christian.[42]

John Locke challenged this concept of essence, and argued that it had two forms. One he labeled nominal, which "is the idea of the property or properties the possession of which justifies the application of a given name,"[43] and the other he called real as understood by "those who look on all natural things to have a real but unknown constitution of the insensible parts, from which flow those sensible qualities which serve us to distinguish them one from another, according as we have occasion to rank them into sets under common denominators."[44] According to Locke, Aristotle was wrong to conflate the meaning (or properties) of an expression with the nature (or essence) of the object so named or expressed. A dog has meaning precisely because we ascribe certain properties to it, yet that label does not in and of itself tell us anything about the real nature of a dog. The same logic had been used by theologians with respect to discovering the real essence of man, although Locke rejected it outright and argued that the most one can know about an object is its nominal essence. Most Christians, on the other hand, rejected Locke's empiricism and deferred to the Holy Scripture to legitimate their beliefs.

Yet in colonial and post-revolutionary America (and even up to this day), popular essentialism accepted the theological as opposed to the empirical position, and ascribed a "real" essence, in the Aquinian or Lockean sense, to human beings if not all objects in the material world. Only with the advent of Darwin's theory of natural selection would the certitude of real essence be challenged in any serious way. But eighteenth- and early nineteenth-century Americans knew nothing of natural selection. The United States was then an agrarian society in which Christian values remained predominant, including a general belief that material objects had "real" essences. What could have come more naturally to the farmer than the knowledge that a pig was a pig precisely because it had the physical properties and the essence of a pig? The same held true for people; and among people, between male and female, black, white, or "red." These distinctions were not only traditional, they conformed to "modern" science. As recently as 1735, Karl von Linne (Linneaus) developed a rudimentary scientific system of binomial classification for fauna and flora based on the empirical observation of fixed physical characteristics that seemed to support this theological position. Each (sensible) object had specific properties derived from its unique character that in turn was a reflection of its true (insensible) essence: cow, pig, horse, penis, vagina, man, woman, goat, fly, rake, sty, corn, chicken, and so on. The (sensible) form and function of each object was absolute and could be shared by no other. The question of what constituted behavior in conformity with an entity's insensible essence was often problematic but as long as the white Euro-American male maintained political, economic, and social power, that was proof in and of itself to demonstrate that white males had a natural essence that placed them over women and people of color. Similar to the argument proffered by Aquinas, white males had the properties that were consistent with their true nature and a reflection of their superior essence. Under this circumstance, it would be absurd to include any whose rightful properties suggested the nature of an inferior essence, particularly as it pertained to rationality, freedom, and the capacity for self-government. The struggles over emancipation and women's liberation magnified these points and their successes actually helped to undermine the viability of essentialism itself, although that was ultimately reserved for the homosexual of the late twentieth century.

To be sure, when popular essentialism is mixed with belief in a hierarchy of status, race, sex, and gender, a highly stratified, conservative society results in which everyone had his or her place, and to be out of place was anathema. While it is true that early American society was generally less fixated with the concept of hierarchy than its European counterpart, it was nevertheless a society in which such stratification existed. Blacks, Native Americans, females, and males each had their ascribed social position based on what was then considered their essential characteristics. In truth, even as the Founders wrote of equality, their notion of it was essentially tribal and functionally pertained only to those who were of the right white-European stock. As for the others, oppression was their lot. According to de Tocqueville:

> Among these widely differing families of men [in America], the first which attracts attention, the superior in intelligence, in power, and in enjoyment, is the white or European, the MAN pre-eminent; and in subordinate grades, the negro and the Indian. These two unhappy races have nothing in common; neither birth, nor features, nor language, nor habits. Their only resemblance lies in their misfortunes; both suffer from tyranny; and if their wrongs are not the same, the originate at any rate with the same authors.
>
> If we reasoned from what passes in the world, we should almost say that the European is to the other races of mankind, what man is to the lower animals;—he makes them subservient to his use; and when he cannot subdue, he destroys them. Oppression has at one stroke deprived the descendants of the Africans of almost all the privileges of humanit... Oppression has been no less fatal to the Indian than to the negro race...[45]

Regarding white women, however, de Tocqueville congratulated the United States for adhering to the "natural" divisions of sex. He rejoiced that in America, unlike in Europe, women were finally free to engage in activities appropriate to their sex and not cross the gender barrier, to the detriment of both male and female:

> In Europe there are people who, confusing the divergent attributes of the sexes, claim to make of man and woman creatures who are, not only equal, but actually similar. They would attribute the same functions to both, impose the same duties, and grant the same rights... it is easy to see that the sort of equality forced on both sexes degrades both, and that so coarse a jumble of nature's works could produce nothing but feeble men and unseemly women.
>
> This is far from being the American view of the sort of democratic equality which can be brought about between man and woman. They think that nature, which created such great differences between the

physical and moral constitution of men and women, clearly intended to give their diverse faculties a diverse employment; and they consider that progress consists not in making dissimilar creatures do roughly the same things but in giving both a chance to do their job as well as possible... They have carefully separated the functions of man and of woman so that the great work of society may be better performed.[46]

Yet, never content to accept their outsider status, women and people of color fought back and demanded full political and social inclusion in spite of massive resistance by the white male elite. Essentialism and exceptionalism would nevertheless come together in early antebellum America to forge a very conservative national ideology that resisted inclusion. But as the nineteenth century developed, the conservative ethnically based republicanism of the founding generation gave way to a rising tide of popular democratic liberalism that was fueled by economic growth and the mass religiosity of the Second Great Awakening. This challenged the old gentry's alleged ideological monopoly, but did not destroy it. Exceptionalism and essentialism continued to inspire the popular imagination even as America clearly became a more diverse nation.

This great people with its virtuous national ethic and generally optimistic outlook on the human condition was also a nationalistic people who, at least during the age of President Jackson, were destined to extend the benefits of the emergent national ideology beyond America's established borders:[47]

> The far-reaching, the boundless future will be the era of American greatness. In its magnificent domain of space and time, the nation of many nations is destined to manifest to mankind the excellence of divine principles; to establish on earth the noblest temple ever dedicated to the worship of the Most High—the Sacred and the True.
>
> For this blessed mission to the nations of the world, which are shut out from the life-giving light of truth, has America been chosen; and her high example shall smite unto death the tyranny of kings, hierarchs, and oligarchs, and carry the glad tidings of peace and good will where myriads now endure an existence scarcely more enviable than that of beasts of the field.[48]

American democracy was thus the highest stage of history and in accordance with God's plan, destined to expand even if that meant running over Native Americans and "liberating" portions of the corrupt Catholic country of Mexico. By the 1840s, American expansion westward was looked upon by those sympathetic to the extension of republicanism as a vehicle through which the "swelling" masses would be able to maintain their freedom and autonomy and thus keep the Revolution alive. Texas, Oregon, and the northern parts of Spanish Mexico were targeted for annexation, in part because they were obviously West, in part because of ongoing Anglo-Saxon emigration there, and in part because of their perceived strategic importance, both domestically and internationally.

Domestically, a slave-free Oregon and California might not only provide vast amounts of natural resources and wealth to their emigrant populations and the nation as a whole, they might also reduce the protests of New England Protestant abolitionists, and thereby offset the claims of southern pro-slavery interests eyeing Texas. Internationally, the United States could strengthen itself against both Spain and England by increasing dramatically its total land mass and access to raw materials, and by asserting moral superiority due to the extension of the "blessings" of liberty and democracy to the newly annexed regions—the exclusion of Blacks and indigenous people notwithstanding. No less important for the South, the new areas, especially Texas, might increase the political power of the slave-owning states over those of the abolitionist North and their sympathizers and possibly tip the balance against northern commercial interests.

If expansion meant different things to those of the North or of the South, Republican, Democrat, or Whig, it was nevertheless legitimated by all sides as part of a divine plan for future American development, and was thus practically unassailable. Although the nature of that future would differ by region and party faction, the national ethic justified claims to manifest destiny, and played an important psychological and propagandistic role in rationalizing American expansion over native populations. Not everyone was comfortable with how claims of divine providence and white male supremacy were used to cover up sheer greed and overt racism, but for the most part, any qualms that existed were often folded into a sense of resignation to providential movement. It was unfortunate that some were left behind, but that, too, was part of God's plan.[49]

The Mexican American War of 1846–1848—which saw Mexico drop all its claims against Texas and cede more than 500,000 square miles of its territory in modern California, Utah, Nevada, parts of New Mexico, Arizona, and Wyoming to the United States—was the culmination of mid-nineteenth-century Manifest Destiny. The immediate problem was slavery, and the contradiction this posed to the belief in the continued extension of liberty and the development of a moral society was not lost on the abolitionists even as it was readily accepted by the slave holders. The Civil War, however, put a stop to slave holding and revitalized the American sense of mission, now under Northern Protestant tutelage and clearly more national in scope than had been the case during the antebellum period. With the War over, Northern elites and middle-class urbanites concerned themselves with ensuring that America remained exempt from the laws of historical growth and decline and thus liberated, as it were, from history itself:

> The Character of our nation is highly complex. It includes many elements, influences, and tendencies of different degrees of strength and importance... some of the influences are wholesome and vital, ... others are of the nature of a disease and depress the national strength, tending, so far as they are effective, to disorder and the decay of society... We have been confronted by problems and dangers which we had thought could never arise in the path of a nation with institutions like ours. Not only had we come to regard our system of government as superior to all others, but we trusted still more to that wonderful perfection and vitality of character which we believed we ourselves as a people to possess... We rejoiced in our exemption from the ills and dangers of European society.[50]

Chapter 2

The Rise of an Urban Middle-Class in the Post–Civil War Era

Historians generally refer to the period between 1870 and 1900[1] as the Gilded Age, named after an 1873 novel published by Mark Twain and Charles Dudley Warner in which the era is satirized for its economic excesses and political abuses.[2] In their not so subtle preface, the authors apologize for their inability to find appropriate examples to illuminate their book because,

> It will be seen that it deals with an entirely ideal state of society; and the chief embarrassment of the writers in this realm of the imagination has been the want of illustrative examples. In a State where there is no fever of speculation, no inflamed desire for sudden wealth, where the poor are all simple-minded and contented, and the rich are all honest and generous, where society is in a condition of primitive purity and politics is the occupation of only the capable and the patriotic, there are necessarily no materials for such a history as we have constructed out of an ideal commonwealth.[3]

A Nation in Transition

In reality, of course, the Gilded Age is associated with greed and political corruption, which, while true, is only part of the story. More importantly, this was when modern industrial America was born, and the process was messy, chaotic, and often overwhelming. Urbanization, industrialization, rapid population growth, and class formation came together during this period to create a country quite different from what it had been before the Civil War. In 1860, the United States had a total population of 31.5 million of whom 4.6 million lived in cities of 10,000 or more, while 3 million lived in 25 cities of over 50,000. Forty years later in 1900, the population was 76 million, 24 million of whom lived in cities of 10,000 or more, and 16. 8 million in 78 communities of over 50,000. In 1860, 25 percent of all Americans lived in urban centers of

Table 2.1 Urban growth in centers of 2,500 or more, 1860–1900[5]

	Urban	Rural	Total
1860	6,217,000 (25%)	25,227,000 (75%)	31,440,000
1870	9,902,000 (28%)	28,656,000 (72%)	38,558,000
1880	13,184,000 (26%)	36,970,000 (74%)	50,154,000
1890	20,693,000 (33%)	42,253,000 (67%)	62,946,000
1900	30,160,000 (40%)	45,835,000 (60%)	75,995,000

Table 2.2 Average age in 1900[7]

	White	Black
Female	48.7	33.5
Male	46.6	32.5

Table 2.3 Median age in 1900

	White	Black
Female	22.9	19.5
Male	23.8	19.5

2,500 or more, and by 1900 the percentage had increased to 40 percent, or approximately 30 million people (see table 2.1).[4]

But in addition to being more urban, the United States was also a youthful country. By 1900, 28 percent of Americans were between the ages of 15 and 29, while roughly 36 percent were between 1 and 14, thus 64 percent of the population was under 30 (see table 2.2).[6] Average life expectancy was 47.3 years, but when broken down by sex and race, an enormous disparity between black and white became evident.

The median age for all Americans in 1900, however, was 22.9 years, but unlike life expectancy, the differences between race and sex were less (see table 2.3).

Immigration contributed significantly to the ethnic diversity and population growth that were hallmarks of this era. Between 1870 and 1900, approximately 12 million immigrants arrived in the United States,[8] and after 1890, an increasing number of them came from Central and Eastern Europe replacing those who had come from the "traditional" locations of Scandinavia, England, English Canada, Ireland, and Germany.[9] In 1880, for example, the United States received 457,000 immigrants. Out of these, about 312,000 came from Northern Europe (to include

Germany), while 38,000 came from Eastern Europe; 6,000 from Asia (mostly China); 100,000 from Canada; 1400 from the West Indies; and 18 from Africa. In 1900, 448,000 immigrants entered, of whom 103,000 came from Northern Europe and Germany; 321,500 came from Eastern and Southern Europe; 18,000 from Asia; 5000 from Canada; 30 from Africa; and 400 from Australia.[10] The "new" immigrant of 1900 accounted for 66 percent of all immigrants, up from 35 percent in 1890, 8 percent in 1880, and just 2.5 percent in 1870.[11] These latest arrivals tended to be "darker" than the native born, and not Protestant, but rather Russian or Eastern Orthodox, or Jewish, and in the case of the Italians, Catholic. Needless to say, English was not their first tongue. Statistically, about two-thirds of the new arrivals were between 15 and 40 years of age and approximately 60 percent of them were males,[12] and on an average 75 percent were unskilled.[13] More than half of the immigrants settled in the urban communities of the Northeast and North Central states[14] to the consternation of native-born whites who viewed the new immigrants as a threat to their way of life.[15] By 1900, 60 percent of the population of the twelve largest urban centers, approximately 5.6 million,[16] were foreign born or of foreign parentage and lived in ethnic enclaves.[17]

In the Northeast, out of a total population of 21 million in 1900, 75.7 percent of the inhabitants, or 15.7 million, were native-born whites of Northern Europe extraction; 4.7 million (22.3 percent) were foreign born, and 385,000 (1.8 percent) were African American. In the North Central states, the total population was 26.3 million, with 4.1 million (15.5 percent) foreign born, and 550,000 (2 percent) African American. The South, with a population of 24.5 million, had only 563,000 (2.5 percent) foreign born, and 8 million (34 percent) African American. Out West, the total population was a mere 4.3 million, and 761,000 (16 percent) were foreign born while only 132,000 (3 percent) were African American.[18] Nationally, the total percentage of foreign born over time was surprisingly stable, as table 2.4 suggests.[19]

Table 2.4 Percentage of native-born white, foreign born, and African American in total population (by decade, 1870–1900)

Year	Total population	Native-born white	Foreign born	African American
1870	39,000,000	28,000,000 (72%)	5,567,000 (15%)	4,800,000 (13%)
1880	50,100,000	37,000,000 (74%)	6,679,000 (13%)	6,570,000 (13%)
1890	62,622,000	46,000,000 (73%)	9,249,000 (15%)	7,460,000 (12%)
1900	76,000,000	56,000,000 (74%)	10,341,000 (14%)	8,820,000 (12%)

Gilded Age America was, thus, a predominantly rural nation of northern European ethnics undergoing steady urbanization in response to industrialization. The new urban centers were home to a large, youthful immigrant population of unskilled male labor who came from regions outside the traditional Northern European homelands of the native-born white families. Economic opportunity was the magnet that motivated the new immigrant and accelerated the historical processes of urbanization that were visible even before the Civil War. The opportunities were real and highly visible across the entire production spectrum from railroads to machinery, lumber, paper, iron, steel, oil, coal, textiles, tobacco manufacturers, and even magazine production. Between 1871 and 1910, over 200,000 miles of track were laid and railroads crisscrossed the United States, with the heaviest concentration in the upper Midwest and in the Northeast, between New York and Chicago. In 1880, the United States produced about 2.5 tons of steel, but by 1890 it had overtaken England in the production of pig iron, and by 1900 produced four times as much as the United Kingdom. In 1914, the United States was the undisputed king and produced almost 35 million tons, an amount that only increased during the Great War. Similar growth was experienced in the national oil industry that was 90 percent owned by John D. Rockefeller in 1880. Between 1878 and 1900, the gross national product more than doubled, from 7.4 to 18.7 billion, an increase from $170 per capita to $246.[20] Furthermore, as industrialization required technological innovation, the number of patents issued nearly doubled from 13,518 in 1870 to 24,644 in 1900.[21]

This remarkable economic expansion was financed with capital from increased savings, an increase in domestic consumption due to the growth of disposable income by the middle class, and investment from Europe, most notably England. An adequate labor force composed of native and immigrant workers, access to cheap resources, and technological innovation combined with capital, pushed American industrialization forward in spite of a general period of deflation that lasted from the 1870s to the 1890s, intense labor unrest, and the two economic panics of 1873–1879, and 1893–1897.[22] Indeed, as early as 1880, the number of nonfarm workers was greater than farm workers and increased thereafter, as did the number of women in the workplace whose employment rose at a faster rate than men, from 1.9 in 1870 to 5.3 million in 1900, or by a factor of almost 2.8 (see table 2.5).

Unemployed or dispossessed manual farm-workers as well as nonmanual workers were drawn to the large urban centers because this is where the new jobs were, especially the white- and blue-collar jobs

Table 2.5 Gainful workers 1870–1900 (in millions)[23]

Year	Total workers	Farm	Nonfarm	M	F
1870	12.92	6.85	6.07	11	1.92
1880	17.39	8.58	8.80	14.7	2.64
1890	23.3	9.9	13.38	19.3	4.0
1900	29.0	10.9	18.16	23.75	5.3

that supported a budding industrial America. The economy had become more diverse and specialized, giving rise to a need for unskilled, semi-skilled, and skilled manufacturing jobs as well as a different sort of worker who managed, supervised, taught, sold, thought, traded, designed, or otherwise expended "brain" power to steer the industrial economy along its path. Teachers, office workers, architects, business managers, salespeople, bankers, investors, accountants, doctors, bookkeepers, and attorneys are representative of the specialized occupations that arose in great numbers during the Gilded Age in response to the new economy. Unlike the manufacturing sector where the jobs were learned on the shop floor and the positions filled by immigrants and the rural dispossessed, the new "white collar" employment often went to the sons and daughters of the burgeoning white, urban middle-class and required some formal education at either a college, secondary school, or a women's normal school in addition to on-the-job training. These new jobs were highly desirable because they conferred social privilege by virtue of their income potential and association with the traditional Protestant Anglo-Saxon gentry of the American Northeast, and were often favored by workers themselves over the blue collar, manual labor of the factory or workshop.[24]

Social distinction based on work and income was certainly not new. Contrary to the romantic myth that all work had equal value, manual labor had consistently been looked down upon by the nonmanual sector of the economy as early as prerevolutionary America when the merchant and professional elites ranked themselves socially above those who worked with their hands for a living or ran small businesses.[25] During the Jacksonian era of "mass democracy" in the 1830s, nonmanual workers reasserted their claim to social superiority because they did not have to rely upon the sweat of their brow for a living.[26] Republican ideology of the day eschewed all such "artificial" distinctions, however, and rejected the necessity and wisdom of class distinction. All work was good and honorable, and as de Tocqueville noted,

> American servants do not feel degraded because they work, for everyone around them is working. There is nothing humiliating about the idea of receiving a salary, for the President of the United States works for a salary. He is paid for giving orders as they are for obeying them. In the United States professions are more or less unpleasant, more or less lucrative, but they are never high or low. Every honest profession is honorable.[27]

Between the Jacksonian era and the Gilded Age, class distinctions intensified and were predicated more frequently upon race, income, consumption levels, and the manual/nonmanual, rural/urban dichotomies. By the 1880s an entirely new professional, managerial, and commercial white, urban middle-class had come of age complete with its own ideological assumptions that it inherited from the Northeast antebellum gentry. Although small in comparison to the population as a whole, the middle class gradually exerted a great deal of influence by virtue of its increasing importance as educated professionals in the expanding national economy. Values that had been primarily regional before the Civil War were nationalized and democratized by this growing class as it took modernization, urbanization, and industrialization into account. The emerging ideology was now modified by science and the addition of "good character" to produce a national ethic that consisted of the three interlocking principles of exceptionalism, scientific essentialism, and character. Each one supported the other and together they established the general value system of the white Anglo-Saxon Protestant urbanite who formed the backbone of the bourgeois elite.[28] Even though this system was adhered to by only a minority of workers, acceptance of it signified "middle class" and implied success.

The Biological Hierarchy

A significant distinction that separated this value system from that of the antebellum period was the development of "scientific" essentialism, the pseudoscience of social Darwinism as epitomized by the phrase "survival of the fittest," coined by Herbert Spencer. A misuse of Darwin's revolutionary scientific theories on the evolutionary principle of natural selection, social Darwinism, was a conservative, "evolutionary" concept that purported to explain the natural political, social, and economic inequalities among and between people. According to the logic of social Darwinism, those who are (the most) successful in society or in any particular field are so because they are the most naturally "fit" to be where they are. Conversely, individuals who are at the bottom of society are naturally "unfit" to be anywhere else. It makes no sense to intervene to help those at the bottom because no amount of help will allow the naturally unfit to survive or be successful in a competitive environment of the most fit. To help the unfit is to artificially assist them and that is unnatural in so far as the unfit will never, by virtue of their naturally unfit condition, amount to anything but being unfit, thus why waste the resources and risk the possibility that the unfit may one day artificially populate the world rather than go the way of the dinosaur?[29]

Social Darwinism was frequently invoked by white males to support their overtly racist and sexist attitudes toward women and people of color by keeping them in their "place," although it was also invoked to support a plethora of contested power relationships such as management over labor, the able-bodied over the disabled, or the mentally well over the mentally ill. In short, social Darwinism was used by those in positions of political, social, or economic power to deny that same power to those on the outside by virtue of their alleged, "inherently unfit" natures. African Americans, for example, had an essence that was real and very different from white Europeans, "The Negro is a different being from the white man, and therefore, of necessity, was designed by the Almighty Creator to live a different life."[30] Blacks were lazy, nonproductive, dangerous, immoral, and clearly subordinate:

> They are vicious as well as idle and non-productive, and every one of them a disturbing force—a dangerous element—which, in conjunction with those hideous wretches maddened with a monstrous theory like those miscreants at Harper's Ferry, are always liable to be made instruments of fearful mischief... he is a social monstrosity—and though his subordinate status nature renders him less likely to commit great crimes than the superior white man, the tendencies to petty immoralities are almost universal.[31]

"Scientific" biology was enlisted to confirm what was "known" through informal observation, and thus give essentialism the stamp of scientific legitimacy:

> The central fact deducible from the results of this investigation into the traits and tendencies of the colored population of this country, is plainly and emphatically the powerful influence of race in the struggle for life... the mixture of the African with the white race has been shown to have seriously affected the longevity of the former and left as a heritage to future generations the poison of scrofula, tuberculosis and most of all,

syphilis. This racial inferiority has in turn brought about a moral deterioration such as rarely met with in civilized countries...[32]

The Northern European white race, however, had an essence that was just the opposite. It alone had the capacity to form great states, political civilization, and express genius:

> If we regard... the history of the world from the point of view... of political institutions, we cannot fail to discern that all great states... have been founded and developed by the... Aryan race. Indian America has left no legacies to modern civilization; Africa has as yet made no contributions; and Asia... has done nothing except in imitation of Europe for political civilization. We must conclude that American Indians, Asiatics and Africans cannot properly form any active, directive part of the political population which shall be able to produce political ideals. They can only receive, learn, follow the Aryan example... Only the race-proud Teutons have preserved the Aryan genius for political civilization; and while guarding jealously their own type of that genius, they have supplemented it with those elements of permanent value that belong to the Greek and Roman types. I consider, therefore the prime mission of the ideal American Commonwealth to be the perfection of the Aryan genius for political civilization upon the basis of a predominantly Teutonic nationality.[33]

The differences between the two races were clear and open to public scrutiny; all one had to do was look. This logic was universalized, and was found in popular images of the world's indigenous peoples who were capable of manifesting only the putative "barbarian" virtues.[34] In the United States, Custer made this point explicit in his discourse on the character of the Native American:

> Nature intended him for a savage state; every instinct, every impulse of his soul inclines him to it. The white man might fall into a barbarous state and afterwards, subjected to the influence of civilization, be reclaimed and prosper. Not so the Indian. He cannot himself be civilized; he fades away and dies.[35]

Jews, Chinese, Latinos, immigrants, and criminals fared no better. "The Jew... has no character,... he is steeped in libertinism, in infidelity, in every kind of profligacy which tends to harden the heart and to deaden the feelings of humility—no less than to stifle the sentiments of true honor;"[36] "The Mongolians... differ from our own race by as strongly marked characteristics as do the Negroes... their moral standard is as low as their standard of comfort... [and] they practice all the unnamable vices of the East and are as cruel as they are cowardly;"[37] "The Indian and Spaniard were alike in natural indolence, love of luxury, fondness for amusement, and hatred of menial occupations . . . For continuous application of those faculties of body and mind which alone achieve permanent greatness, the Latin races were children beside the Anglo-Saxon . . .;"[38] "Only a short time ago, the immigrants from southern Italy, Hungary, Austria and Russia made up . . . one percent . . . today the proportion threatens to become fifty or sixty percent. The entrance into our country . . . of such vast masses of peasantry, degraded below our utmost conceptions is a matter which no intelligent patriot can look upon with out . . . alarm . . . They are beaten men from beaten races representing the worst failures in the struggle for existence."[39] Criminals "form a variety of the human family quite distinct from law-abiding men. A low type of physique indicating a deteriorated character gives a family likeness due to the fact that they form a community which retrogrades from generation to generation."[40]

Science was enlisted to support the innate differences between men and women as well. Unfortunately Darwin had contributed to this mindset because he, too, believed in innate, essential differences between the sexes predicated upon sexual selection.[41] Men and women really were different, and not just in the realm of reproduction. Mental distinctions, based on biological differences, were all too evident:

> With respect to differences of this nature between man and woman, it is probable that sexual selection has played a highly important part. I am aware that some writers doubt whether there is any such inherent difference; but this is at least probable from the analogy of the lower animals which present other secondary sexual characters . . . Woman seems to differ from man in mental disposition, chiefly in her greater tenderness and less selfishness . . . Man is the rival of other men; he delights in competition and this leads to ambition which passes too easily into selfishness . . . It is generally admitted that with woman the powers of intuition, of rapid perception, and perhaps of imitation are more strongly marked than in man, but some at least, of these faculties are characteristic of the lower races and therefore of a past and lower state of civilization . . . The chief distinction in the intellectual powers of the two sexes is shewn by man's attaining to a higher eminence, in whatever he takes up, than can woman—whether requiring deep thought, reason, or imagination or merely the use of the senses and hands.[42]

Darwin even extended his discussion on innate differences to race, and argued that such differences as do exist between higher and "lower" races are the product of sexual selection:

> ... it has however, been shewn that the races of man differ from each other and from their nearest allies, in certain characters which are of no service to them in their daily habits of life, and which it is extremely probable would have been modified through sexual selection. We have seen that with the lowest savages the people of each tribe admire their own characteristic qualities—the shape of the head and face, the squareness of the cheekbones, the prominence or depression of the nose, the colour of the skin, the length of the hair on the head... For my own part, I conclude that of all the causes which have led to the differences in external appearance between the races of man and to a certain extent between man and the lower animals, sexual selection has been the most efficient.[43]

In *The Mismeasure of Man*, Stephen Jay Gould argues that this type of scientific essentialism as it relates to the myth of inborn characteristics derived from the Platonic tradition is nothing more than the desire to assign worth to individuals or groups by means of biological determinism, which holds that "shared behavioral norms, and the social and economic differences between human groups—primarily races, classes, and sexes—arise from inherited, inborn distinctions and that society, in this sense, is an accurate reflection of biology."[44]

In other words, distinctions were construed as essential and biologically determined, and those scientists who researched these differences were themselves subject to cultural constraints that informed the subject of their research in the first place, and as such they "have no special claim upon scientific truth."[45] Thus, during the Gilded Age, scientists demonstrated their prejudices in two ways: first in the type of questions they asked, and second, by their methodology, which would only confirm their belief in scientific essentialism. Gould's discussion of the nineteenth century's scientific study of brain size and psychological testing on people of color and women to demonstrate their alleged inferiority to the white male confirm this point. According to Gunnar Myrdal in his book, *An American Dilemma* regarding biological and medical arguments about human nature:

> They have been associated in America, as in the rest of the world, with conservative and even reactionary ideologies. Under their long hegemony, there has been a tendency to assume biological causations with out question, and to accept social explanations only under the duress of a

siege of irresistible evidence. In political questions, this tendency favored a do-nothing policy.[46]

Inherent Virtues

Under these circumstances, it should come as no surprise that male and female gender roles were determined to be innately biological and not cultural in origin, thus to cross them or mix them up constituted an erroneous confusion of biological determinism and therefore popular scientific essentialism. Due to their biological makeup, women were passive, passionate, prone to nervous disorder, inclined to gossip, intuitive, very emotional, physically weak, and subject to hysteria under pressure. Their constitutions were such that they lacked the ability to participate in the professions, business, or politics. Since caretaking was an essential biological imperative of women, caretaking was woman's work and a female virtue. A woman's role in society was therefore determined by her unique nurturing essence, and that would allow her to be responsible for the moral development of those under her charge, as well as for the domestic happiness of her family in the "cult" of domesticity. She hired servants, obtained furnishings, established correct decor, chose the appropriate diet, watched the children, taught correct behaviors, civilized the husband, and maintained the family's public and private appearance. It was her duty to guide and mold the middle class itself.

Furthermore, women would use their assigned biological status as moral caretakers to become engaged in the various purity and moral reform campaigns of the period and in this manner impact all of society, not just the middle class. The Women's Christian Temperance Union directed by Frances Willard from 1879 to 1899 is a case in point.[47] Nevertheless, the common assertion that women were different from men in an essentially determinate way contributed to the creation of segregated "women's work." Women were to be kept apart from the world of men and were prevented from entering the "male" professions. This form of segregation would be challenged, of course, and set the intellectual stage for the women's rights movement at the end of the century associated with Elizabeth Cady Stanton, Susan B. Anthony, and others.[48]

But by the same logic of biology, men had an altogether different essence from women. It was more rational as well as more muscular, aggressive, predatory, competitive, power hungry, and physical. Although more strength was supposed to imply strong character, men also had a tendency to be coarse and engage in sexual promiscuity, drinking, and cursing. It was believed that women would modify this behavior, and to the extent that men took an active interest in domestic life, it did. Yet males had strong constitutions and a highly developed biological sense of competitiveness that suited them perfectly for the rough and tumble world of business, sports, or a taxing career in the professions.

Success, however, also depended upon the development of "good character," a concept that was the direct descendant of the moral education of the antebellum period but that was now reconsidered in light of one's true biological nature. First and foremost, a person had to live by a set of gender specific virtues that established the middle-class social identity. Variously enumerated as morality, prudence, integrity, reason, thrift, frugality, industry, propriety, justice, honesty, freedom, clarity, temperance, and restraint, these "old fashioned," masculine oriented Protestant virtues came to define the virile middle-class in the new industrial order. To be effective, the virtues were to be internalized when young,[49] and through self-discipline[50] acted out over a lifetime. What could be more appropriate in a competitive, capitalist economy where discipline was critical? In 1884, T. L. Haines published *Work and Wealth*,[51] one among many thousands of Gilded Age books dedicated to the development of good character as a means to personal success. In his opinion, nothing else was more important:

> Character is a fortune. It pays a better dividend than bank or railroad stock. The young man who goes forth into the world with an unimpeachable character, can never suffer permanent defeat. The blows which he receives from his competitors will bound back from his character, and all the injury they inflict will be upon those who give them. In every emergency, it is the man of character who is sought. Those lacking this beautiful jewel, may, for a time, crowd themselves forward and so enjoy prominence in business and social affairs; but when the crisis comes, when government is threatened, when society is menaced, when it is a special honor to be prominent, character is scrutinized and only he whose character is spotless is selected to lead.[52]

Women, too, had to be of good character consistent with their sex in order that her "great work" be accomplished:

> Character is worth of soul, wealth of heart, and diamond dust of mind. To acquire this is her first work, so as to be able to pass through life and do the great work of woman. There is much in starting right. A stumble in the start often defeats the race, while a good strike at the onset often wins the victory.[53]

Good character was never gender neutral and each sex was obliged to do that which was appropriate to itself. As Haines pointed out:

> The young man and the young woman constitute the characters in the drama of life. His realm is that of power, while hers is that of love; that is, his strength is power while hers is love. He is power and thought; she is love and thought. In strength of intellectual effort into which they have entered together, they have been a match for each other ... Though equal in this respect, they are different. Woman is quicker, more sagacious and intuitive; man is more plodding, analytical and argumentative. But in the realm of love, she wears the crown; he in the realm of power. The difference adapts each to the other, and when united, makes each stronger, more powerful and more useful.[54]

By the end of the nineteenth century, a small revolt began against what was perceived as the feminization of American civilization by virtue of the doctrine of separate spheres and the cult of domesticity. Led by internationalists such as Theodore Roosevelt, they actively sought out the essential "muscular" virtues of action, aggression, and struggle:

> In speaking to you ... wish to preach, not the doctrine of ignoble ease, but the doctrine of the strenuous life, the life of toil and effort, of labor and strife; to preach that highest form of success which comes, not to the man who desires mere easy peace, but to the man who does not shrink from danger, from hardship, or from bitter toil, and who out of these wins the splendid ultimate triumph.[55]

In *Barbarian Virtues*, Matthew Jacobson quotes Theodore Roosevelt's 1899 communication to psychologist G. Stanley Hall about the problem of demasculinization brought about by too much civilization, "Over-sentimentality, over-softness, in fact washiness and mushiness are the great dangers of this age and of this people. Unless we keep the barbarian virtues, gaining the civilized ones will be of little avail."[56] Roosevelt's concern related to the then ongoing debates about annexation and the hesitant steps the United States had taken to use Hawaii and the territories it had won from Spain in the Spanish American War to establish an overseas empire. The time had come to put aside the artificialities of culture and return to the more fundamental virtue of man that was in accord with his true nature.

Economics and Equality

In contrast to the period's fixation with essentialism, Americans also appeared to project an aura of equality that was so admired by both de Tocqueville in the 1830s and the noted English observer James Bryce in the 1880s:

> The United States are deemed all the world over to be preeminently the land of equality. This was the first feature which struck Europeans when they began, after the peace of 1815 had left them time to look beyond the Atlantic, to feel curious about the phenomenon of a new society. This was the great theme of De Tocqueville's description, and the starting point of his speculations.[57]

Bryce enthusiastically reported that Americans went out of their way to reject social distinctions between and among themselves based on any "recognized order,"

> There is no rank in America, that is to say, no recognized stamp, marking one man as entitled to any social privileges, or to deference and respect from others. No man is entitled to think himself better than his fellow, or to expect any exceptional consideration to be shown by them to him. There is no such thing as a recognized order of precedence, either on public occasions or at a private party...[58]

This was, after all, the lure of immigration that had seen millions of foreigners enter the United States, particularly after the Civil War. Nevertheless, such equality as existed was less the reality of all citizens than the propagandistic assertions of native-born white males threatened by the unprecedented concentration of wealth and power that came to symbolize the era. Such assertions reflected a romantic vision of America's promise in an age of intensified economic competition where not everyone was successful. We are all equal, the argument ran, but how is it that only a few have access to such enormous amounts of wealth and political clout? In a society where all people were truly equal, distinctions based on class, race, or gender would be nonexistent, yet that was a pipe dream, and for some, not even desirable. Andrew Carnegie expressed this position best in 1889 when he wrote:

> The price which society pays for the law of competition like the price it pays for cheap comforts and luxuries, is also great; but the advantages of this law are also greater still, for is to this law that we owe our wonderful material development, which brings improved conditions in its train. But, whether the law be benign or not, we must say of it, as we say of the change in the conditions of men to which we have referred: It is here; we cannot evade it; no substitutes for it have been found; and while the law may be sometimes hard for the individual, it is best for the race, because it insures the survival of the fittest in every department. We accept

and welcome, therefore, as conditions to which we must accommodate ourselves, great inequality of environment, the concentration of business, industrial and commercial, in the hands of a few, and the law of competition between these, as being not only beneficial, but essential for the future progress of the race.[59]

Economic power depended upon such distinctions, and anything less smacked of socialism. True equality was actually inconsistent with the American ethos of laissez faire economic competition, exceptionalism, essentialism, and social Darwinism, all of which rejected equality. Once again, Andrew Carnegie's words are apt:

> Objections to the foundations upon which society is based are not in order, because the condition of the race is better with these than it has been with any others which have been tried. Of the effect of any new substitutes proposed we cannot be sure. The socialist or anarchist who seeks to overturn present conditions is to be regarded as attacking the foundation upon which civilizations itself rests . . . To those who propose to substitute communism for this intense individualism the answer, therefore, is: The race has tried that. All progress from that barbarous day to the present time has resulted from its displacement. Not evil, but good, has come to the race from the accumulation of wealth by those who have the ability and energy that produce it . . . We might as well urge the destruction of the highest existing type of man because he failed to reach our ideal as to favor the destruction of Individualism, Private Property, the Law of Accumulation of Wealth, and the Law of Competition; for these are the highest results of human experience, the soil in which society so far has produced the best fruit. Unequally or unjustly, perhaps, as these laws sometimes operate, and imperfect as they appear to the Idealist, they are, nevertheless, like the highest type of man, the best and most valuable of all that humanity has yet accomplished.[60]

Yet the disparities of income and material well being could not be disregarded, and middle-class Americans argued that if the United States were not to sink into class warfare or degenerate into a bona fide oligarchy, society had to reform. Such, for example, was the message of the Populist Party when in the preamble of their 1892 platform it was stated, "The fruits of the toil of millions are boldly stolen to build up colossal fortunes for a few, unprecedented in the history of mankind; and the possessors of those, in turn, despise the Republic and endanger liberty. From the same prolific womb of governmental injustices we breed the two great classes—tramps and millionaires."[61]

Conservative social Darwinists were skeptical about social reform in so far as their essentialist assumptions prevented them from lending a helping hand to the "naturally" lazy, "degenerate," "inferior," or "unfit." Reformers such as John Dewey and George Herbert Mead, on the other hand, had no such misgivings because they accepted the Darwinian concept of evolution and were willing to acknowledge the persistence of change and the fluidity of social status within society. Social reformers, including women and people of color, would use this line of argumentation to effect change and in the process contribute to the decline of essentialist thinking.[62]

For the most part, however, middle- and upper-class white American men were united in their belief that the United States was a unique and exceptional place where the historical "law" of corruption and national decline could be suspended. The key was to clearly understand the causes of corruption, then devise and implement strategies that would insure continued growth and development rather than decay and degeneration. The consequence was an ideology of order, stability, and propriety that would mitigate an urban world that was complex, changing, highly competitive, very threatening, and always vulgar. The new white middle- and upper-classes appreciated ordered change because it allowed for what they believed was progress, improvement, and wealth accumulation without the unpredictability of industrialization. The ideology thus developed a structured system of beliefs and behavioral norms that if internalized and followed properly provided direction, order, and personal fulfillment. This would be a difficult but not impossible task requiring inspired leadership guided by science to assure national greatness for generations to come. This vision was optimistic and visionary, if not self-serving, since women, poor people, people of color, and the socially marginalized such as the homosexual and prostitute, were considered unfit for inclusion. Indeed, it was on the backs of these people that the late nineteenth-century national ideology of exceptionalism, essentialism, and good character was constructed.

Chapter 3

Nineteenth-Century Gay America

> When I peruse the conquer'd fame of heroes and the victories of
> mighty generals, I do not envy the generals,
> Nor the President in his Presidency, nor the rich in his great house,
> But when I hear of the brotherhood of lovers, how it was with them,
> How together through life, through dangers, odium, unchanging
> long and long,
> Through youth and through middle and old age, how unfaltering,
> how affectionate and faithful they were,
> Then I am pensive—I hastily walk away fill'd with the bitterest envy.[1]
> —Walt Whitman, 1860

Random Sightings

From the Pacific to the Atlantic and everywhere in between, America in the period before the Gilded Age was no stranger to same-sex sexuality. Although it was not until the end of the century that a homosexual identity was recognized, in large measure based upon German claims associated with Karl Heinrich Ulrichs and Richard von Krafft-Ebing, sexual activity between members of the same sex was frequently recorded. From the inception of the European colonial experience in the New World through the Revolutionary era and beyond until mid-nineteenth-century America, various forms of same-sex sexual contact between individual men and women were observed and commented upon even as they were condemned as sins against God and the "natural" order of the universe. Reports of same-sex sexual activity focused on what were construed as individual lapses of moral judgment "driven by the innate corruption of fallen humanity,"[2] and consisted of negative observations by explorers, settlers, clergy, or the courts, and were usually described as acts of "sodomy," "unnatural filthiness," or "buggery." In 1642, for example, Governor William Bradford wrote in his history, *Of Plymouth Plantation*, that "Marvelous it may be to see and consider how some kind of wickedness did grow and break forth here . . . Not only incontinency between persons unmarried, for which many both men and women have been punished sharply enough, but some married persons also. But that which is worse, even sodomy and buggery (things fearful to name), have broken forth in this land oftener than once."[3] Descriptions of this sort were fairly common throughout the seventeenth century as was the presence of draconian sodomy statutes that frequently stipulated the death penalty if same-sex sexual activity could be proven.[4] In so far as this attraction was perceived as a sin against God, no positive descriptions existed, and no records have been found in which individuals who expressed such feelings wrote favorably in support of their own behavior.

During the eighteenth century and well into the nineteenth, British colonial and later American thinking about same-sex sexual attraction mirrored that of the seventeenth century. Sexual contact between men, and less frequently between women, when reported, was quite hostile. In 1778–1779, for example, Thomas Jefferson wrote in section XIV of "A Bill for Proportioning Crimes and Punishments" that "Whosoever shall be guilty of rape, polygamy, or sodomy with man or woman, shall be punished; if a man, by castration, a woman, by boring through the cartilage of her nose a hole of one half inch in diameter at the least."[5] In a clarification note on the word sodomy, Jefferson goes on to state that "Buggery is twofold. 1. With mankind, 2. with beasts. Buggery is the Genus, of which Sodomy and Bestiality, are the species. 12. Co. 37. says, 'note that Sodomy is with mankind.' But Finch's L.B. 3.c. 24. 'Sodomiary [sic] is a carnal copulation against nature, to wit, of man or woman in the same sex, or of either of them with beasts.' "[6]

In a similar negative vein comes a report from the period of 1824–1826 in which same-sex activity between men and boys in prison was observed and condemned, not because of issues related to the abuse of power between an adult and a minor, but rather as an example of unnatural behavior,

> I have seen boys in Prison, of a very tender age, who had no natural deformity, who were among the most unnatural and deformed objects, which I ever saw. The peculiar skin, the strained and sunken eye, the distorted mouth and head, and the general expression of the countenance; as if God had impressed the mark of the beast upon them, for unnatural crime; were things, which I did not understand, till I learned, that the SIN OF SODOM IS THE VICE OF PRISONERS, AND BOYS ARE THE FAVORITE PROSTITUTES.[7]

Native Americans, too, found their place in the extant literature on same-sex activity, and not surprisingly, descriptions by Europeans were condemnatory. Most observers of this sort, be they soldiers or missionaries, Spanish, French, British, or American, ascribed the homoerotic behavior of the Native Americans to their alleged barbarism and savagery, bereft as they were of the guiding light of Christianity. During the long period of European exploration between the sixteenth and seventeenth centuries, anthropological studies of indigenous populations were relatively unsophisticated, and observers were quick to apply their own cultural biases to any behaviors they found objectionable. When discovered and observed, same-sex behaviors among the indigenous populations of Native America was resoundingly censured without ever inquiring into the possible social and cultural functions they may have played in any particular society. This was as true for the Spanish in the sixteenth century as it was for the Americans three centuries later. Thus we read the comments of the Spanish explorer Cabezza de Vaca upon his release from five years of captivity among native Floridians, sometime after 1533,

> During the time that I was thus among these people I saw a devilish thing, and it is that I saw one man married to another, and these are impotent, effeminate men and they go about dressed as women, and do women's tasks, and shoot with a bow, and carry great burdens, ... and they are huskier than the other men, and taller.[8]

Two hundred and fifty years later, the Jesuit priest Pedro Font could write while on an expedition with Juan Bautista de Anza to California in 1775–1776,

> Among the women I saw some men dressed like women, with whom they go about regularly, never joining the men. The commander called them amaricados, perhaps because the Yumas call effeminate men maricas. I asked who these men were, and they replied that they were not men like the rest, and for this reason they went around covered this way. From this I inferred they must be hermaphrodites, but from what I learned later I understood they were sodomites, dedicated to nefarious practices. From all the forgoing, I conclude that in this matter of incontinence there will be much to do when the Holy Faith and the Christian religion are established among them.[9]

During the first half of the nineteenth century, the pattern repeated itself. In 1820, for example, the American explorer Edwin James wrote of the Omaha in his book, *Account of an Expedition from Pittsburgh to the Rocky Mountains in the Years 1819 and 1820*, "Among their vices may be enumerated sodomy, onanism, & various other unclean and disgusting practices... but to the honor of humanity, it may be remarked that those abominable traits of character are not generally conspicuous among them."[10] In 1826, however, there is one report that appears to contradict the typically negative reaction to same-sex sexuality. In a letter between the later well-known southerners James H. Hammond and Thomas J. Withers, dated May 15, 1826, Withers writes, "I feel some inclination to learn whether you yet sleep in your Shirt-tail, and whether you yet have the extravagant delight of poking and punching a writhing Bedfellow with your long fleshen pole—the exquisite touches of which I have often had the honor of feeling?"[11] It is difficult to know precisely how this letter was intended to be interpreted, and for that reason it stands alone among pre–Gilded Age references to (presumably) same-sex attraction. The tone of the letter, however, is a departure from the traditional in so far as the author evinces a certain joy in what otherwise had been described as vile. Nevertheless, same-sex eroticism continued to be condemned, although among the Mormons its presence between males appears to have been tolerated even as it was criticized, at least up until the mid-twentieth century. The position of the Mormons in this respect, however, was unique in the nineteenth century,[12] and appears not to have been repeated elsewhere, although there are numerous references to sodomy in court records across the country suggesting the presence of same-sex behaviors was far from rare.[13]

For the most part, observations of same-sex attraction were limited to men but not exclusively so. Colonial records discovered by Jonathan Katz demonstrate that women, too, were known from an early date in American history to engage in same-sex sexual activities. In 1642, for example, Elizabeth Johnson, was sentenced by a court in Massachusetts Bay because of her "unseemly practices betwixt her and another maid."[14] Likewise Sara Norman and Mary Hammon were accused in 1649 of "lewd behavior each with [the] other upon a bed."[15] There is also limited evidence to suggest that Native American women "passed" as men within their respective societies, some of whom participated in same-sex sexual activities.[16] Instances of white women "passing" as men attempting to escape the restrictions of their sex by participating in the world of men were also known to exist. More frequently, however, women were acknowledged as participants in extremely close friendships that were often quite passionate. As Lillian Faderman has pointed out in her book, *Surpassing the Love of Women*, such romantic relationships were not considered necessarily improper if only because women were seen "as kindred spirits who inhabited a world of interests and sensibilities alien to men."[17] Nevertheless, when explicit sexuality became an issue, as was the situation with Jeanne Bonnet of San Francisco in the 1870s,[18] or in 1892 when Alice Mitchell murdered her female lover Freda Ward,[19] then much ink was spilled over the evil of lesbianism. Even discounting these highly publicized events, many male doctors during the last decades of the nineteenth century began to question the sexual proclivities of those female activists who participated in the women's movement, and ascribed their behavior to unnatural lesbian degeneracy.[20] Women were thus negatively labeled because they challenged male privilege and in so doing allegedly engaged in unnatural acts contrary to their female essence.

Literature and the Arts as Expressions of Same-Sex Attraction

Yet, in spite of the generally negative reception of same-sex attraction by the American public, around the middle of the nineteenth century one begins to find literary images that celebrated same-sex attraction in a myriad of situations even though the notion of a specific, homosexual identity in opposition to a heterosexual one remained unstated.[21] In this period of transition to the Gilded Age—by which time a homosexual identity had been objectified—numerous writers, such as Walt Whitman, Herman Melville, and Bayard Taylor, presented rather romantic images of same-sex attraction. In contrast to the observations of earlier recorders, these new images, whether they were drawn from empathy or fanciful flights of the imagination, presented a quite different understanding of the homoerotic. No longer a sinful expression or moral lapse, homoeroticism was the necessary consequence of honest reflection into one's deepest emotional longings for closeness and spiritual unity. These new images suggested that the evil associated with homoerotic desire was of less importance than the desire to forge pure, unadulterated relationships and overcome the sense of emotional and personal separation so pervasive in industrializing America. That some of these writers might also have been "homosexual" only enhanced their ability to create other than crude caricatures of their love for members of the same sex. In "A Squeeze of the Hand," chapter 94 of Melville's 1851 epic Moby Dick, this point is more than adequately expressed,

> Squeeze! squeeze! squeeze! all the morning long; I squeezed that sperm until I myself almost melted into it; I squeezed that sperm till a strange sort of insanity came over me; and I found myself unwittingly squeezing my co-laborers' hands in it, mistaking their hands for the gentle globules.

Such an abounding, affectionate, friendly, loving feeling did this avocation beget; that at last I was continually squeezing their hands, and looking up into their eyes sentimentally; as much as to say,—Oh! my dear fellow beings, why should we longer cherish any social acerbities, or know the slightest ill-humor or envy! Come; let us squeeze hands all round; nay, let us all squeeze ourselves into each other; let us squeeze ourselves universally into the very milk and sperm of kindness.[22]

So it was with Walt Whitman, and in the Calamus section of the *Leaves of Grass*, homoeroticism is often quite explicit, as the quote that opened this chapter makes clear. Read, too, in "City of Orgies" how Whitman rejoiced in the male cruising that enticed him in New York,

> City of orgies, walks and joys,
> City whom that I have lived and sung in your midst will one day
>   make you illustrious,
> Not the pageants of you, not your shifting tableaus, your spectacles,
>   repay me,
> Not the interminable rows of your houses, not the ships at the
>   wharves,
> Nor the processions in the streets, nor the bright windows with
>   goods in them,
> Nor to converse with learn'd persons, or bear my share in the soiree
>   or feast;
> Not those, but as I pass O Manhattan, your frequent and swift flash
>   of eyes offering me love,
> Offering response to my own—these repay me,
> Lovers, continual lovers, only repay me.[23]

One also reads of a deep yearning between two men for each other in Bayard Taylor's 1873 novel, *Joseph and His Friend: A Story of Pennsylvania*. Joseph, who is about to be married, is confronted with the longing of his unmarried companion Philip,

> ... I can be nearer than a brother. I know that I am in your heart as you are in mine. There is no faith between us that need be limited, there is no truth too secret to be veiled. A man's perfect friendship is rarer than a woman's love, and most hearts are content with one or the other; not so with yours and mine! I read it in your eyes, when you opened them on my knee: I see it in your face now. Don't speak: let us clasp hands.[24]

Literature of this sort was not always written by men. In 1887, for example, Mary Wilkins Freeman penned a short story for *Harper's Bazaar* entitled "Two Friends." This is a poignant story of an endearing relationship between two women, and while not erotic in the manner of

Melville or Whitman, the story manages to convey the deep love and enduring commitment of two women throughout their lives. At the end of the story, when one of the women, Abby, is literally about to die, her friend Sarah is prodded to confess that sometime earlier in their relationship, she, Sarah, had managed to drive Abby's one-time suitor, John Marshall, away. Piqued by Sarah's odd behavior, Abby inquires of her friend,

> "What have you been keepin', Sarah?"
> Then Abby listened. Sarah told. There had always been an arch curve to Abby's handsome mouth—a look of sweet amusement at life. It showed forth plainly toward the close of Sarah's tale. Then it deepened suddenly. The poor sick woman laughed out, with a charming, gleeful ring.
> A look of joyful wonder flashed over Sarah's despairing face. She stood staring.
> "Sarah," said Abby, "I wouldn't have had John Marshall if he'd come on his knees after me all the way from Mexico!"[25]

A Community Forms

During the Gilded Age, however, the homoeroticism of the romantic novelists was superceded by the growth of homoerotic communities, particularly within large cities such as New York. In opposition to the isolation of the novelist, the new communities were places where both men and women might develop an entire subculture that publicly catered to their needs and desires. An example of this was a New York hot spot named Paresis Hall where in the late 1800s, men who enjoyed other men sexually felt free to gather and indulge their desires in spite of the protestations of the police and clergy. According to Earl Lind, aka Jennie June, a late nineteenth-century homosexual cross-dresser,

> Paresis Hall bore almost the worst reputation of any resort of New York's Underworld. Preachers in New York pulpits of the decade would thunder Philippics against the "Hall," referring to it in bated breath as "Sodom!"
> But there existed little justification for the police's "jumping on" the "Hall" as a sop to puritan sentiment. Culturally and ethically, its distinctive clientele ranked high. Their only offense—but such a grave one as to cause sexually full-fledged Pharisees to lift up their own rotten hands in holy horror—was, as indicated, female impersonation during their evenings at the resort ... But the "Hall's" distinctive clientele were bitterly hated, and finally scattered by the police, merely because of their con-genital bisexuality [in modern terms "homosexuality"].

On one of my earliest visits to Paresis Hall—about January, 1895—I seated myself alone at one of the tables. I had only recently learned that it was the androgyne headquarters—or "fairie" as it was called at the time. Since Nature had consigned me to that class, I was anxious to meet as many examples as possible . . . In a few minutes, three short, smooth-faced young men approached and introduced themselves as Roland Reeves, Manon Lescaut, and Prince Pansy.[26]

Paresis Hall did not stand alone, and locations that catered to the homoerotic could be found across New York and the country. Indeed, portions of New York were so famous for saloons in which "fairies" congregated that they became popular destinations of middle-class gawkers who went out for a night of "slumming."[27] Although New York had perhaps the largest congregation of the homoerotically inclined, communities were found as far west as San Francisco, and in some cases, "on the road." In St. Louis, for example, a homosexual man who wrote under the name of Claude Hartland records successfully cruising some of that city's main streets in the late 1890s, "I met a young man one evening on the corner of Sixth and Olive streets, who was affected as I am and we knew each other at sight. I spent that night at his house and we had a most delightful time. He was gentle, refined and very interesting, and we soon became fast friends."[28] In *Studies in the Psychology of Sex*, the British sexologist Havelock Ellis concluded his 1917 American edition with an appendix entitled "Homosexuality Among Tramps" by the apparently pseudonymous "Josiah Flynt." In this essay, the author described an investigation he made of American tramps, the "out-of-works," in the last decade of the nineteenth century. Here, too, homoeroticism was present, if not pervasive. "Concerning sexual inversion among tramps, there is a great deal to be said . . . Every hobo in the United States knows what 'unnatural intercourse' means, talking about it freely, and, according to my finding, every tenth man practices it, and defends his conduct."[29]

Not all Gilded Age homosexuality was as overt as Paresis Hall, Claude Hartman, or Ellis's tramps. In *Oscar Wilde's America*,[30] author Mary Warner Blanchard notes that the presence of what we today might label "gay chic" enveloped portions of the United States soon after the arrival of Oscar Wilde in 1882. While not explicitly homosexual, the response to Wilde among the countercultural elite expressed a sensibility and an aesthetic that embraced a softer, more feminine code of behavior and dress while rejecting the traditional muscular and masculine ethic that pervaded American society at the time. To be sure, Wilde was lampooned in the mainstream press across the country for his lectures on the decorative arts as well as for his trademark silk stockings, patent leather shoes, wilting lily, and feminine pose.[31] Nevertheless, Wilde managed to ingratiate himself to many American artists, not the least of whom were Walt Whitman and America's first great public photographer of the male nude, the Bostonian F. Holland Day. Indeed, it was Day's infatuation with Wilde that would eventually lead to his ostracization by later photographers, yet during his prime in the 1890s, Day incorporated much of Wilde's androgynous male aesthetic into his photos of the male nude. In contrast to the rigid, stuffy and patriarchal images of the American male that were then so much in vogue, Day's photographs exhibit a curvaceous, tender male sensuality that invited the viewer to explore and imagine, invoking a sexuality never before seen in America or in American photography.[32] Such images were homoerotic, to say the least, and as such they remain the first such images in American history to express the homosexual aesthetic of their creator, F. Holland Day. It is of interest to note that Day, along with one of his best friends, Adam Cram, the author of *The Decadent: Being the Gospel of Inaction* (1895), were members of a Boston countercultural male occult society, the Visionists, suggested by some, perhaps erroneously, to be a haven for male "perversion."[33]

Confirmation of the existence of the homoerotic exists from outsider observers as well, although these descriptions more often than not were quite negative in tone. Nevertheless, even these highly critical descriptions point to thriving subcultures during the period of the Gilded Age. Most frequently, these descriptions were made by members of the scientific community looking in without any real understanding of the dynamics of these particular subcultures, a pattern similar to the European intrusions into the traditional Native American cultures. Thus, for example, we read the comments of a psychologist when he described a community of "inverts" in New York,

> Coffee-clatches, where the members dress themselves with aprons, etc., and knit, gossip and crochet; balls, where men adopt the ladies' evening dress, are well known in Europe. "The Fairies" of New York are said to be a similar secret organization. The avocations which inverts follow are frequently feminine in their nature. They are fond of the actor's life, and particularly that of the comedian requiring the dressing in female attire, and the singing in imitation of a female voice, in which they often excel.[34]

Or in Washington, DC where according to one physician we learn,

> Only of late the chief of police tells me that his men have made, under the very shadow of the White House, eighteen arrests in Lafayette Square

alone (a place, by the way, frequented by Guiteau [Charles Guiteau, assassin of James Garfield]) in which the culprits were taken *in flagrante delicto*, Both white and black were represented among these moral hermaphrodites, but the majority of them were negros.[35]

While the physician, Irving Rosse, makes no explicit reference to a community per se in Washington, it is quite evident that Lafayette Park was a well-known cruise location for those seeking a homosexual sexual outlet. Furthermore, that this location was integrated suggests the presence of a black community as well, a notion that is given further credence by C. H. Hughes, a St. Louis neurologist. In a postscript in the *Alienist and Neurologist* to his October 1893 article entitled "Erotopathia—Morbid Erotism," Hughes wrote,

> Apropos of my paper on "Erotopathia," I am credibly informed that there is, in the city of Washington, D.C., an annual convocation of negro men called the drag dance, which is an orgie [*sic*] of lascivious debauchery beyond pen power of description. I am likewise informed that a similar organization was lately suppressed by the police of New York City.
>
> In this sable performance of sexual perversion all of these men are lasciviously dressed in womanly attire, short sleeves, low-necked dresses and the usual ball-room decorations and ornaments for women, feathered and ribboned head-dresses, garters, frills, flowers, ruffles, etc., and deport themselves as women. Standing or seated on a pedestal, but accessible to all the rest, is the naked queen (a male), whose phallic member, decorated with a ribbon, is subject to the gaze and osculations in turn, of all the members of this lecherous gang of sexual perverts and phallic fornicators.
>
> Among those who annually assemble in this strange libidinous display are cooks, barbers, waiters and other employees of Washington families, some even higher in the social scale—some being employed as subordinates in the Government departments.[36]

One can discern from depictions such as these the existence of not only large communities of sexual "perverts," but something of their organization as well, particularly the rather sophisticated development of homosexual ritual, the drag ball, and all the unique behaviors that surround it, such as the type of attire and the public glorification of the penis. Furthermore, that such an extravagant event would take place required the existence of a large and established network of homosexual men who communicated with each other on a frequent basis, perhaps by word of mouth, or perhaps even by flyer or letter. It is no small matter to pull off any large party for a diverse crowd, but to do so for a drag ball complete with an exquisitely choreographed centerpiece suggests both a high level of communication and a community that has existed long enough for there to be a consensus about what everyone will enjoy. A naked man standing on a pedestal with a bow around his penis confirms not only a consensus of desire, but of humor and presentation as well. These are not sentiments that were made up overnight, but took time and the establishment of what we now label as an identity, in this instance the identity of a male who regales a festooned penis in spite of whatever social and official opprobrium such enjoyment might lead to. This further suggests that over and above what police presence there may or may not have been, there were a sufficient number of homosexually inclined men in whose presence one felt comfortable enough to attend a drag ball in the first place.

Thus in spite of the social marginalization homosexuals were subjected to by the pen of the physician or in the mind of the so-called better classes, homosexuals were pervasive, particularly within large metropolitan areas such as New York, Chicago, and St. Louis. For the most part, those so inclined lived out their lives as a subculture in the twilight zone of the inner city, generally hidden from full view and often, but not always, mingling with the newly emergent urban underclass. To be sure, the prevalence of same-sex attraction across the United States fueled the public's interest in the first place, although few investigators accepted the condition as normal even as the members of this enigmatic but apparently energetic subculture resisted outside efforts to stigmatize them. As the Gilded Age progressed, therefore, homosexuals were both silent and heard, private and public, unseen and seen.

The visibility of the American homosexual depended most obviously upon one's perspective. From the point of view of the inner-city homosexual, homosexuality was a common enough, if an incompletely understood, phenomenon. One had to be careful, it was true, but most major American cities had large concentrations of homosexuals with whom one might choose to associate—or not. For the medical community, homosexuality was a growing problem that defied rational explanation concentrated in, but not limited to, the metropolis. For the general nonhomosexual public, be it rural, suburban, or urban, homosexuality was not a generally well-known condition even if one knew of the existence of homosexual acts or of locations where those who committed such acts might congregate. On this, the police and city authorities concurred. Among those who felt themselves attracted to members of the same sex, the reactions were decidedly mixed. Some, such as the writers and partygoers discussed earlier, celebrated their love, be it on the pages of a manuscript or standing on top of a pedestal.

Others, however, were afraid of their feelings even as they acted upon them, and felt inclined to seek out professional assistance to help them overcome or, at the very least, control their urges. In either case, homosexuality was not tolerated by the general public, and indeed, its very presence was threatening to a society going through the throes of modernity and the social turmoil with which modernization was associated.

CHAPTER 4
A PERIOD OF TURMOIL AND CHANGE

> The central or fundamental philosophical truth which underlies the mental and moral culture which the age requires is the truth of the moral order of the universe. Human life belongs to an actual order, a cosmos, not a chaos; and this order is a moral order, and tends to and prefers truth, justice, and righteousness. The opposite error, which has misled a large portion of American society, is the opinion that the moral order to which man's life belongs is subjective only; that nothing belongs is true or right in itself, but only as it seems so to us; that there is no real standard of human conduct; only a conventional one; and that if men would generally agree to it the relations and nature of right and wrong might be reversed. This is what is really fatal in unbelief in our times, not the rejection of the creed of my church or yours, but the loss of the perception and assurance of the truth that the laws of nature and the inevitable working of the forces of the universe are hostile to falsehood and injustice.[1]

As Americans reviewed the years between 1865 and 1901, they could only shudder. If the Civil War had been fought to renew God's covenant and truly create a more perfect union, it had ended on a note of nihilistic martyrdom: the assassination of President Lincoln. Over the course of the next 36 years, the country would live through the additional turmoil of the impeachment of President Johnson; the assassination of James Garfield in 1881; and in 1901, the murder of President McKinley. Yet three assassinations and one impeachment were only the tip of an iceberg: violence persisted in the Indian Wars of the West, conflict in Hawaii, the Spanish American War, and the labor strikes of the 1870s, 1880s, and 1890s, while the economic dislocations of industrialization were exacerbated by the panics of 1873 and 1893. Slums, tenements, disease, vice, and a "dangerous class" of undesirables were endemic in the new city centers. The urban upper- and middle-classes looked on in horror as prostitution, alcoholism, drugs, gang violence, murder, urban riots, illiteracy, and poverty threatened the very fabric of society itself. Women, rural farmers, and African Americans rocked the status quo, while political and economic corruption at the highest levels made a mockery of progress and perfection.[2] Racists and nativists made no attempt to hide their disdain for ethnic minorities, and agitated for immigration reform, the exclusion of Asians, segregation of African Americans, and destruction of Native American culture. If these issues were not enough to confuse and bewilder, God appeared to come under attack after Darwin's publication of *Origins of Species* in 1859 and in 1873, the *Descent of Man*. For white Protestant America, both rural and urban, it seemed as though the country was falling apart and something had to be done.

Numerous remedies were offered and each one targeted specific problem areas. In 1872, for example, political reformers were able to shut down William M. "Boss" Tweed in New York. In 1873, Anthony Comstock of New York formed his Society for the Suppression of Vice and in that same year, Congress passed the infamous Comstock Law that outlawed the mailing of "obscene, lewd or lascivious" articles. The next year, 1874, Frances Willard founded the Woman's Christian Temperance Union to end the social evils associated with alcohol, and by 1877 the Social Purity Alliance had begun to take form, the goal of which was to outlaw prostitution and purify society in accordance with the moral perfectionism of a secularized Protestant Christianity. In 1879, Henry George severely criticized American poverty in his book, *Progress and Poverty*, and called for a single tax on the incremental value of land. In the 1880s, evangelists Dwight L. Moody and Ira B. Sankey conducted enormously popular revival meetings across the United States and on college campuses. Richard Ely attacked classical laissez faire economics in 1884, and in 1885 he founded the American Economic Association and urged governmental intervention in economic affairs. In the late 1870s and into the 1880s, Washington Gladden helped ignite the Social Gospel Movement, to which Walter Rauschenbush lent a helping hand several years later.[3] By the 1880s, settlement houses were established in the slums of American cities to provide community services, and in 1889, Jane Addams set up Hull House in Chicago, while in 1892 Robert Woods established South End House in Boston, and in 1983 Lillian Wald established Henry Street Settlement in New York. Between 1885 and 1895, American purity reformers finally succeeded in creating a mass social purification movement to morally reconstruct the United States, and in 1895, the American Purity Alliance was established from local and regional purity alliances to do just that. Finally, in the 1890s and lasting until World War I, the Progressive movement sought to effect major political and moral reforms across the nation and thereby reassert America's claim to moral superiority that it had abandoned only temporarily during this period of unbridled industrialization and economic integration.[4]

Science as the New Authority

Gilded Age modernization was obviously creating enormous problems that threatened the very fabric of American society as understood by those who adhered to the principles of a national ideology. In a nation as ethnically, socially, religiously, philosophically, and economically diverse as the United States, what possible source of authority could be invoked to support that ideology and still be considered valid across these national divisions? Increasingly, the educated elites turned to science as the key to locating universally binding principles to which a majority of people, in spite of their very real differences, might agree. That science could be invoked is not surprising given America's industrialization, which depended upon the fruits of scientific research and development. Who could argue with the presumption of the universality of scientific principles, which in the world of a commercial republic had immediate and real applications, from the invention of the steam engine to the use of electricity?

God was important, to be sure, but His presence was often overshadowed by the marvels of applied science. Furthermore, in the wake of Darwin, the origin of species by natural selection explained the evolution of humankind without reference to God, and indeed, His immediate presence was perhaps not needed at all according to this new paradigm. Some Protestant scientists such as Louis Agassiz rejected Darwinian evolution outright,[5] but after 1875, most people, including Protestants, sought some form of accommodation to the revolution in evolutionary thought. The core concepts of natural selection and the transmutability of species, however, were not well received because of the negative implications for essentialism, because deviations from type can "never touch the underlying essence," and had to be eliminated.[6] Traditional Protestant Christianity, popular essentialism, and social Darwinism were thus challenged by the implications of Darwinism, which were inimical to Americans who believed in an underlying order and structure of the material and immaterial worlds.[7] What was good about Darwinism, on the other hand, was that it placed man back into a created but natural world, the knowledge of which was open to rational scientific investigation. If the link between man and God had not been definitively broken, one was now free to pose fully naturalistic questions about society without intrinsic reference to sin or salvation. Science had come of age. It could be counted upon to give some insight into the natural origins of the human species and had the potential to provide the economy a competitive edge, thus contributing to a better quality of life for all Americans.

Late nineteenth-century America could not exist without science in spite of the challenges it posed to the traditional religious sources of order and authority. Science therefore had to discover the immutable laws of nature that could be substituted for the laws of God so that principles of the national ideology could be confirmed and firmly established outside the purview of the theologians. As sectarian Christianity was no longer sufficient to be that source, science would have to do— even if that meant limiting one's understanding to the "physical" knowledge of the material world. In an industrial America on the cusp of a consumer revolution, this was not such a difficult turn of mind. The United States was rapidly developing into a materialist society in which economic and political self-interest, not religion, predominated public and private discourse. Therefore, scientific knowledge of the physical laws of the material world was critical to success even if that success contributed to clear-cut distinctions, as well as contradictions, between the world of God and the world of man.

Nevertheless, Americans were not yet ready to drop essentialism from their imaginations. The Universe had a purpose, and the job of the scientist was to confirm what that was. The answer Americans received was evolutionary progress. Although Darwin had opened the door to natural selection, which when properly understood turned the notion of biological progress on its head, evolutionary social thinkers like Lewis Henry Morgan and Herbert Spencer replaced the ambiguities of natural selection with theories of the linear directionality of evolutionary cultural change and progress. The United States was a case in point. Had it not become more civilized, more moral, and thus more advanced over the course of its almost three-hundred-year presence in the New World? Of course it had, or so evolutionists like Morgan believed. Teleological perfectibility was not an artifact of the past relegated to archaic Christian theology. It had been updated, modernized, and reintegrated into nature producing the quite natural evolutionary process of linear cultural progression that moved from lower to higher and that mimicked the medieval chain of being even as it was reinserted into the natural world of humankind. Christianity did not disappear, to be sure—and many scientists remained Christian—but after Darwin, science began to repudiate any claims to know the world of God and was content instead to know the order and structure of the social and physical world.

It was within this context that American science became interested in the social behavior of humans in order to ascertain those laws that, if followed, would allow humans to construct a better society consistent with the principles of the national ideology. Rather than question the principles upon which the ideology rested, American scientists assumed their efficacy, and attempted to discover the social structures and laws that were conducive to the realization of these principles and the fulfillment of America's earthly mission, "Social Science is the Healer, the life-thrilled Messianic Healer of the human race. It is the herald on the misty mountain top, proclaiming, through all this burdened earth, that the KINGDOM OF MAN IS AT HAND."[8] The Kingdom of Man might be earthly, but it called for no less faith than Christianity. If science was to be successful as the ultimate knowledge broker and "healer," it had to establish its authority separate from, and perhaps over, the churches. To do this, it had to demonstrate that its knowledge was fundamental to human happiness, and nowhere could this be more apparent than its practical application to the economic and physical well-being of the American public, particularly when human lives might be saved or the pain of illness reduced. For the social sciences in particular, this suggested the ability to facilitate the civic harmony of America's pluralist society. Were this to occur, it would indicate that equilibrium between the individual, society, and the natural laws governing social behavior had been achieved to produce a smoothly functioning society that was naturally moral. Social harmony and morality were thus linked to the existence of naturally occurring laws and structures that governed social behavior, a belief system that continued to reflect the enduring pull of essentialism.

Although nineteenth-century scientists frequently approached morality from a Christian perspective, they asserted the ability of modern science, not speculative philosophy, to discover the conditions under which the presence of a natural morality was operative. The Greeks might have been correct in their assessment of the relationship between natural law and mankind, the pre-Christian version of the Kingdom of Man, but they certainly were not modern for all that. The educated Gilded Age middle- and upper-class gentry, on the other hand, could rest easy in their knowledge that science had proven what early philosophers could only speculate about, and to the extent that these Americans believed the pronouncements of the social scientists, evolutionary change and progress, not natural selection, were real. The key was to make sure that the appropriate rules that governed change were obeyed, and in the 1880s and 1890s, American social scientists went about the task of discovering them in order to "subject history to scientific control":[9]

> For American social scientists these new attitudes toward nature and history had a special meaning. Faced with mounting evidence of historical change and no longer able to call on providential power, they had to confront the possibility that changes could alter the exceptionalist course of American History. They began what would prove to be a long effort to accommodate to that possibility. They admitted the erosion of some of those peculiar characteristics what made American different from Europe and united American history more systematically to the universal course of natural law and Western historical development. But on a more fundamental level, they remained wedded to the exceptionalist vision... They redrew the lines of American uniqueness and turned natural law and historical principle into unchanging bases for the established course of history. So far as possible, change was contained and history rendered harmless. Indeed, the sense of crisis that pervaded the Gilded Age was itself the product of the exceptionalist historical consciousness not yet accommodated to the necessity of change. Fears of the decline of the Republic and apocalyptic images of impending doom and reborn millennial hope still shaped the historical imagination of these social scientists...[10]

The United States was, thus, both part of the historical processes of change and exempt from them. The job of the social scientist was to discover the laws that insured the "evolutionary" victory of a Liberal, Protestant, Republican, capitalist America and reverse the frightful slide into chaos. In this manner the United States would not only enjoy the fruits of modernization, but also maintain its promise of freedom, now and in the future.

The Authority of Science

Science did not work in a vacuum, and to be successful it required the assistance of the educated middle- and upper-class white professionals who together with industry could effect reform and preserve America's national ideology from the trash bin of history.[11] Linked by education, patronage, and birth, the new elites coalesced into a transnational aristocracy with the intent of making America a better place, "Already aware of themselves as a kind of republican natural aristocracy and as Whiggish moral stewards, they emerged in the Gilded Age as both the conscience of the capitalist class and the voice of 'right reason' to the nation at large."[12] And they could do this because they based their claims to authority on the universally binding principles of science, of which only they were the practitioners and thus all the more elite:

> The basis of their new authority was to be modern scientific knowledge. As clerical leadership became increasingly discredited, the cosmopolitan gentry were uniquely placed to offer themselves as a modern alternative. In contrast to the politicians, labor leaders, and the businessmen who raised divisive claims, the gentry could call on the authority of modern science to command agreement. Science allowed them to speak with the voice of universal rationality, which bestowed special authority on its elite class of practitioners.[13]

This was an aristocracy, moreover, that for the duration of the Gilded Age developed a course of action which masculinized the new construction of American exceptionalism and gave it a "muscular" face that appealed to the northeastern gentry's traditionally gendered sense of virtue and morality. The scientific enterprise was conducted in gendered terms and was appraised not according to the feminine ideal of romantic intuition as found in literature or antebellum transcendentalism for that matter, but rather by means of a male ideal of observable, empirical, and quantifiable hard fact as justified by common sense realism and scientific method. Yet before any of this could be realized, American education and science had to undergo the painful process of reform. Scientific education had to become more rigorous, and nonscientific education had to break away from its association with moral philosophy and religion. In short, American higher education had to be secularized and modernized so that it might serve the interests of the new educated elites rather than the vested interests of an older antebellum religious establishment whose attitudes and values were closer to Jonathan Winthrop and Thomas Jefferson than Charles Darwin and John D. Rockefeller.

To be sure, the Gilded Age experienced a tremendous amount of educational reform that specifically addressed these issues. Colleges were secularized and science curriculums were strengthened. The vision of the educated elites was of an American commercial republic that might not only be modern with respect to its industries and the scientific constructs that supported them, but also with respect to the social values that drove this new industrial order. Social scientists understood that if the exceptionalist paradigm that had guided America from its inception were to survive, it had to be reconfigured to conform to scientific principles unheard of just fifty years earlier. It was with this idea in mind that the American Social Science Association was organized in 1865, and in the 1870s, the modern field of sociology was organized under the guiding hands of Lester Ward and William Graham Sumner.[14] For America to remain that one special place in a modern and dynamic world where the rule of historical decline was broken, scientific insights into how the United States might overcome history were critical.

The social sciences were not the only sciences concerned about America's future and others were quick to follow, one of which was medicine that by virtue of its subject matter, attempted to investigate the physical ills of society and cure them. The Civil War had shown both the strengths and weaknesses of medicine, but now medicine had to reform itself if it, too, wanted to be more effective and contribute further to the overall health of the American people. Sick citizens were incapable of sharing in America's manifest destiny, so it was natural that the American medical community be included in the exceptionalist quest for perfectibility. The future strength of the United States depended not only upon its industrial might, moral fiber, and social behavior in conformity with the natural laws, it also depended on its physical health as determined by the best research in the world. A sick population was a weak population that put the future in jeopardy. No state could achieve economic, social, cultural, or political greatness if its citizens were diseased or dependent for wellness upon herbs and laudanum. Just what constituted disease, and how one went about effecting a cure would engage American medicine throughout the Gilded Age, no less than the discovery of the laws that governed humans in society.

The Gilded Age was a complex period during which modern America was born. The new industrial order, led by northern capitalists, was to transform the United States and in the process, give rise to a crisis of authority that was gradually resolved by science instead of religion. While Americans as a whole never became atheistic, they accepted this new authority because it was rational, allegedly universal, practical, and it worked, as a consequence of which the United States became more powerful and potentially the greatest industrial nation in the history of the world. It was precisely because of America's practical application of science that Americans now considered themselves the rival to Great Britain and, more importantly, the last repository of freedom in the world. But nineteenth-century Americans did not automatically accept the authority of science. It had to prove itself, and one field that self-consciously attempted to do that was medicine—which, while it had made some strides during the Civil War, was still considered by most Americans as nothing but amateur sectarian quackery. If medicine was to be accepted by all Americans, and especially the middle- and upper-class public as a valid profession that could contribute to America's destiny in a positive way, then it had to appeal to and be accepted by those who composed the new aristocracy of upper and middle educated professionals. In order for this to occur, medicine had to undergo a remarkable transformation from a hodgepodge of self-serving sects into a respected institution worthy of the public trust and private investment.

Chapter 5

Nineteenth-Century American Medicine

The Victorians were burdened, as no other generation before them, with the weight of their own image. Self-conscious, class-conscious, race-conscious, and nation-conscious, they struggled to gain the highest planes of achievement. Aware of their responsibilities not only to past generations, but to future ones as well, they dutifully bore the obligations with which they were blessed. Children of the industrial age, and descendants of the Enlightenment, they could admit no pessimism, no nihilism, no medieval gloom to impede their steady march onward. White, Anglo-Saxon, and Christian, they saw their destiny ordained by their inheritance; they were the leaders to be followed, the examples of civilization's highest hopes, to be envied, admired, and imitated. This self-image could admit no fault, for their highest duty lay not in themselves, but to future generations. For the Victorian men and women who bore the brunt of this effort, nothing that benefited class, nation, or race was too daring or too difficult.[1]

American medicine experienced a great amount of change during the Gilded Age and although still very much in a state of flux by 1900, it was beginning to take on the appearance of a modern science whose practitioners were clearly members of the middle and upper classes. This development was relatively slow in coming, and did not happen without a great deal of effort by doctors who were determined to raise the low status ascribed to medicine by professionalizing it. Indeed, as late as 1891, American theological schools had a total endowment of $18,000,000 while the medical schools were at a paltry $500,000![2]

The field of medicine was anything but sophisticated during this period as Americans were more interested in industrialization and making money. Shortcomings included rivalries between regular physicians, herbal homeopaths, and "healing" botanists, or "eclectics"; poor educational resources and instruction; a generally low level of medical knowledge and skill; a second rate rural health-care system; and an elite, urban medical community of dubious medical training with wealthy middle- and upper-class clients.[3] These shortcomings were exacerbated by the rampant commercialism of many of the medical schools. Between 1860 and 1900, regular medical schools grew at an astonishing rate from 53 to 126,[4] the bulk of which were proprietary. Unaffiliated with any college or university, these proprietary institutions were essentially degree mills whose sole purpose was to make money for the owners by appealing to those who had little money and who wanted a quick medical education, although few actually graduated. Education was necessarily a secondary concern that unfortunately contributed to the disrepute in which many Americans, especially rural Americans, held doctors. On the other hand, the larger and wealthier medical schools attempted to separate themselves from the minor schools and pushed for more rigorous standards such as the three-year graded curriculum that was initiated at Harvard in 1871 and by 1889, had reached 33 or one-third of all medical schools.[5]

By the late nineteenth century, educational reform was initiated by all the leading medical colleges to improve the level of medicine taught and to pressure the smaller, ill-equipped proprietary colleges to shut down. The assistance of the American Medical Association (AMA) was enlisted, and those colleges that did not conform to new educational standards risked expulsion from the Association. The AMA had no sanctions over the expelled institutions however, and thus expulsion had little practical effect except with respect to prestige and fundraising potential. One of the most significant reforms was in the area of education, and since some of the best and most advanced was offered in Europe, many Americans went there to learn what they could. Europeans, especially the Austrians, were leaders in specialized medical education and during the last decades of the century, the Germans came of age after their unification in 1871. Indeed, German scholarship had long been recognized as superior to American, and even before the Civil War, Americans made their way to Göttingen, Berlin, Halle, or Leipzig where they learned about the new elective system, the lecture, the seminar, graduate studies, and clinical research in the sciences.[6] These innovations proved to be so popular that when the American students returned to the United States, the innovations were gradually adapted to the American college system. Of all the new educational methods learned in Europe, the most important for the development of American higher education proved to be the lecture, the seminar, and the elective system.[7]

For American medical education, however, the most important innovation was laboratory-based research. In the period immediately after the Civil War, two-thirds of the medical schools—the best and most wealthy—conducted clinical or hospital instruction but without benefit of research. Unfortunately, most American doctors, including the elite, had little real knowledge of the basic medical sciences. Even as late as 1910, Abraham Flexner in his groundbreaking report on the quality of American medical education, reported that but for only a handful of colleges,[8] scientific education was "inert."[9]

> Scientifically, then, these schools may be called inert. They rarely cultivate any research at all; their faculties are generally composed of active practitioners whose training has rarely been modern . . . very rarely has the full-time teacher opportunity to work ahead. His time and energies are bespoken by heavy routine, unenlightened by competent or organized force of assistants and helpers. In general, school positions are valued as professional stepping stones, not as scientific opportunities; laboratories are often slovenly and except during class hours, entirely abandoned.[10]

Nevertheless, for a few expensive medical colleges such as Johns Hopkins, Michigan, or Harvard, it was the Austro-German postgraduate model of advanced specialized studies with its emphasis upon sound scientific training in a laboratory environment that prevailed. Although this model was expensive and functioned best with small enrollments, the educational benefits were enormous and included greater individualized training, more flexibility, and uniformly based scientific study. Unlike the predominant didactic educational model of traditional American medical education, the new model was intended to provide hands-on research that would enhance critical thinking, teaching, and ultimately the practice of medicine itself.[11]

American doctors went to Europe because that is where the first clinical laboratories for scientific research were located. Initially France, but gradually extending to Germany and Austria, the clinic provided graduate and postgraduate students an opportunity to conduct the sort of hands-on research in a variety of specialties that was as yet generally unavailable in the United States. Pathology, histology, chemistry, neurology, psychiatry, pharmacology, pediatrics, ophthalmology, laryngology, and bacteriology were but some of the fields in which Americans were weak and for which there were dedicated clinics where experimental research was conducted.[12] In so far as American medicine stood to gain from such expertise, and to the extent that an industrializing America would benefit from new discoveries in medicine, the European laboratory experience became a magnet for Americans.[13]

And it was a strong magnet at that, attracting some 15,000 American graduate and undergraduate students between 1870 and 1914.[14]

Those primarily drawn, however, were male postgraduate physicians from New York, Boston, Philadelphia, and Pittsburgh who were interested in clinical specialties not available in the United States and who would develop a considerable reputation and much influence in their day. Ophthalmologists were the first to seek out the European clinics, and they were followed in turn by those in specialties such as obstetrics, surgery, and laryngology. While medical research clinics were found throughout the German speaking areas of Central Europe—as in Heidelberg, Strasbourg, Leipzig, Breslau, and others—it was primarily to Vienna and Berlin that the Americans were drawn, especially after 1870. Both capitals were known as centers for research in pathology, gynecology, nervous diseases, and general medicine; and both offered the physician a wide array of possibilities to expand ones medical knowledge. Of the 15,000 students who went to Europe during this period, for example, approximately 10,000 went to Vienna, 3,000 to Berlin, and the remainder dispersed throughout all of Central Europe.[15]

The Push for Respectability and Authority

The clinics of Vienna and Berlin were in high demand because of their expertise and quality. For over fifty years, but especially between 1870 and World War I, these clinics provided Americans with the best in experimental medical education available. Such was, after all, their ultimate function, the results of which would be applied practically to the general public. Thus, unlike American medical education with its emphasis on observation and healing, the German and Austrian models of postgraduate education stressed the theoretical and in this manner pushed the limits of medical knowledge forward. The research clinic became such a popular educational model that it was eventually imported to the United States where it was initially introduced at Johns Hopkins in 1893.[16]

For most American doctors, legitimacy, authority, and influence were fundamental goals and the only way these could be achieved was through the success of the profession, and that was predicated on curing the sick or preventing illness in the first place. Since the research clinic might open the door to both, it was perceived as an extremely valid reform. But in spite of this reform effort, the overall status of the physician during the Gilded Age was insecure. The vast majority of doctors were not wealthy, although some had great wealth or treated those who did. Indeed, many doctors had other jobs so that they could support themselves and their families. Furthermore, with the proliferation of

Gilded Age proprietary medical institutions, most doctors had a poor or mediocre education at best, be it medical or otherwise. Yet, not unlike the urban white-collar worker, physicians believed they stood above the manual laborer. Similar to the white-collar worker, the doctor identified with the middle class and thus could mentally separate himself from the rabble, the poor, and the mass of the uneducated. There is one important distinction, however. Urban white-collar workers did not generally claim the ability to prevent illness, heal the sick, or be able to bring one back from the brink of death. Only the physician laid claim to these miracles and because he did, respectability and propriety were all the more important, and many tried to align themselves with the socially and economically prominent,

> We have in our cities, great and small, a much larger class of physicians whose principle object it is to obtain money, or rather the social position, pleasures, and power, which money only can bestow. They are clear headed, shrewd, practical men, well educated, because "it pays," and for the same reason they take good care to be supplied with the best instruments and the latest literature . . . They write and lecture to keep their names before the public, and they must do both well, or fall behind in the race. They have the greater part of the valuable practice, and their writings, which constitute the greater part of our medical literature, are respectable in quality and eminently useful.[17]

To be a "professional" was thus contingent upon where one was employed, and the closer one was to the socially prominent, the more "professional" one became. In spite of this mentality, the medical profession continued to support educational reform, specialization, new licensing procedures, and worked to expand the jurisdiction of the AMA into a confederation of state medical societies. In short, the American medical community was determined to raise the social status of the doctor by developing a corporate consciousness to replace an older competitive one that had informed the field for the bulk of the nineteenth century.[18] One aspect of medicine's new found corporate consciousness was adherence to the middle-class ideology of good character, common-sense essentialism, and American exceptionalism. This was observed by the rejection of recruits from the "lower" classes or those judged to be immoral; the resistance to women, Jews, and people of color;[19] and a strong push to shut down proprietary colleges. Of course not all of the 110,000 physicians in 1900 agreed with this agenda, but in fact, the more successful within the medical community did. They segregated themselves by means of exclusive local medical societies as a consequence of which the most important members of the medical profession by the turn of the century were northeastern white males of considerable wealth, power, and influence who could afford to enroll in the clinics of Vienna or Berlin and hobnob with the most famous physicians Europe had to offer.[20]

Neurasthenia

Far from being political, economic, or social revolutionaries, these elitist doctors considered themselves to be part of the eastern Establishment. Indeed, they often used the authority of medicine to support important moral positions, and were perceived by the public as a sort of secular priest whose duties included the ritual healing of a society made sick by the unrestrained indulgences of modern life. Neurasthenia, or nervous exhaustion, is a case in point. The term was coined in 1869 by the New York neurologist George M. Beard to categorize a variety of nonspecific emotional disorders such as fatigue, insomnia, or depression, which he noticed in his patients. Unable to locate its pathology, Beard turned to leading American and European intellectuals such as Herbert Spencer and Thomas Edison for help, and eventually concluded that neurasthenia was an American disease caused by urban living, economic competition, and the climate of the northeastern United States. Victims were most frequently white Euro-American professional and businessmen who engaged in the competitive market place, or white middle- or upper-class women who, because of pressures exerted upon their "delicate" nervous systems by housework and other wifely chores, suffered hysterical breakdowns. American life, Beard believed, was thus ultimately responsible for this disease because its cultural evolution had outpaced individual evolution, and Americans were expending too much brain power trying to catch up to the increased pace of civilization. As proof, Beard argued that the institutions of modern life such as the telegraph, the railroads, the press, science, and personal liberty conspired to increase the mental demands on Americans thereby draining them of their nervous forces to the point of exhaustion. In short, neurasthenia was the price Americans had to pay for civilization and progress,[21] and it was eagerly confirmed by several of Beard's colleagues within the American Neurological Association such as Charles Dana, S. Weir Mitchell, and Henry Lyman. By the turn of the century, nervous exhaustion had become a respectable if not quite common condition and was considered by physicians and patient alike to be America's preeminent mental disorder, at least until the advent of Freudian psychoanalysis.[22]

Most frequently, neurasthenia was cured by rest and absence of those factors that led to the expenditure of nerve force. Most importantly, physicians became moral educators who warned their patients to avoid the evils of modern urban environment and return to a more traditional lifestyle of moderation consistent with the middle-class ethos:

> Clearly the "American disease" was attributed to a multiplicity of causes that were inextricably associated with American society in the late nineteenth and early twentieth centuries... But the overwhelming concerns of the physicians who treated neurasthenia were, first, the fear of change and its ultimate consequences for the nineteenth way of life. The competition of the market place and university, the mass production of the factory and the public school, the beckoning call of the city with its opportunities for vice as well as profit—all conspired against emotional health. Physicians sounded a warning that has been a theme of traditionalists throughout history, namely, that old ways are best and that change, if unavoidable, should at least be gradual... Because neurasthenia, once acquired, could seldom be completely cured, physicians assumed the role of teachers or even missionaries to educate their fellow Americans on the prevention of neurasthenia.[23]

For women, this meant a return to the more traditional female activities associated with separate spheres and the cult of domesticity. Neurasthenia asserted that the female intellect was less developed than the male and that the female brain was subservient to the reproductive system. Thus, if women became engaged in activities disassociated from the reproductive tasks to which their intellects conformed, the exhaustion of nerve force resulted. The only appropriate cure for female neurasthenics, therefore, was to be found in a return to those responsibilities for which she was biologically suited, a not so subtle iteration of female essentialism.[24]

The history of neurasthenia and the physicians who treated it reflected the medical community's role in support of the national ideology. They had diagnosed a novel disease that was attributed to the chaotic conditions of an overcivilized urban America, and had developed a cure that required men and women to return to more "traditional" gender-based roles in order to save both their sanity and their civilization. In this capacity, those who treated neurasthenia became moral guidance counselors whose job it was to help white upper- and middle-class Americans overcome the crisis of modernity and return to those values and behaviors that had made the United States great in the first place. A rejection of these recommendations, on the other hand, was counterproductive because as men and women literally withered away from nervous exhaustion and a lack of nerve force, civilization was at risk of degenerating into a state of unbridled barbarism and moral anarchy. George Beard was especially worried about this because he thought he had already discovered evidence it was occurring in those individuals he diagnosed in 1884 as suffering from sexual neurasthenia, or "sexual exhaustion," "There is a special and very important and very frequent clinical variety of neurasthenia (nervous exhaustion) to which the term sexual neurasthenia (sexual exhaustion) may properly and conveniently applied."[25] Sexual neurasthenia, according to Beard, was primarily a disease of the male because female nervous exhaustion was long known to be a disorder of the reproductive organs, the cure for which had been long established. This was not the case with men and what had hitherto been diagnosed as the several diseases of "genital debility," such as impotence, spermatorrhoea, "irritable testes," masturbation, and sexual gratification with a member of the same sex were now known to be symptoms of sexual exhaustion ultimately caused by the stress of civilization:

> The causation of sexual neurasthenia, as of all other clinical varieties, and of modern nerve sensitiveness in general, is not single or simple, but complex; evil habits, excesses, tobacco, alcohol, worry and special excitements, even climate itself—all the familiar excitants being secondary to the one great predisposing cause—civilization.
>
> This form of neurasthenia, like all other forms, is more common in America than in any other country, mainly on account of the dryness of our air and violent extremes of heat and cold, and opportunities and necessities of a rising civilization in a new and immense continent.[26]

Of all forms of sexual neurasthenia, masturbation and "excess sexual intercourse" were particularly heinous because they inevitably led to love of one's own sex and sexual perversion. Each of these activities contributed to the exhaustion of the sexual organs that in turn induced indifference, then hate, of the opposite sex and culminated in the love of one's own sex that would then be inherited by offspring to create congenital sexual perversion:

> Violent and excessive exercise of any function finds relief only in the opposite condition—in perversion... Exhaustion of the sexual organs, through excess or masturbation, brings on at first indifference to the opposite sex, then positive fear or dread of normal intercourse; confirmed, long-standing masturbators of either sex care little or not at all for the opposite sex; are more likely to fear than to enjoy their presence, and are especially terrified by the thought of sexual connection... The subjects of these excesses go through the stages of indifference and of fear, and

complete the circle; the sex is perverted; they hate the opposite sex, and love their own; men become women, and women men, in their tastes, conduct, character, feelings, and behavior ... when the sexual debility becomes organized in families, then children may be born with this tendency; hence the congenital cases of sexual perversion ... .[27]

Although Beard's concern with self-abuse and sexual excess was anything but unusual and reflected an attitude that had a long-established pedigree in the West, his cures for the condition were unique. Since American civilization had led to the exhaustion of the vital nerve force in the first instance, the only realistic cure was to recreate conditions not as nerve draining, a return to the great outdoors and a rejection of the urban environment of the late nineteenth century:

> and it is quite safe to assume, reasoning deductively and inductively from a general knowledge of the nervous, from observation among savages and semi-savages, among the negroes and among the strong, healthy farming population in all civilized countries, that those who live out-doors and have well balanced constitutions of the old-fashioned sort are not annoyed by sexual desire when they have no opportunities for gratification, nor to the same degree as the delicate, finely-organized lads of our cities and of the higher civilization.[28]

Similar to Roosevelt's interest in the "barbarian" virtues, Beard's call for a return to the wild in the name of American civilization projected a moral position that was shared by members of his profession and that supported the national ideology. Beard may have been more outspoken in his advocacy than most, but his faith in physicians as moral agents was no less ubiquitous within the medical community. Beard understood that morality was dependent upon the state of one's physical well-being, and that good health was therefore essential for good morality, both at the individual and at the national level.

Medical Specialization and Medicine as a Moral Guide

Although the moral and scientific authority of the physician in general was yet to be nationally recognized, and much more professional reform was to be undertaken, medicine increasingly perceived itself as the agent of national rejuvenation. For many doctors, this was the key to their success as moral leaders since, "They placed themselves at the center of national life, claiming to be the moral vortex of the century's power and progress, whose attitudes on religion, training of the will, exercise and diet, intellectual employment, amusement, and marriage helped to build national character."[29] But this demanded more than mere guardianship of the national ideology; it required that the medical profession become an active propagandist on its own behalf. Along with moral purity writers, therefore, the physician expounded the propriety of ordered morality over chaos to ensure progress and the continuation of American civilization.[30] Nevertheless, not all members of the American medical community were engaged solely in the quest for status, or guardianship of the nation's future. Some, in fact, were also deeply concerned with research, medical competency, and specialization. Although not particularly welcomed by the general practitioner who feared the economic competition a good specialist might bring, specialization was nevertheless a fact of life during the Gilded Age. Four general reasons account for their development: (1) the growth of a valid body of medical knowledge after the Civil War large enough to support a specialty; (2) a huge increase in the urban population during this same period sufficient to support a specialist's case load; (3) the financial rewards that accrued to the successful urban practitioner; and (4) the establishment of the specialty hospital and specialty medical society. The hospital allowed for the treatment of patients under controlled conditions, and the medical societies allowed for the communication of knowledge by means of conferences, journals, and symposia, all of which served as vehicles for the national and international promulgation of specialty knowledge.[31] By the 1880s, in fact, medical specialization was an accepted fact of life in urban America even as it was criticized for crowding out the general practitioner and for being too "luxurious":

> Within the last thirty years departments of the healing art that were embraced within the narrowest limits have widened into vast fields that engage the labors of the most intelligent and industrious to comprehend them. This has been accomplished by the division of labor whereby men of talent by devoting themselves to a single branch of medicine have been enabled to develop it to an extent otherwise impossible. But while by this division of labor an infinite amount of good has been accomplished, which would have been impossible had all been general practitioners, there is now danger lest, all being specialists, none shall be general practitioners. Indeed in some of our large cities specialism is now carried to such an extreme, and the human body is so nicely mapped out and divided, that there is only left to the general practitioner or family physician the umbilicus. In country districts where from necessity the physician has to treat all diseases, and consequently where specialism is an impossibility, the family doctor still holds his own; but in our large cities and densely populated districts specialism revels in tropical luxuriance.[32]

Medical specialization was part of the larger trend of economic specialization that by the end of the century had become synonymous with professionalization. Since the Gilded Age was characterized by an explosion of new knowledge, doctors who wanted to be perceived by the general public and medical colleagues as modern and professional developed an expertise and became associated with a clinic or hospital. Initially modeled on the German and Austrian experiences, medical specialization would continue to increase in tandem with domestic educational reforms and the growth of national medical specialty societies. In spite of grumbling from general practitioners, the ranks of specialists grew rapidly and they dominated the elite national and local medical societies such as the American Medical Association and the New York Medical and Surgical Society. Specialists were also to be found in increasing numbers on the faculties of medical colleges, and on the staffs of hospitals, clinics, and dispensaries. Equally as important, specialists now had the financial and social support of numerous wealthy clients who paid handsomely for their services.[33] The age of the scientific expert had arrived and in the case of American medicine the expectations were high, and nowhere was this more evident than in the struggle between neurology and psychiatry over the issues of scientific authority, legitimacy, prestige, and influence.[34]

Chapter 6
The Debate Between Alienism and Neurology

By 1900, psychiatry had reached a dead end. Its practitioners were concentrated for the most part in asylums, and asylums had become mainly warehouses in which any hope of therapy was illusory. Psychiatrists themselves had a rather poor reputation among their medical colleagues as the dull and the second-rate, just a step, if that, above the spa-doctors and the homeopaths.[1]

As a specialized medical field, psychiatry is relatively new. Although it has roots in the custodial asylum of medieval Europe, it was only during the Enlightenment that mental illness was looked upon as a proper subject of scientific investigation.[2] Asylums were built throughout Europe, but especially in England, France, and the Germanies, both to house patients and to study their symptoms in the hope of effecting cures. In the main, those who studied mental illness fell into two general camps. One group argued that mental illnesses were a product of some sort of a nerve defect, and was probably centered in the brain. The other side argued that its origins were "psychosocial" and caused by the inability of the depraved individual to adjust to the strains of life. For the most part, the European scientists favored the biological theory over the "psychosocial," and throughout the early nineteenth century, most asylum research was conducted along those lines.[3]

In the United States, the biological nerve model was initially just as popular and is associated with the late eighteenth-century figure of Benjamin Rush whom the American Psychiatric Association labeled the "father of American Psychiatry."[4] And as in Europe, the asylum was the preferred institution in which the mentally ill were to be studied and hopefully cured, so that by the 1840s, asylums were designed to be places where the best scientific treatment could be received.[5] In 1844, the Association of Medical Superintendents of American Institutions for the Insane was organized to facilitate the sharing of new information garnered from this research, but by 1869, therapeutics were abandoned altogether in favor of asylum warehousing of which the Willard State Hospital in New York State was a prime example.

To be sure, much of what psychiatry then claimed to know about mental disease was the result of the observation of patient behaviors within an institutional setting. When mental patients were observed engaging in activities that were deemed inappropriate, asylum psychiatrists suspected that the mental illness was a result of brain lesions that might have been created spontaneously or by the constant repetition of bad habits due to the depravity of a naturally weakened will. Diagnoses of this sort were not especially limited to American physicians, and indeed, were well-established "facts" during the nineteenth century in both the United States and in Europe. Thus, rather than acknowledge the possibility that some allegedly illicit activities, such as masturbation or same-sex attraction were normal, a psychiatrist often assumed they were either the cause or the result of insanity. Based upon this logic, doctors developed elaborate descriptions of aberrant behaviors that stemmed from an ambiguous mental illness caused by lesions or depravity. A classic example is that given by Allen W. Hagenbach, M.D., Senior Assistant Physician, Insane Hospital, Cook County, Illinois. In the first paragraph of the article, "Masturbation as a Cause of Insanity" published in the October 1879 edition of the *Journal of Nervous and Mental Disease*, Hagenbach tells the reader in no uncertain terms:

> The frequency with which masturbation is practiced by the insane . . . shall be my excuse for recording a few facts in connection with masturbatic insanity, as they have presented themselves during the past three years in the wards of the Cook County Hospital for the Insane. I shall endeavor to show that masturbation is an exciting cause of insanity, also the relations they bear to each other, and enumerate some peculiar physical conditions associated with the disease.[6]

A detailed analysis of the inmates ensues that draws attention to their lower-class origins, then proceeds to prove the direct relationship between males who masturbated and the onset of several types of insanity, one of which he labeled "corrupted sexual feelings" as a consequence of a continued indulgence in the bad habit. In this instance, not only did masturbation cause insanity in a 21-year-old male patient, it also caused a specific type marked by effeminacy and "morbid attachments for persons of his sex":

> He confesses that he masturbated frequently, since fourteen years of age, but is unwilling to make any efforts at reform . . . He is very effeminate

in all his habits; constantly carries an open and shut fan, delights in ladies' small talk, spending most of his time in needlework, arranging his toilet for the weekly dances, and other equally effeminate employments. The corrupted sexual feelings, such as forming morbid attachments for persons of his sex, are quite marked, and it became necessary to remove several patients to different wards to separate him from the object of his regards.[7]

Hagenbach concluded his essay with a series of true statements deduced from his asylum observations, thus proving his initial thesis:

In conclusion I think I am justified in making the following deductions:

I. That masturbation is an exciting cause of insanity.
II. That in a small percentage, certain physical conditions are present due to the vice and may prove valuable aids in confirming a diagnosis.
III. That the general health of the masturbator is always impaired.
IV. That the diagnosis in the first stage usually is difficult, and comparatively easy in the second stage.
V. That the diagnosis is always unfavorable unless the practice is discontinued.[8]

Given the then commonly held belief that masturbation culminated in madness or death anyway, Hagenbach's methodology and conclusions come as no surprise. Nevertheless, it was precisely this sort of methodology that proved deeply held predispositions which so offended many in the American medical community. Outside the asylum, the situation was much the same. A new generation of biologically oriented "alienist," as psychiatrists were then called, failed as well to successfully apply the findings of modern biology to mental disease. This failure was not their intent, of course, and psychiatry was initially looked upon favorably and with great hope. Scientists on both sides of the Atlantic were optimistic, and engaged in systematic medical research to "lay bare the relationship between mind and brain."[9] In the main, Germany dominated the field throughout the nineteenth century, and provided the educational model for Europe. Great emphasis was placed on research and teaching in the areas of genetics and biology, and university-affiliated clinics were established in support of these twin goals.[10]

As has been previously mentioned, the state of late nineteenth-century American medicine was poor, and biological psychiatry was not exempt from this overall backward status. In 1892, Adolf Meyer immigrated to the United States from Switzerland, and sought to change this situation. First at the University of Chicago, then the Illinois Eastern Hospital for the Insane in Kankakee, the Worcester Asylum in Massachusetts, the Pathological Institute in Washington, DC, and finally at Johns Hopkins in 1910, Meyer attempted as a professor of psychiatry to apply the German educational model of biological research and teaching to mental disease within the university atmosphere. For all of his efforts, American psychiatry, with the exception of his department at Johns Hopkins, resisted these reforms and continued to maintain a separation between research and teaching that was unthinkable in Germany.[11] In the end, though, it was not American resistance to German educational models that doomed biologically oriented psychiatry, it was the arrival of a new German school of thought associated with Emil Kraepelin.

A New Biological Approach

As opposed to the lesion theory of mental illness, Kraepelin emphasized illness within the context of a person's lifetime history. He believed that there were several varieties of mental illness, each one different, and knowable by means of a systematic study of large numbers of cases. This novel approach became quite popular in Europe and in the United States where it was adopted by Adolf Meyer himself in 1896, thus initiating the end of the older biological model. Yet before it died, the theory of degeneration would influence Gilded Age neurologist and psychiatrist alike. Introduced in 1857 by the French alienist Benedict-Augustin Morel, the degeneration theory asserted that some illnesses, especially the mental ones, were inheritable, and as they passed from generation to generation, they got worse and threatened the very fabric of society itself:

> The degenerate human being, if he is abandoned to himself, falls into a progressive degradation, He becomes . . . not only incapable of forming part of the chain of transmission of progress in human society, he is the greatest obstacle to this progress through his contact with the healthy portion of the population.[12]

For many psychiatrists and neurologists, degeneration seemed plausible, particularly for those scientists who also subscribed to the then popular notion of the inheritance of acquired characteristics. Developed in 1809 by the French naturalist Jean Baptiste Lamarck in his work *Zoological Philosophy*,[13] Lamarckian inheritance was quite popular among American and British physicians at the turn of the century. Referred to as neo-Lamarckians, these scientists asserted that once a characteristic like an illness was acquired, say alcoholism or insanity, it was transmitted to the next generation. If degeneration theory was added to the mix, the disease was not only inherited, it became worse in successive generations, and under these circumstances, isolation or elimination through the prevention of reproduction was the only proper medical response.

The scientific results of those who supported neo-Lamarckian theories of inheritance lent support to the general theories of physical, social, and cultural degeneration that became popular among the middle and upper classes both within Europe and the United States during the Gilded Age. In the aftermath of Darwin and during a period of rapid industrialization, degeneration offered a simple, yet plausible explanation for the myriad social ills associated with rapid economic change. The pressures of modern life threatened social stability, and those with weak constitutions, such as the poor, women, and people of color were particularly susceptible because as they were subjected to the stresses and strains of modernity, their nerves would weaken leading to improper behaviors that would in turn be inherited. In 1877, Richard L. Dugdale made this point quite clear with the publication of his book *The Jukes: A Study in Crime, Pauperism, Disease and Heredity*. This was the study of a poor rural family that, over the duration of seven generations, had produced a plethora of social misfits including prostitutes, beggars, bastards, and thieves, each generation worse than the one before. The book was a best-seller on both sides of the Atlantic and became an icon for the emergent eugenics movement, the purpose of which was to prevent degeneracy through sterilization.[14] Indeed, the field of criminal anthropology was established by the Italian Caesare Lombroso to both study the phenomenon of inherited degeneracy and devise methods for dealing with it.[15] The notion of "natural born criminal" thus entered the scientific imagination, and was picked up throughout the medical community where it was particularly well received. According to G. Frank Lydston, one of America's leading Gilded Age criminal anthropologists:

> America has for many years furnished conditions peculiarly favorable to degeneracy. The strenuous life of the average American, certainly of every ambitious citizen, has many aspects bearing upon degeneracy in general and vice and crime in particular. Lust for wealth, desire for social supremacy, ambition for fame, love of display, late hours, lack of rest excitement, the consumption of alcohol, especially women—these factors combine to cause what Beard termed a distinctively American disease. The body social is growing more and more neuropathic. In the train of this widespread neuropathy comes degeneracy, with all it evil brood of social disorders.[16]

Between 1893 and 1909, no less than nine major American works on criminal anthropology were published.[17] In the main, the message was the same: there existed a class of individuals with a criminal essence who differed physically and psychologically from the rest of society. Pauperism, alcoholism, consumption, imbecility, sexual perversion, illegitimacy, and "insanity" were but a few of the identified conditions that were inherited. Degeneration could be found in any social class, although pauperism, alcoholism, and illegitimacy in particular were associated with individuals who were economically less well off than the middle and upper classes and who lived in the inner cities of North America, especially along the eastern seaboard. In so far as these individuals tended to be the new immigrants, the inborn criminal was frequently identified with the darker Eastern European, the Jew, the Italian, or the African American.[18] From time to time, however, the inborn criminal type could be found in rural communities where a "social residuum" of tramp families similar to the Jukes could be found.[19] Not only did individuals from these backgrounds have the traditional phenological essence that set them apart from the northeastern gentry, they also contained within their midst a criminal essence as well. Women were not exempt, and those who engaged in nongender conforming activities were equally assigned a degenerate, criminal essence. G. Frank Lydston, was quite clear on this point,

> The exceptional strong-willed woman is unfortunately a degenerate with virile tendencies, and often strong criminal propensities. Conscience and moral sense, and especially moral bias from religious suggestions, are keen in women, but not strong, because dominated by a hyper developed ego, unstable and powerful emotions, a defective appreciation of altruism, and a weak will. Centuries of dependence upon the stronger individuality of man has had much to do with woman's psychology. Her relatively weak cerebral organization is, in a sense, a physiologic atrophy from disease. This is explanatory of the lack of individualism in women,— i.e. their psychic uniformity. Exposure, since the human family began, to this lack of stimulus to cerebral independence has resulted in what is practically a psychic dead level. With the advent of the "new Woman," a change has begun, but alas! the increased brain capacity which woman must surely acquire must inevitably be paid for in infertility and physical degeneracy.[20]

Although some biologically oriented psychiatrists and many nerve doctors accepted degeneracy theory and the inheritance of mental illnesses, the general public did not. To be labeled either a depraved degenerate or insane was tantamount to total social marginalization and possible commitment to an asylum. Nowhere was the rejection of these labels more visible than among the educated white middle-class that preferred instead to be diagnosed with neurasthenia, George Beard's "disease" of the nerves. It will be recalled that this disease was presented to the public as being caused by environmental factors, and thus the victim would have no fear of the taint of heritable degeneration. This resulted in what Edward Shorter has characterized as a "flight from psychiatry,"[21] a "deception of the public to the effect that [mental] illness meant a disorder of the nerves when in fact the brain was meant."[22] Yet for nerve doctors, there was reward enough in the increased business they received as patients assiduously avoided the worlds of the psychiatrist and the asylum, which by now had become synonymous.

The Rise of Neurology

Nineteenth-century neurology attempted to differentiate itself from psychiatry, even though distinctions were frequently blurred, and in the Gilded Age medical community where medical education was spotty at best, one was free to label one's expertise. In the absence of effective professional policing of the specialties, such was frequently the case and many physicians dealt with both simultaneously.[23] Nevertheless, neurology accorded itself a specialized field of medicine that studied the anatomy of the nervous system, whose true practitioners had been trained in pathology and internal medicine. By today's standards, however, neurology was in its infant phase, and more often than not simply referred to one who was a specialist in the catchall conditions of "nervous exhaustion" and diseases of the nerves. Nevertheless, neurology as was then known had a fairly long and distinctive pedigree in Europe, where three distinctive schools developed among the French, the English, and the Germans. The German School took its roots from Moritz Romberg (1795–1873), a professor of neurology at the University Hospital in Berlin who was the first to write a systematic treatise on clinical neurology. The French School is associated with Jean Martin Charcot (1825–1895), who in 1882 was appointed professor of diseases of the nervous system at the University of Paris. In England, Jabez S. Ramkill and Charles Edouard Brown-Sequard were the first pioneers, but it was only with John Hughlings Jackson (1835–1911), William Gowers (1845–1915), and David Ferrier (1843–1928) that British neurology gained prominence.[24]

In the United States, neurology was initially a subset of general medicine, although some early doctors, such as Benjamin Rush (1745–1813),

Amariah Brigham (1798–1849), and the forementioned Charles Edouard Brown-Sequard (1816–1894) made significant contributions.[25] The actual founders of American neurology, however, are considered to be Silas Weir Mitchell (1829–1914) and William Alexander Hammond (1828–1900). S. Weir Mitchell was the scion of a wealthy Philadelphia family, the seventh physician in three generations. He made an early name for himself investigating injuries to the nervous system caused by gunshot wounds inflicted during the Civil War. After the War, Mitchell became less interested in medicine, and became a highly successful private "consultant in the nervous diseases," specializing in female hysteria and neurasthenia. Although Mitchell never gave up entirely his research into the physiology of the cerebellum and wrote numerous papers on clinical neurology, his work was increasingly oriented to the relationship between American life and the nervous diseases. He is best known for the development of the "rest cure," an elaborate regimen that combined bed rest, diet, physiotherapy and "moral therapy." In spite of his public involvement in alienism, he was highly critical of it, and in an 1894 address before the American Medico-Psychological Association, he scolded the asylum psychiatrist for his isolation:

> Once we spoke of asylums with respect, it is not so now. We neurologists think you have fallen behind us, and this opinion is gaining ground outside our ranks, and is, in part at least, your own fault. Where are your careful scientific reports? You live alone, uncriticized, unquestioned, out of the healthy conflicts and honest rivalries which keep us [neurologists] up to the mark of the fullest possible competence.[26]

Throughout his career, Mitchell was never able to secure an academic appointment although he was awarded many honorary degrees from universities such as Bologna, Edinburgh, Harvard, Johns Hopkins, and Princeton. During the course of his life, he was also well received by the highest elements of American society and became friends with the likes of Charles Francis Adams, Andrew Carnegie, Oliver Wendell Holmes, Simon Flexner, William James, Francis Parkman, and others.[27]

William Alexander Hammond, Mitchell's friend and neurological collaborator, was the other individual responsible for the development of American neurology. He was the son of a wealthy Annapolis physician, studied medicine at New York University where he graduated in 1848, enlisted in the Armed Forces as an assistant surgeon, and in 1860, accepted an appointment as professor of anatomy and physiology at the University of Maryland. During the Civil War, in 1862, President Lincoln appointed him as Surgeon General at the age of 34, but he was unjustly drummed out of the service in 1864 over a conflict with Secretary of War Edmund Stanton. His tour of duty was nevertheless noted for the reforms and innovations he instituted, among which were the Army Medical Museum and the compilation of the Medical and Surgical History of the War of Rebellion. After he left the army, Hammond went to New York City where he established a medical practice specializing in neurology and psychiatry, and in 1871 he published the first American textbook of neurology, *A Treatise on the Diseases of the Nervous System*. In 1874 he was appointed lecturer in neurology and psychiatry at the College of Physicians and Surgeons, and in 1876 he was appointed professor of nervous and mental diseases at the Bellevue Hospital Medical College. In addition to authoring numerous texts on neurology, he also edited medical journals, for example, the *Quarterly Journal of Physiological Medicine and Medical Jurisprudence* and the *New York Medical Journal*. Hammond is best remembered medically as a pioneer in the area of neurological symptomatology and as a champion of the importance of the neurological sciences.[28]

Together, Mitchell and Hammond helped pioneer neurology as an important medical specialty in the United States, which allowed it to grow and prosper. But before this could be accomplished, the specialty had to be professionalized, and that process began with the establishment of the American Neurological Association in 1875. A growing body of knowledge, better technology, large cities such as New York with more doctors and more white middle- and upper-class patients with more symptoms willing to pay for the services of a specialist but unwilling to be committed to an asylum provided an excellent atmosphere for neurology to establish itself as a professional, singular field of medicine. This development was not without its detractors, however, because some doctors, most notably the asylum psychiatrist and family practitioner, were threatened by the range of nervous illnesses over which the neurologist claimed dominance and that had traditionally been their areas of responsibility. But neurologists were unimpressed and accused asylum psychiatry of being ignorant about the nervous system when it came to the origins of mental illness, and dismissed it as secondary to neurology. According to Edward Spitzka, one of America's leading neurologists of the Gilded Age,

> It has long been a subject of comment and surprise, that nothing worthy of notice has proceeded from our insane asylums, in the fields of pathology and clinical observation. The exceptions to this rule are so few that they just serve to prove it. There are nearly a hundred asylums in this country, many of which have opportunities for making from thirty to

fifty autopsies annually, and a few, as many as a hundred or more. These autopsies, if systematically and properly made, would furnish valuable and suggestive data, not only in nervous and mental, but also in general pathology. One is justified, in view of this unpardonable waste of material, to employ the strongest terms of censure in characterizing the apathy and ignorance manifested by those concerned in this dereliction of scientific duty. Even where autopsies are performed, they are usually made to satisfy purely formal considerations, such as an occasional coroner's inquest.[29]

No ordinary physician, Spitzka was born in New York City in 1852, attended the College of the City of New York, and studied medicine at New York University. Upon graduation in 1873, he moved to Europe where he married a German and for the next three years studied embryology, morphology, and psychiatry in Berlin, Leipzig, and finally Vienna, where he became an assistant in embryology at the University of Vienna.[30] Upon his return to the United States, he entered into general practice in 1876 and soon became a surgeon at Mt. Sinai Hospital and the consulting neurologist to the North Eastern Dispensary, then to the Syndham Hospital, during which time he developed an interest in evolutionary and biological degeneration. He was so highly regarded by his peers that during this period he received the prestigious W. A. Hammond prize of the AMA and another prize in international competition from the British Medico-Psychological Association for his essay "The Somatic Etiology of Insanity."[31] His fame and expertise were such that he was especially requested to testify for the defense of Charles Guiteau, the assassin of President Garfield.[32] Between 1881 and 1884, he was the editor of the *American Journal of Neurology and Psychiatry*; from 1883 until 1884, the president of the New York Neurological Association; and from 1882 until 1887, professor of comparative anatomy in the Columbia University Veterinary College as well as professor of nervous and mental diseases and of medical jurisprudence at the New York Post Graduate Medical College. After leaving this post, he became the vice-president of the Section of Neurology of the Ninth International Medical Congress held in Washington, DC, and in 1890 he was elected president of the American Neurological Association. In 1904, he was appointed chairman of the Section on Neurology of the Congress of Arts and Sciences in St. Louis, and by the time of his death on January 3, 1914, he was regarded as one the most important and innovative neurologists in the United States.[33]

Spitzka was openly hostile to mental asylums and their weak record of scientific research into the etiology of mental illness. In his now famous address, "Reform in the Scientific Study of Psychiatry," delivered before the New York Neurological Association on March 4, 1878, Spitzka denounced asylum physicians and their superintendents as nothing but greedy charlatans whose research amounted to nothing more than fraud and chicanery paid for by public money. Asylum physicians were, he said, poorly educated in the field of medicine, more interested in politics and in their pocketbooks than research into the etiology of mental illness, isolated, and untrustworthy in their research on mental illness,

> From all which I have just stated, our mature conclusion must be, that the average medical superintendent of insane asylums, not appointed on the strength of general and scientific culture, deficient in anatomical and pathological training, without a genuine interest in their noble specialty, untrustworthy as to their reported results, and not in communication with the general medical profession which every liberal and broadminded physician naturally seeks, are the *last* individuals in this world to whom the responsible duty of training the embryo practitioner in an important specialty should be entrusted.[34]

Patient welfare was of uppermost importance to Spitzka. He was deeply upset about the conditions of the asylums, the abuses to which the patients were subjected, and their lack of medical care once committed. He was particularly concerned about the lack of research into the etiology of insanity and the total absence of anything approaching a true theory of mental illness. What he saw instead was the imposition of false theories upon which injurious treatment was administered to the detriment of the patient's well being, "It is the application of a false theory, which not only deprives the sufferer of proper treatment, which he has a right to claim, but subjects him to wrong and injurious treatment, and especially to neglect of remedies in the beginning, when the disease is in its curable stage."[35] As a doctor who considered himself "one of the advisers of society,"[36] Spitzka pleaded for the more humane treatment of the mentally ill as well as more scientific insight into their illnesses. With proper medical diagnosis came proper treatment, not the least of which was to be sent home to be under the benign influence of family and friends rather than the "insanity" of an asylum:

> We conscientiously believe that the principles of proper treatment demand, that many cases of chronic mania, of paralytic insanity and of terminal dementia, cases which can be best treated at home, should not be sent to asylums, and that other patients in asylums should be dismissed as soon as it becomes evident that it can be done without risk and to their benefit. The surroundings of his family, the occupation of his

vocation, often have a far better influence on the patient than the grated windows, crib-beds, bleak walls, gruff attendants, narcotics and insane surroundings of an asylum.[37]

The problem, Spitzka argued, was that medically untrained asylum superintendents were mostly concerned with their social status and had monopolized the field of nervous disorder through the exclusion of non-asylum physicians by any means possible, thus leaving the true neurologist without the "material essential" for their teaching and research:

> As you are well aware, it is only under exceptional circumstances, if ever at all in America, that the teacher of nervous diseases can command the material essential to a thorough clinical and pathological demonstration of insanity.
>
> This is chiefly on account of a feeling among a number of asylum superintendents that they can claim to monopolize the sciences of psychiatry, to exclude every non-asylum physician from this field, and that they alone are entitled to teach this subject in our medical schools. *A priori* there can be no fairer proposition than this: that he who has devoted his life-time to a given specialty, ought to have the first voice and the high privilege of instruction in that specialty. If capable, zealous, and honest scientists establish a monopoly in scientific matters, even a monopoly may be endurable. But I would most strenuously object, that every one who may have happened to possess the requisite social and political influence, to receive an asylum position, is therefore to be considered a psychiatrist. Such as conclusion, based on an acceptation of a discreditable status quo, has been the great bane of American psychiatry, and I regret to say has been diligently fostered by that narrow circle of asylum physicians which furnishes the *ex cathedra* statements on the Asylum Association.[38]

To overcome these obstacles, neurologists went about the business of organizing themselves into a voluntary association, the express purposes of which were to extend both their field of inquiry and their authority within society. Specialization was an important element in the larger process of professionalization designed to secure the status of the neurologist and simultaneously convince the public that neurology was superior to psychiatry and the general practitioner in the area of nerve disease. Psychiatry was thus projected as nonscientific and subjective while neurology was touted as a modern scientific endeavor that could heal without the stigma associated with institutionalization in a madhouse. More authority, more money, better science, and a higher social status would hopefully be the result.[39]

On June 2, 1875, the first meeting of the American Neurological Association was held in the lecture room of the Young Men's Christian

Association, and William Hammond was voted by the eighteen neurologists present as the first chairman; S. Weir Mitchell, the first president. Over the course of the next several years, all of the best and brightest of American neurology became members, including A. McLane Hamilton, J. S. Jewell, George Beard, E. C. Seguin, James Putnam, E. C. Loring, John Shaw, Edward Spitzka, S. V. Clevenger, Charles Dana, and E. H. Clarke to name a few, and by 1900, membership included most of the research neurologists in the United States. Whereas psychiatry had by now reached its nadir, neurology had succeeded in developing a specialty that demanded respect from the physician and the public alike. This demand was readily evident at the trial of Charles Guiteau, assassin of President Garfield, where Spitzka and a young neurologist named James G. Kiernan led the charge for the defense.

The Insanity Defense

On July 17, 1881, Guiteau, an allegedly deranged office seeker, shot Garfield twice, and on September 19, the President died of his gun wounds. At the trial held immediately after Garfield's death, the defense presented an insanity plea that was immediately rejected by the prosecution, which argued that according to the then infamous M'Naghten rule, a law adapted by the British in 1843 and accepted by the American courts shortly thereafter, a "defendant was to be considered responsible if he was aware of the nature and consequences of his act and knew it was forbidden by law."[40] To the extent that Guiteau took full responsibility for his actions and was therefore demonstrably sane by all accounts, he was responsible and must be found guilty. The defense, on the other hand, rejected this proposition and argued instead that Guiteau was indeed insane by virtue of a congenital defect and therefore had no control over his actions, even though he might reasonably have known what he did was wrong, which no one doubted. In support of their position, the defense called, among other witnesses, Drs. Kiernan and Spitzka.

Born in New York City in 1852, Kiernan was an 1874 graduate of the medical department of the University of New York. He became an assistant physician at the New York City Asylum for the Insane and an officer of the New York Neurological Society. While a member of this Society, Kiernan made a name for himself as a scientific modernizer in the Spitzka mold, and lobbied for reforms in both neurology and psychiatry. Eventually, Kiernan would become a medical court specialist, and frequently testified in trials that dealt with mental illness, the most noteworthy of which was his presence at the Guiteau trial. Among his many memberships, honors, and teaching positions, Kiernan was a fellow of the Chicago Academy of Medicine; honorary president of the Section of Nervous and Mental Disease of the 1893 Pan American Medical Congress; honorary member of the Chicago Neurological Society; a professor of mental and nervous diseases at the Milwaukee Medical College; and in 1903–1904, a professor of neurology at the Chicago Post-Graduate School.[41] He died in 1923.

Kiernan was called as the first expert defense witness for Guiteau in early December, 1881. In a response to a hypothetical question posed by the defense regarding an unnamed individual who ostensibly suffered from "strong hereditary taint" and who also behaved exactly like Guiteau before, during, and after the assassination of the President, when asked if this person was sane or insane at the time of the shooting, Kiernan replied, "Assuming this to be true, I should say the prisoner was insane."[42] The defense then turned the witness over to the prosecution for a cross-examination that was designed to discredit both Kiernan and his theory of irresponsible insanity by reason of hereditary taint. The cross-examination witness was followed by a series of prosecution and defense redirections in which the prosecution was determined to debunk Kiernan's hereditarian theory that Guiteau had been unable to control his behavior even though he knew what he was doing. Kiernan stuck to his understanding that there was an innate or primary form of insanity such that one was born insane and one would die insane. Underneath this line of reasoning, Kiernan's point was clear: a criminal behaved the way he did because his heredity prevented the exercise of free-will thus precluding individual responsibility for acts committed. Upon further questioning, the prosecution was able to get Kiernan to establish that at least 20 percent of the population in virtually any walk of life suffered from this form of insanity, a position the prosecution used to ridicule Kiernan, after which the cross-examination was wrapped up.[43]

Undaunted, the defense continued to draw upon medical witnesses whose views were similar to Kiernan. Finally, and after some prodding, Edward Spitzka agreed to take the stand a few days after the prosecution had examined numerous witnesses who declared that Guiteau suffered from "depravity and not mental illness."[44] Contrary to the position of the prosecution experts, and quite consistent with those of Kiernan, Spitzka was open about his belief that Guiteau was insane. In the October 29 edition of the *Medical Record*, Spitzka had written under the pseudonym "Philalethas":

> There is not a scintilla of doubt in my mind, that if Guiteau with his hereditary history, his insane manner, his insane documents and his insane actions were to be committed to any asylum in the land, he would be unhesitatingly admitted as a proper subject for sequestration... A thorough study will convince an impartial and competent jury of medical examiners... that he was never anything else, that his crime was the offspring of insanity, and that in every act he will betray the characteristic features of querulent monomania. They will also conclude that, inasmuch as his insanity is not the result of his own vices, but based on a defective organization inherited from a diseased ancestry, anything like responsibility, complete or partial, is out of the question.[45]

During his testimony, he remained adamant in his position, and at one point went so far as to ridicule the prosecutor who had tried to impugn Spitzka's reputation because the famed neurologist had at one time served as a professor of comparative anatomy at the Columbia Veterinary College:

> Prosecutor: Q. You are a veterinary surgeon, are you not?
> Spitzka: A. In the sense that I treat asses who ask me stupid questions, I am.[46]

In the end, Spitzka let it be known that in his expert opinion, Guiteau suffered from a "congenital malformation of the brain" and was born with "so defective a nervous organization that he is altogether deprived of that moral sense which is an integral and essential constituent of the normal human mind."[47] For their part, the prosecution attempted to rebut Spitzka by examining numerous well-known psychiatrists who denied that Guiteau was insane or that there was any such disease as hereditary insanity, even if one might be able to accept the existence of a hereditary tendency to insanity if born with a defective "nervous organization."[48]

Here then, in the trial of the assassin of President Garfield, the rancorous debate between the modern neurologist and the asylum psychiatrist unfolded. The former wedded to a deterministic theory of the inheritability of insanity that precluded responsibility, the later wedded to his theory of depravity and the influence of environment as causative agents for insanity. These two divergent positions would be later reflected in the debates over the origins of sexual perversion, and homosexuality in particular. By the last decade of the nineteenth century, however, the debate had clearly shifted in favor of the hereditarians Kiernan and Spitzka.

The Professionalization of Neurology

In the main, American neurologists were initially concentrated in the east, primarily in New York, Philadelphia, and Boston where they had access to wealth and status. In 1888, for example, the Vanderbilt family donated money to establish an outpatient clinic at the prestigious New York College of Physicians and Surgeons, the center of early neurological developments.[49] Over the next twenty years, neurology spread westward to St. Louis and Chicago, where the Chicago Neurological Association was established in 1898. Eventually, neurological studies were established in locations such as the University of Maryland, Baltimore; the Medical College of Virginia; the Albany Medical College of New York; the University of Michigan at Ann Arbor; and the Detroit College of Medicine. Until after the turn of the century, little neurological research of prominence was conducted west of the Mississippi, and during the last twenty years of the nineteenth century, the northeast remained the vital hub of research and publishing.[50]

The new specialty was self-consciously proud of its reliance upon science and worked hard to convey this point to the public. Although it was true that late nineteenth-century neurology and psychiatry were often intermixed in practice, the methodology of the neurologist was supposed to be based on real science to the benefit of everyone concerned.

Yet for all their claims to scientific objectivity, the Gilded Age nerve doctors were no more able to see beyond their narrow class interest and the ideology that informed it than were the asylum doctors. If the observation of poor and working-class asylum patients provided psychiatrists the materiel for their scientific insights, then the same can be said of the neurologist who treated his upper- and middle-class clients on an outpatient basis. The most significant difference was that nerve doctors catered to the prejudices and pretensions of their wealthier and more educated patients, while the asylum physician catered to their own prejudices about mental illness and the actions of the lower classes as they were observed in an institutional setting. Many physicians in both arenas, moreover, subscribed to the theory of degeneration, and wove it into their explanatory narratives. In the world of psychiatry, for example, degeneration of mind led to degeneration of the will, and hence, of morality. Human depravity, brain lesions, and possibly even a bad environment might have contributed to this condition. For some neurologists like Spitzka, for example, aberrant mental and criminal behaviors were considered congenital conditions caused by the inheritance of structural or functional degeneration that led, in turn, to an assortment of behaviors for which the individual was not to be held personally responsible.

These distinctions would have major consequences when it came to the diagnosis, etiology, and treatment of "corrupted sexual feelings." As opposed to the traditional psychiatrist-alienist who considered this condition a symptom of a degenerative disease that inevitably led to madness and institutionalization, the modern nerve doctor transformed it into the symptom of a degenerative condition over which the individual had no control and that should, therefore, be rightly treated on an outpatient basis. As corrupted sexual feelings were ultimately caused by the strains and stresses of modern civilization, sexual inverts were neither mad nor mentally ill. In fact, just the opposite was true. Many sexual inverts were quite well adjusted, intelligent, and creative, if not overtly neurasthenic. Although the object of their desire was inverted—and thus perverted—as individuals, they were otherwise quite normal and understood that if they were to get around in society, they had to disguise their true feelings. This was hardly the sign of mental illness. In so far as inverted sexual perverts were not to be personally held responsible for their unfortunate condition, blame was assigned elsewhere, most frequently the degenerative effects of modern civilization itself. The implication was that society had somehow gone awry, and that the condition of corrupted sexual feeling was merely a symptom of a more fundamental social pathology. It was within this context that the neurologist sought to discover the origins of this pathology and possibly find a remedy so that the national ideology of exceptionalism, essentialism, and good character would survive and the nation would not decline into a miasma of degeneration.

Yet in spite of this general attitude, the study of sexual inversion remained hostage to the debates between psychiatry and neurology over authority, legitimacy, and scientific method. Each field borrowed easily from the other in an attempt to develop the most comprehensive and scientific theory available to explain the etiology of this "new" disease. All parties looked far and wide for explanations, turning first to Europe where the disease had been initially diagnosed, then to the situation at home, where the disease was beginning to increase in alarming proportions. The physician's response ran the entire gamut from a naturally occurring behavior among the barbarians and savages in their midst, to the degenerative madness of the lower classes, and to the degenerative effects of neurasthenia within the higher social orders of an advanced civilization. Not once in any of these debates was same-sex sexual attraction considered a normal variation of human sexual behavior; its pathology was simply assumed. But the question remained: what were the origins of this pathology, or deviation from the essential norm of male and female attraction? As psychiatry's popularity waned in the last years of the nineteenth century, neurology stepped forward and provided the most scientific analyses available, most often derived from the insights of their colleagues in Germany and Austria.

Chapter 7
The German Discovery of the Homosexual

Congenital contrary sexual instinct occurs only in predisposed (tainted) individuals, as a partial manifestation of a defect evidenced by anatomical or functional abnormalities, or both . . . The majority of Urnings are in a painful situation. On the one hand, there is an impulse toward persons of their own sex that is abnormally intense, the satisfaction of which has a good effect, and is natural to them; on the other, is public sentiment which stigmatizes their acts, and the law which threatens them with punishment. Before them lies mental despair,—even insanity and suicide,—at the very least, nervous disease; behind them, shame, loss of position, etc. It cannot be doubted that, under these circumstances, states of necessity and compulsion may be created by the unfortunate natural disposition and constitution. Society and the law should understand these facts. The former must pity, and not despise, such unfortunates; the latter must cease to punish them,—at least, while they remain within the limits which are set for the activity of their sexual instinct.[1]

The medicalization of same-sex attraction first took place within the neuro-psychiatric community of Berlin on the eve of German Unification. In 1869, Karl Westphal (1833–1890), a professor of neuro-psychiatry at the Charite Hospital of Berlin University, wrote an article for the journal *Archiv für Psychiatrie und Nervenkrankheiten* in which he addressed two cases. The first one concerned a woman who dressed as a boy and was attracted to women, while the other case dealt with a man who dressed and acted as a woman. The term he used to describe the unusual behavior he observed was *conträre Sexualempfindung*, or contrary sexual feeling, the origins of which he believed were congenital. Westphal argued this condition was usually pathological, and should be the concern of the physician rather than the court, where victims of this phenomenon traditionally found themselves.[2]

In coming to this limited diagnosis, Westphal was influenced by the writings of Karl Heinrich Ulrichs (1825–1895), a self-proclaimed lover of men and the first major figure in the nineteenth-century German homophile movement. Between 1864 and 1871, the Kingdom of Prussia under the leadership of Otto von Bismarck unified the German states of Central Europe. One of those states was the Kingdom of Hanover, Ulrichs' home. Hanover, unlike Prussia, had no laws that regulated consensual sex among adults and thus sex between males was legal. When the German Empire was pronounced on January 17, 1871, a new constitution had to be drafted, and Ulrichs was determined that it not include paragraph 143 of the Prussian penal code that criminalized sex between members of the same sex. Between 1864 and 1880, Ulrichs wrote twelve tracts known as the *Riddle of "Man-Manly" Love* in which his argument for the biological innateness of same-sex attraction was put forward. It was his belief that if lawmakers understood that same-sex attraction was as natural and normal as opposite-sex attraction, they would be more inclined to reject paragraph 143 outright.

According to Ulrichs, it was a well-known fact that there are men who are attracted to other males as other men are attracted to females. Ulrichs labeled these men "Urnings,"

> 1) It is a fact that there are individuals among us whose body is built like a male, and at the same time, whose sexual drive is directed toward men, who are sexually not aroused by women, i.e., are horrified by any sexual contact with women.
> 2) I have termed these individuals Urnings . . .[3]

Furthermore, and contrary to what some may have believed, the condition of the Urning was inborn,

> There is a class of born Urnings, a class of individuals who are born with the sexual drive of women and who have male bodies. They are a variety of man whose Uranina love is congenital.
> By congenital, is meant sexual, organic, and mental inheritance, not an inherited disease and not such inheritances as pyromania, kleptomania, and alcoholism, but rather an inheritance such as Dionings [heterosexuals] receive in their drives toward women and vice versa.[4]

Because Urning love is congenital, it is natural, and to punish it would be absurd,

> The infamy of the prosecution of Urnings is cruel, unjust and senseless . . . This persecution is as senseless as—if you will allow the comparison—punishing hens for laying eggs instead of chicks or cows for bearing calves instead of laying eggs.

The present-day persecution of man-manly love is just as foolish as the persecution of heresy and witchcraft.[5]

Richard von Krafft-Ebing (1840–1902), a Viennese neurologist who would become the most significant medical researcher of same-sex attraction by the end of the century, was another well-known physician Ulrichs enlisted in his struggle to have the state decriminalize same-sex sexual activity. Already in the 1860s, Krafft-Ebing had written about the need for scientific investigation into sexual behaviors that had traditionally been the purview of the courts. In 1867, after Ulrichs had become aware of this research, he sent him some of his own publications hoping they could add additional insights into same-sex behaviors. They did, and in a letter to Ulrichs some years later, Krafft-Ebing acknowledged his indebtedness:

> The study of your writing on love between men interested me in the highest degree... since you... for the first time spoke openly about these matters. From that day on, when—I believe it was in 1866—you sent me your writing, I have devoted my full attention to this phenomenon which at the time was as puzzling to me as it was interesting: it was the knowledge of your writings alone which led to my studies in this highly important field.[6]

Ulrichs was not able to have the offensive section of the Prussian penal code deleted, although other individuals, specifically the Austro-Hungarian writer Karl Maria Kertbeny who is credited with inventing the word homosexual in 1869,[7] worked very hard and quite publicly to that end. Krafft-Ebing, on the other hand, succeeded in moving homosexuality out of the shadows of vice and into the light of science and medicine.

Born in Mannheim, on August 14, 1840, Krafft-Ebing grew up in Heidelberg, and began his studies in psychiatry and neurology in the early 1860s at the Illenau asylum in Baden. In 1864, he relocated to Berlin where for the next several years he was an advisor on psychotic abnormalities to the municipal court, and in 1872 he was appointed professor of neuro-psychiatry at the University of Strasbourg. A year later, he resigned and moved to Graz, Austria, where he directed the Sanitarium Marigrumin and became a professor of psychiatry at Graz University. During this period of his career Krafft-Ebing did research into sexual abnormalities, and developed an interest in Auguste Morel's theories of degeneration that he thought were verified by the behaviors of the asylum's inmates, prompting him to write in his 1879 text,

Lehrbuch der Psychiatrie,

> [In degenerates] it is specially frequent for sexual functioning to be abnormal, in so far as there is either no sexual drive at all, or it is abnormally strong, manifesting itself explosively and seeking satisfaction impulsively, or abnormally early, stirring already in early childhood and leading to masturbation. Or it may appear perversely, meaning that the kind of satisfaction is not oriented to reproduction.[8]

In 1886 the first German edition of his *Psychopathia Sexualis with Especial Reference to the Antipathetic Sexual Instinct: A Medico-Forensic Study*, was published. More than a compendium of sexology, Krafft-Ebing's book was also a summation of years of personal research into the nonconforming sexual behaviors of inmates and walk-in patients. The original intent was to provide courts with the most up-to-date scientific information about the "psychopathology" of sexual behaviors so that they might make intelligent, informed, and rational decisions about the disposition of sexual criminals, for as he noted in the preface to the 1892 English translation of *Psychopathia Sexualis*:

> The purpose of this treatise is a description of the pathological manifestations of the sexual life and an attempt to refer them to their underlying conditions . . . The importance of the subject for the welfare of society, especially forensically, demands, however, that it should be examined scientifically. Only he who, as a medico-legal expert, has been in a position where he has been compelled to pass judgment upon his fellow-men, where life, freedom, and honor were at stake, and realized painfully the incompleteness of our knowledge concerning the pathology of the sexual life, can fully understand the significance of an attempt to gain definite views concerning it. Even at the present time, in the domain of sexual criminality, the most erroneous opinions are expressed and the most unjust sentences pronounced, influencing laws and public opinion.[9]

The end result was an exhaustive study that soon became the standard reference tool for alienists and neurologists in Europe and the United States who were concerned with the subject of aberrations of the sexual "instinct."

The Sexual Instinct

By the late nineteenth century, most natural scientists and physicians assumed that much animal and human behavior was the product of inborn instincts or "drives" over which the individual had little or no control. Although the concept was not new, it was given a certain scientific legitimacy in the eighteenth century by H. S. Reimarus in his studies of animal behaviors and then refined by Charles Darwin throughout his career. By the end of the century, scientists on both sides of the Atlantic believed they had made significant discoveries into the nature and origins of instincts, which could help explain human and animal behavior alike.[10] One of the most obvious and important instincts was the sex instinct, which drove species to propagate by means of sexual reproduction, the lack of which would lead to extinction. By this standard, any form of non-procreative sex was a perversion of the sex instinct because it would not lead to reproduction and the survival of the species. Christian natural law as developed by Thomas Aquinas and applied to sexuality was now reinvented as a scientific theory of instinctual and essential drives, the thwarting of which was a perversion of the biological ends for which the reproductive organs had evolved.

For Krafft-Ebing, this meant that all human sexual behaviors that fell short of the propagation of the species were aberrations of the sexual instinct. As a trained neurologist, he made it his life's work to discover how such perversions arose and rectify them because if left unattended, they put humanity at risk. Unlike other inborn human drives, the sexual drive when properly expressed not only propagated the species, it was also channeled to create the cornerstone upon which true love, beauty, and morality rested:

> The propagation of the human species is not committed to accident or to the caprice of the individual, but made secure in a natural instinct, which, with all-conquering force and might, demands fulfillment. In the gratification of this natural impulse are found not only sensual pleasure and sources of physical well-being, but also higher feelings of satisfaction in perpetuating the single, perishable existence, by the transmission of mental and physical attributes to a new being. In coarse, sensual love, in the lustful impulse to satisfy this natural instinct, man stands on a level with the animal; but it is given to him to raise himself to a height where this natural instinct no longer makes him a slave: higher, noble feelings are awakened, which, notwithstanding their sensual origin, expand into a world of beauty, sublimity, and morality.[11]

Krafft-Ebing also believed that sexuality was the most powerful factor in social life. If properly employed according to its true nature and essence, it led to the exertion of strength, the acquisition of property, the foundation of the home, and the awakening of altruism, first toward the beloved, then the children, and ultimately, to humanity itself. The downside, however, was the ability of the sex instinct to be employed contrary to its true purpose, and degenerate into powerful passions and gross vice to the overall detriment of civilization and morality. Control of the sex instinct was therefore necessary, and that was only accomplished in the more highly evolved Christian cultures of the West, where the equality of a "bond of love" between man and woman had been elevated to a "religio-moral institution." Savages and primitives, who were found in Australia, the Philippines, or in Polynesia, simply held females in common and used them for their own lustful purposes, thus perverting the natural end of the sex instinct. This was also the case with Islam, which according to Krafft-Ebing had kept a woman from any participation in public life and turned her into a "means of sensual gratification and procreation; while, on the other hand, the virtues and capabilities of the Christian woman, as housewife, educator of children, and equal companion of man, have been allowed to unfold in all their beauty."[12]

Although Krafft-Ebing placed great emphasis on Christianity to help control the sex instinct, and was convinced that Europe had "progressed" over the centuries from its own barbarous and decadent past, he was worried that as modern cities increased demands upon the nervous system, decadence, sensuality, and effeminacy would result and undermine the "morality and purity" of family life. Under these new circumstances, "real love" could not exist, and the natural sex-instinct of man to woman and woman to man would be perverted into love that was not genuine, thus stretching further the bonds that held society and civilization together. This condition was exacerbated by what Krafft-Ebing believed was the less intense sexual appetite of the female who if not "normally developed mentally and well bred," would turn the whole world into a brothel in which marriage and family would be impossible.[13]

Yet for all his concerns, Krafft-Ebing was no moral reformer. He remained a neurologist dedicated to the study of the aberrations of the sexual instinct in order to shed light upon their origins so that the courts would have access to the most up-to-date information possible before rendering judgment over those who had committed sexual crimes. Krafft-Ebing argued that sexual pathologies were caused by stress upon the central nervous system, an unfortunate side effect of civilization. In some instances, nervous stress upon individuals in past generations had been so great that it led to functional degeneration that was inherited by successive generations culminating in, among other things, a degenerate, congenital perversion of the sexual instinct. Of all the sexual perversions that Krafft-Ebing believed were derived from degeneration, male "congenital" same-sex attraction was one of the most interesting because in his mind—similar to the position of Ulrichs and Kertbeny—this type was improperly singled out for special treatment by the laws of Germany. Degenerates who committed abnormal sex acts should be the responsibility of the medical community while delinquents who committed immoral sex acts were the responsibility of the courts. Fairness and justice required that each be treated differently, otherwise the state ran the risk of causing unnecessary injury to society and possibly a loss of faith in the institution of law itself. This was especially true with congenital perverts who were otherwise perfectly responsible people but for their reversed sexuality. Under the legal regime of the period, these individuals had to remain either celibate or secretive because if they were discovered, they were subjected to a host of legal and social sanctions that often led one to madness or suicide. If it could be medically demonstrated that some forms of same-sex attraction were involuntary, then those so afflicted could be placed into the hands of the physician.

In order to prove his point, Krafft-Ebing read the then current literature on the subject, and interviewed hundreds of individuals who had engaged in same-sex sexual activities. He then classified those interviewed according to whether or not he felt their aberrant sexual behavior was "congenital" or "acquired," distinctions that correspond with the modern concepts of "nature" versus "nurture." For the most part, diagnoses were predicated upon the patient's own insights, thus the distinctions that Krafft-Ebing drew were less the result of medical research than the consequence of an individual's self-assertion. Be that as it may, these categories were almost universally adopted, and remain the standard models for any discussion about the origins of homosexuality in use to this day under the rubrics "nature" or "nurture."

Accordingly, the acquired sexual perversion of same-sex attraction was the result of bad habits or influences that had the cumulative effect of turning an individual away from normal sexual behavior, "develops upon a sexuality the beginnings of which was normal, as a result of very definite injurious influences, and thus appears as an acquired anomal ... Careful examination of the so-called acquired cases makes it probable that the predisposition also present here consists of a latent homo-sexuality, or at least bi-sexuality, which, for its manifestation, requires the influence of accidental exciting causes to rouse it from its slumber."[14] Most frequently, Krafft-Ebing associated this condition with males in prisons or asylums, on ships, in boarding schools, and in the military. With women, this was often the case when they were in asylums or at boarding schools. Gratification was generally temporary and "there is an immediate return to normal sexual intercourse as soon as obstacles to it are removed."[15] Nevertheless, some individuals apparently resisted a return to normal sexuality because of hereditary "taint" or neurasthenia "induced by masturbation, abstinence or otherwise" in which case the acquired habit was transformed into a contrary sexual instinct that ranged from a temporary and "simple reversal of sexual feeling" to the "delusion of a transformation of sex . . . resulting in a mental disease—paranoia."[16]

Congenital homosexuality, on the other hand, was a biological perversion of the sexual instinct the origins of which were to be found in an "abnormal psycho-sexual constitution" that Krafft-Ebing believed was clinically a "functional sign of degeneration" and a partial manifestation of a "neuro-psychopathic state, in most cases hereditary."[17] Individuals so afflicted developed the sexual apparatus appropriate for their sex but were physically and mentally attracted to members of their own sex with greater or lesser degrees of attraction. Not unlike Alfred Kinsey sixty years later, Krafft-Ebing developed a sliding scale of homosexual desire, from limited homosexual attraction, to predominant attraction, to "the entire mental existence . . . altered to correspond with the abnormal sexual instinct," and finally to a literal transformation such that "the form of the body approaches that which corresponds to the abnormal sexual instinct," without, however, becoming a "hermaphrodite."[18]

While these four categories were meant to be inclusive of all forms of congenital homosexual behavior, Krafft-Ebing adopted Ulrichs' nomenclature and labeled those who were exclusively homosexual "Urnings," and the rest he referred to as "psycho-sexual hermaphrodites." Although the latter engaged in sexual activity with members of their own sex, their "character and mental personality" were not "seriously" affected by such activity because somewhere inside of them there existed a residuum of heterosexuality, even if very faint and latent. Urnings, on the other hand, were "ab origine" inclined to persons of the same sex exclusively such that their love of one another was the exact opposite of the natural sexual instinct. If heterosexual love felt normal and natural for a man and a woman, then, as Krafft-Ebing noted, Urning love also felt normal and natural and was not in any manner considered by those involved as a perversion. And just as a normal man wanted beautiful and feminine women, Urnings sought out handsome, masculine men.

Nevertheless, Krafft-Ebing considered Urning love to have been a caricature of real love, all the more so since he believed Urning lovers exaggerated their love for each other through excess passion and emotion. And because any form of congenital homosexuality was a "functional sign of degeneration" with neuropathic "taint," other "peculiarities" were present even in the most "normal." Among those peculiarities that Krafft-Ebing interpreted as manifestations of a "taint" were the early onset of sexual activity; an exaggeration and exhalation of "psychical" love between members of the same sex; "additional" [unstated] functional and anatomical evidence of degeneration; neuroses, such as hysteria, neurasthenia, and "epileptoid states"; "psychical" anomalies described as brilliant endowments in art, music, or poetry, possibly leading to "pronounced conditions of mental degeneration (dementia, moral insanity)"; and finally, a family history of neuroses, psychoses, and degeneration. Yet in spite of these debilitating conditions, Krafft-Ebing also noted that most of the patients he treated were happy in their perversion and "unhappy only in so far as social and legal barriers stand in the way of the satisfaction of their instinct toward their own sex."[19]

Neurasthenia, neuropathic taint, and degeneration were actually the indirect causes of homosexuality, and as a neurologist, Krafft-Ebing was quite interested in the specific neurological origins of this condition. In his research, he initially borrowed from Ulrichs and others who suggested the immediate biological cause of homosexuality was a "disturbance of cerebral organization" resulting in the pathological condition of a female brain in the body of a person with male sexual glands. Upon further reflection, however, Krafft-Ebing realized he had a mystery on his hands. Although he was quick to acknowledge the existence of inborn homosexuality, he was unable to locate its specific biological origins, which prompted him to write, "This constitution, as far as its anatomical and functional foundation is concerned, is absolutely unknown."[20] This did not stop him from speculating about the impact of nervous stress on psychosexual development, however, or from expounding upon physical degeneration as necessary and sufficient ancillary causes, but he was never able to find any physical abnormalities that would explain the condition.

Krafft-Ebing was certainly not the only person in Europe during the latter part of the nineteenth century to study homosexuality "scientifically." To be sure, other physicians in Austria, England, France, Spain, Italy, Germany, and Russia invested much time and effort in an attempt to understand the "new" phenomenon. As a medical condition, cases of homosexuality increased exponentially between 1880 and 1900, and no less than fifty physicians across the continent conducted research. American physicians had ample opportunity to learn about this research, either through their education in the European medical schools, or by means of the new medical journals that were published during the period. It was not uncommon for articles by German, Italian, or French doctors to be translated and reprinted in American journals, and in this manner, anyone interested was able to keep up on the latest theories of homosexuality. But the principal European physician Americans were familiar with was Richard von Krafft-Ebing, if for no other reason than his book was the first European study to come out in English translation in 1892.

Other European physicians wrote books or articles that were translated in leading journals, such as the *Journal of Mental and Nervous Diseases*, and Americans would themselves begin to publish articles specifically addressing homosexuality in increasing numbers after 1885; yet for most U.S. physicians, Krafft-Ebing was the most important initial authority on the subject. He established a medical foundation upon which a generation of American neurologists would build and expand as they were called upon to explain and then treat the homosexual person. Unfortunately, much of what Krafft-Ebing understood about the sexual instinct, sex, love, and morality was ultimately derived less from good science than the blinding prejudices of his economic, religious, and social peers. When he was done, Krafft-Ebing had become a champion for the decriminalization of homosexuality even as he reduced the homosexual to a state of physical and moral degeneracy, conditions that were to resonate in the United States during the Gilded Age. By the time Krafft-Ebing renounced degeneracy in 1901, it was of little consequence to most American neurologists who by that time had expanded upon Krafft-Ebing's earlier theories, as a consequence of which American homosexuals remained physical and moral degenerates for decades to come.

Chapter 8
American Physicians Discover the Homosexual

The sexual instinct is one of the strongest forces for good and for evil. Its good effects are seen in happy family life, and a house full of healthy and creditable children. Its ill effects! Whatever things are done by men and women that are incomprehensibly foolish or criminal, there we may predicate that an aberrant or unsatisfied sexual feeling lies at the bottom of the mischief.[1]

In 1867, the New York based *Quarterly Journal of Psychological Medicine and Medical Jurisprudence* reprinted an article from the *London Medical Times and Gazette* entitled "Aberrations of the Sexual Instinct." This was the first of what would become a flood of articles published in the United States over the next two decades that dealt "scientifically" with the delicate subject of abnormal sexual behavior. While this article did not directly discuss the issue of same-sex attraction, it did inquire into the purpose of the sexual "instinct," and concluded that according to Christian "natural history" and "common sense," this instinct was properly expressed in the marriage union, the purpose of which was the procreation and education of children, the avoidance of "incontinence," and the mutual assistance of the marriage partners. If these three specific activities were not "fulfilled," then one suffered from aberrations of the sexual instinct that were manifested in any one of four different fashions: (1) masturbation culminating in hysteria, hypochondria, and "dark crimes which are not to be named of by Christian men"; (2) sexual intercourse without pregnancy; (3) illegitimacy; (4) miscellaneous behaviors that "thwart the natural ends" of the sex instinct—among this last category were free love, celibacy, polygamy associated with the Mormon Church and the followers of John Humphrey Noyes; and (5) "Androgynism," or "the intrusion of one sex into the other's province" such as was found when women demanded "admission to all offices and dignities . . . and the privilege of doing all that man does" and that aimed at occupations incompatible with the duties of maternity and thus "smothered" the "maidenly instincts."[2]

Here was a classic example of essentialism as applied to sex and gender, as well as a not too subtle reminder that it was unwise for the so-called New Woman to aggressively cross the gender boundaries that separated the world of men from the world of women. Although same-gender attraction is alluded to, it is hidden beneath a layer of Christian unmentionables that would take another fourteen years to unwrap and when it was, it was done by none other than the physician Edward Spitzka.

The Americans are Introduced to Krafft-Ebing

Similar to his Austrian counterpart Richard von Krafft-Ebing, Spitzka was deeply concerned about the welfare of his patients and was quite sensitive to their plight. His goal was to help them become well and return to society healed, not to remain trapped in some "brick hell hole strapped to a bed." In this sense, Spitzka was a humanitarian and in comparison to the caretakers of the asylum system, quite a progressive. Nevertheless, Spitzka's progressive and humanitarian impulses were constrained by the economic and essentialist biases of his era and class. It is thus no surprise that the first article in the United States to mention the specific issue of *conträre Sexualempfindung* was in fact a letter-to-the-editor of the *New York Medical Record* on March 28, 1881, by Spitzka.[3] This short letter was written in response to a question posed in an article of the previous week on cross-dressing in the same journal. Entitled "Gynomania," this article appeared in the March 19 edition and discussed the case of a young married man who was definitively attracted to women, but who also liked to dress up in women's clothes and "walk the city streets and even attend church, wearing his new black silk dress caught up on one side as to expose a white fluted skirt, beneath which his high-heeled French boots were visible." Confused as to the etiology of this condition, the author, a certain Dr. H., asked in his conclusion, "Have any of your readers had a similar case within their experience?"[4]

In his letter to the editor the following week, Spitzka responded in the affirmative, and explained that such behavior as outlined in the article "Gynomania" was not frequent, but neither was it uncommon and that such a condition had been researched by French and German "alienists." In particular, Spitzka explained that Westphal, under the label "*Contraere Sexualempfindung* [sic]," and the neurologist Krafft-Ebing had done much research on similar cases and had determined that men who felt inclined to act as women even during the "normally performed sexual act" suffered from the symptoms of a "degenerative psychosis." There were, Spitzka continued, approximately twenty cases of this perversion described in the German periodicals, but in all probability, a larger number existed. Spitzka then concluded his letter by stating that he had three patients who exhibited similar symptoms and that a "careful search should be made in cases of this kind for a hereditary history, and for anomalies in the offspring."[5]

At this point in his career, Spitzka had not yet made the distinction between same-sex sexual attraction and the behaviors of men that crossed gender lines, such as a man dressing as a woman, but whose sexuality was directed toward women. All behaviors that crossed established gender lines were conflated into the sexual perversion of contrary sexual feeling even though his German and Austrian colleagues, when they used that term in the early 1880s, employed it more often than not to describe same-sex sexual attraction, irrespective of other sexual perversions or of clothing. But at this early date, the term was still fluid enough to encompass almost any form of behavior that violated the strict separation of male and female behaviors in the Victorian and Gilded Age.

In spite of his unfamiliarity with the full reach of Westphal's and Krafft-Ebing's research, it is noteworthy that Spitzka was the first American to take notice of contrary sexual feeling. Shortly after the publication of Spitzka's letter to the *Medical Record*, he published a short article on August 20, 1881, in the *Chicago Medical Review* under the title "A Historical Case of Sexual Perversion." Similar in tone to the "Gynomania" article of March, Spitzka described the cross-dressing habits of New York's colonial governor, Lord Cornbury, as a sexual perversion in which the Governor manifested a degenerative form of mental illness that led to contrary sexual "sensation." This was a phenomenon in which "a male finds himself drawn to males, the female to females, and either feels himself or herself as if a person of the opposite sex." Although there was no evidence that Cornbury was attracted to men, his cross-dressing was sufficient in itself to be construed as a degenerative perversion. Citing Krafft-Ebing, Spitzka further explained that sexual perversions were divided into four specific categories in which (1) "sexual feeling is altogether absent," (2) "sexual feeling is greatly exhaled," (3) sexual feeling appears normal at an abnormal time of life, and (4) "it is simply perverted, this is, not of such a character as to lead to the preservation and increase of the species."[6]

For the second time within the space of a few months, Spitzka had made reference to Krafft-Ebing and employed his theory of perversion and degeneracy to explain this strange new condition. Unlike the "false" theories of the asylum physicians based on slipshod observation, Spitzka believed he had relied upon correct theories of the origins of mental illness based on the best and most modern neurological research conducted by the Germans and the Austrians in their university clinics. Thus, when Krafft-Ebing wrote about the etiology of contrary sexual feeling, Spitzka could accept his finding with little or no disagreement because he knew it had been derived from meticulous research in a scientific environment by a fully trained Austrian neurologist and M.D. and was consistent with his own belief in the existence of hereditary taint.

American neurologists across the country were further exposed to Krafft-Ebing's theories of contrary sexual feeling in early 1882 when the *American Journal of Neurology and Psychiatry* reviewed his work in the section "Progress in Neurology." Although the author of this unsigned piece found the topic of sexual perversion "disgusting," it was still of "anthropological, ethnological and medico-legal" importance and therefore an appropriate subject for scientific research. As of 1882 when the article was published, the author was aware of only seventeen cases of contrary sexual feeling, the bulk of which had been studied by Krafft-Ebing. Because of his great scientific knowledge of the subject, this Austrian neurologist had the greatest insight into the etiology of that sexual perversion, and indeed had "established the unquestionably morbid character of the perversion in a number of cases by calling attention to the coexisting somatic evidences of degeneration." Three of Krafft-Ebing's more recent cases were briefly discussed. The first dealt with a nobleman who had an insane father, and suffered from retarded "mental and physical development." The patient manifested feminine tendencies, avoided females, and became sexually aroused to the point of orgasm by embracing or grasping the hand of a male. The second case was that of a doctor of philosophy who "indulged" in males and suffered from "*originäre Verrücktheit*," or original "monomania."[7] This was a clinical form of mental illness, originally diagnosed by the Germans among whom were Westphal in Berlin and Krafft-Ebing in Vienna, characterized by a "neuropathic" constitution and a hereditary predisposition to mental disturbance. Krafft-Ebing defined the condition as:

> an essential or primary disease . . . almost wholly an affection of a burdened brain . . . characterized by delusions with an absence of an emotional basis, and or conscious intellection of their origin. It is of

a deep fixed character, not terminating in confusion or dementia, but leaves the apparatus of logical thought intact . . . The burdening shows itself largely in inherited taint or if acquired burdening from infantile brain disease."[8]

It was this diagnosis that was applied by Spitzka to Guiteau in his December 1881 testimony. The third case was that of a man who dressed as a woman, and while he did not demonstrate an inheritable taint, he was nevertheless incurable in his perversity and suffered from a nervous defect that left him unable to perform "normal sexual functions." The author then summed up the observations on all seventeen cases, and noted that in thirteen, hereditary taint was present "in the shape of insanity in the ancestry"; in three, the patients were "neurotic and presented positive insane manifestations"; and in one, no cause was determined. The article concluded with a reiteration of Krafft-Ebing's belief that except in cases of child molestation or "paederasty," no laws should be enacted against those suffering from contrary sexual feeling because individuals so afflicted should be allowed to "follow their tendencies to any extent not involving an injury to the rights of others or public scandal."[9] Krafft-Ebing made the distinction between contrary sexual feeling and "paederasty" or anal intercourse between men, on the basis of his conversations with Urnings who claimed that such behavior was unseemly, disgusting, immoral, and totally foreign to their nature. Those who did engage in it were characterized as even more perverted than Urnings whose sensitivities were often shocked by the mere suggestion that they engaged in this form of sexual activity.

Krafft-Ebing was by now well on his way to becoming the leading American source on all things related to contrary sexual feeling. His expertise was given additional legitimacy in the psychiatric community when G. Adler Blumer, an assistant physician at the New York State Lunatic Asylum, wrote the article "A Case of Perverted Sexual Instinct" in the July 1882 edition of the *American Journal of Insanity*. Citing the contributions of Krafft-Ebing to the study of origins of congenital perversions of the sexual instinct, Blumer related the story of a young walk-in patient who suffered from bouts of jealousy over his rejection by a potential male suitor and who by his own word never engaged in the "detestable" act of pederasty.[10] In spite of the man's intelligence, good manners, and high social standing, he had not been able to overcome his condition, leading Blumer to conclude that its origins were consistent with Krafft-Ebing's diagnosis of neuropathic "taint" and should not be a matter for the courts, especially as he was not involved in anal intercourse.

Blumer's diagnosis, while tentative, set the stage for further research and diagnoses.

Krafft-Ebing's name surfaced again shortly thereafter when "The Disease of the Scythians (Morbus Feminarum) and certain Analogous Conditions" by William A. Hammond was published in the August 1882 edition of the *American Journal of Neurology and Psychiatry*. This article was a reprint of a June 23 speech that Hammond had given before the American Neurological Association in which a "peculiar disease" of physical demasculinization among the male inhabitants of the Caucuses was described. Certain men, who Hammond labeled Scythians, suffered from a disease that made them lose the physiological and moral attributes of men and assume the "manners, customs, and occupations of the female sex." Due to long hours of horseback riding, the reproductive organs of these individuals atrophied to the point that they lost the ability for sexual intercourse, forcing them to "fly from the society of men" and seek the company of women where they might "acquire the mental characteristics and instincts of the female sex."[11]

Hammond recounted an analogous situation he had personally experienced as a young medical officer in 1851 when he was stationed in New Mexico at a Pueblo Indian village called Laguna. Not long after he had arrived, he discovered that there were certain males who had mysteriously changed into females and "assumed the garb of women, lived with women, and followed their occupations." These individuals were called *mujerado* or "womanish" by the Indians, and were the subject of much "reserve and mystery." Hammond was able to see one of these individuals and gave him a physical, during which time he discovered that the *mujerado* had large breasts, which the subject said he used to nurse infants, as well as atrophied sexual organs induced by excessive horseback riding, similar to the Scythians. Unlike the Scythians, however, the *mujerado* was used as a ceremonial sex object even though he was impotent, and became a "passive" pederast during "orgiastic" ceremonies held in the spring of each year. Individuals were chosen for the role of *mujerado* based on how masculine they were, and only through a long process of induced demasculinization forced upon them "by the power of tradition, custom, and public opinion" was the transformation completed. Because of this practice and of the sexual impotence that resulted, Hammond concluded that the *mujerado* was not of the same nature as were the cases of contrary sexual feeling described by Krafft-Ebing and others.

For American neurologists at least, the concept of contrary sexual feeling had now been clarified by reference to what it was not, and it was not a condition of sexual impotence, ritual demasculinization, depravity, or the absence of the ability and desire to have sex. Hammond's remarks commanded a great deal of respect precisely because he was considered a significant figure in American neurology and had been President Lincoln's Surgeon General during the Civil War. Hammond's authority as a neurologist was based on his academic success (he was a founder of the New York Post Graduate Medical School) as well as his important and original research into neurological symptomatology, his voluminous publishing record, and his fame as founder of the American Neurological Association and later as its president.

The First American Cases

In October, 1882, an unsigned review of Krafft-Ebing's latest three European cases appeared in the *Alienist and Neurologist* that had the effect of clarifying even further the concept of contrary sexual feeling. All three studies dealt with upper-class white males who were sexually attracted to other men, two of whom were described as thoroughly masculine looking, while one was described as effeminate. The essay concluded with a summary of the evidence gathered from the studies of the known cases to date, and that evidence, the author believed, established a type of individual who was both attracted to a member of the same sex and who behaved in a manner consistent with the opposite sex:

> The sufferers invariably feel towards their own sex as a normally constituted person feels towards the opposite sex, whilst, towards the opposite sex they feel either indifference or else a positive aversion. Their tastes, pursuits, &c., are those of the opposite sex to that to which they belong anatomically.[12]

Here was arguably the first American description, based on Krafft-Ebing's, of clinical contrary sexual instinct in which an individual had specifically expressed a sexual desire for a member of the same sex. From this point on, contrary sexual instinct was a congenital "perverted sexual impulse" in which the individual was sexually attracted toward a person of the same sex as opposites were attracted to each other, and who, in all probability, often suffered from a sexual role inversion whereby the male took on the social attributes of a female, and the female took on all the social attributes of a male. The cause of this condition was taken directly from Krafft-Ebing's research, and ascribed to functional degeneration in persons of a "hereditary predisposition."

Between 1883 and 1889, there were no less than a dozen scientific articles that appeared in American journals in which contrary sexual instinct was discussed. In general, several themes developed that informed the discussion on homosexuality for the next several years, the most consistent of which centered around clinical examples of contrary sexual instinct; its causes and origins; the personal responsibility of the victim for contrary sexual activity; and the extent and completeness of the instinct reversal.

The majority of the examples of contrary sexual instinct continued to be derived from the case studies of the Europeans, especially Richard von Krafft-Ebing, but there were others as well who were cited by the Americans, for example the Germans Westphal, Schmincke, Scholz, and Gock; the Italian Tamassia; and the French alienists Charcot and Magnan. For the most part, contrary sexual instinct was conceptualized as a unique subset of the sexual perversions, that wide ranging catch-all phrase that by now implied virtually any non-procreative sexual gratification or nongender conforming behaviors This included cross-dressing, effeminacy; "excessive" masturbation (once a week or more, although for some, any masturbation at all); lack of sexual desire; "excessive" heterosexual intercourse; heterosexual fellatio and cunnilingus; fetishes (shoes, slippers, dresses, hair); anal intercourse between men and women; masochism with a member of the opposite sex; and, of course, contrary sexual instinct. Because Krafft-Ebing was the authority in these matters, there developed a general consensus regarding the characteristics of contrary sexual instinct regardless of the manner one chose to express this instinct, and according to the case studies of the Europeans, it took on as many different and varied expressions as could be found among opposite sex "sexual perversions." The only consistent characteristic was that the object of desire had to be of the same sex. What was now different was that the American researchers investigated American examples of contrary sexual instinct for an American audience, the express purpose of which was to help American medical doctors recognize this novel condition as it revealed itself in the United States, among a population that suffered from an excess of neurasthenia. How the American medical community would eventually interpret their findings would also be different, in so far as they would later attempt to account for the causes of this unique congenital hereditary predisposition within the context of American exceptionalism.

For the time being, however, American doctors satisfied themselves with simply discovering certified examples of the condition, and if it was rare—approximately 17–20 in all of Europe by the Spring of

1883—then only one verifiable case in the United States was reported in the medical literature as of that date. Although it had been discovered in 1880, it was only in 1883 after the Americans had learned from the Europeans the alleged true nature of what they were dealing with, that they could diagnose the condition properly.[13] In the opening paragraphs of their April 1883 article in *The Journal of Nervous and Mental Disease*, Drs. Shaw and Ferris set the tone of their discovery by quoting the German neurologist Griesinger,

> One is led to peculiar considerations of many revolting aberrations which disgust healthy moral feelings, when we hear an honest, cultured man of good social standing, but with a bad hereditary history however, confess that since his eighth year he has experienced a sexual desire towards his own sex, but has never experienced normal, healthy sexual desire.[14]

Thus, in this same issue it could now be reported that back in 1880 the two doctors had observed a true case of contrary sexual instinct based on their new understanding of the term,

> A German [in the United States], aged thirty-five ... Says he is engaged in mercantile business and occupies a good position. For some time past has had an almost uncontrollable desire to embrace men. Fears that some time this horrible morbid desire may overcome him and he will really embrace some of his fellow clerks. When in the presence of men, he is tormented by the constant erections of his penis and a desire to embrace the men.
> ... The distinguishing features of this phenomenon are so clearly analyzed and arranged by Krafft-Ebing, that we cannot refrain from quoting them in conclusion, and thus once more glance over the subject:
> a. Congenital absence of sexual feeling toward the opposite sex, at times, even disgust of sexual intercourse.
> b. This defect occurs in a physically completely differentiated sexual type and normal development of the sexual organs.
> ...
> f. Sexual desire toward the same sex.[15]

This would of course not be the only case, as additional ones were diagnosed on a more frequent basis then written about in medical journals in order to share the new information within the scientific community and to provide a core of knowledge to facilitate future diagnosis. This process was cumulative, and more information was added to the pool as the years progressed. One of the many notable American neurologists who added to this pool was James G. Kiernan, also of Guiteau fame. Kiernan was a prodigious writer who discussed all manner of diseases of the mind from the perspective of heredity that he applied to the ills of society with the zeal of a reformer. Although Kiernan was first and foremost a physician, Kiernan was also concerned with the stability of American civilization in a period of rapid change. As a neurologist, his area of expertise lent itself to medical hygiene and the effects of an unhealthy mind and body upon society. In this regard, he was a forward-looking medical reformer who sought answers to social decay not in religion but in science and medicine instead. Less concerned overtly with Christian morality than his purity reform peers, he nevertheless understood that if the United States was to be cured of the myriad ills that plagued its urban centers, then medicine would have to dispassionately reveal underlying pathologies. Medical hygiene based upon solid physiological research was thus a prerequisite for overcoming social decay in favor of social advancement. Among his lengthy articles are *"Katatonia"* (1877); *"Psychical Effects of Nerve Stretching"* (1883); *"Syphilis in Its Relations to Progressive Paresis"* (1883); *"Insanity and Cardiac Disease"* (1884); *"Psychological Aspects of the Sexual Appetite"* (1891); *"Psychical Treatment of Congenital Sexual Inversion"* (1894); *"Interaction of Somatic and Psychic Disorder"* (1897); *"Transformation of Heredity"* (1879); *"Responsibility in Sexual Perversion"* (1898); and *"Degeneracy Sigmata as a Basis of Morbid Suspicion"* (1901).[16]

The first two of Kiernan's numerous articles on "sexual perversions" were published in the January and May 1884 editions of the *Detroit Lancet*. In these brief articles, a series reprint of a paper given before the Chicago Medical Society, Kiernan lays out his understanding of "perverted sexual instinct," not in order to shock, he states, but instead to open up the subject to scientific investigation. "The present subject may seem to trench on the prurient, but in medicine the prurient does not exist," since "science like fire purifies everything."[17] After a very brief review of the European and American literature to date, Kiernan summed up his presentation by agreeing that contrary sexual instinct in particular was both morbid and "congenital," but with an added twist. It might be, Kiernan speculated, that this novel sexual instinct was the result of imperfect sexual differentiation and thus a biological "reversion of type," consistent with Charles Darwin's theory of arrested development,

> The original bi-sexuality of the ancestors of the race, shown in the rudimentary female organs of the male, could not fail to occasion functional, if not organic, reversions when mental or physical manifestations were interfered with by disease or congenital defect. The inhibitions on excessive action to accomplish a given purpose, which the race has acquired through centuries of evolution, being removed, the animal in

man springs to the surface. Removal of these inhibitions produces, among other results, sexual perversions...[18]

Kiernan's general argument that the sexual perversions were biological in origin was shared by several prominent American physicians who took up the issue during the 1880s, individuals such as George F. Shrady ("Perverted Sexual Instinct," July 1884[19]); George M. Beard (*Sexual Neurasthenia or Nervous Exhaustion, Its Hygiene, Causes, Symptoms, and Treatment*, 1884[20]); S. V. Clevenger ("The Origin of Sexual Perversions," November 1888[21]); and the neurologist G. Frank Lydston ("Sexual Perversion, Satyriasis and Nymphomania," September 7 and 14, 1889[22]). Over the course of the 1890s, Lydston would become arguably the leading American specialist on the sexual perversion of contrary sexual instinct within the context of "diseases of society."

George Frank Lydston was a most interesting character. Born March 3, 1857, in the gold mining town of Jacksonville, California, as a young boy George was sent to private schools in his home state and in New York. In 1879, he graduated from the Belleview Hospital Medical School of New York, and after a year's internship in the New York Charity Hospital, he found himself a member of the faculty of the College of Physicians and Surgeons in Chicago. There he taught courses in "genitourinary surgery" and became intensely interested in the pathology of crime, the work of Cesare Lombroso, and criminal anthropology, which he also taught at the Chicago Kent School of Law. Concurrent with his academic work, Lydston owned a private practice that was reputed to cater to Chicago's elite, as a consequence of which, it was considered to have been the most lucrative in the city. For most of his career, Lydston was sympathetic to the purity reform movements and in so far as he was interested in eliminating prostitution and in promoting sex hygiene, he was considered a progressive and moral reformer himself. Later, during the Spanish American War, Lydston served as surgeon major to the 2nd Infantry Illinois National Guard, and in World War I, he was an examination physician.

Throughout his career he was a prolific writer of more than one hundred articles and the author of several medical texts, to include *Variocentele and Treatment* (1892); *Social Diseases of the Genito-Urinary Tract, Venereal and Sexual Diseases* (1899, 1904); *Diseases of Society* (1904), a compendium of his past writing on vice and crime; *Sex Hygiene* (1912); and *Impotence and Sterility* (1917). Among his other books are the novels *Over the Hookah* (1896); *A Doctor's Wander Days* (1900); *Poker Jim, Gentleman* (1907); *Trusty 515* (1921); *That Bogey*

Man, the Jew (1921); a play *The Blood of the Fathers* (1912); and the travel guide, *Panama and the Sierras* (1900). In addition to these activities, Lydston founded the Chicago Academy of Medicine, and found time to be active in the AMA, Chicago Medical Society, the American Geological Association, the Society of Colonial Wars, the Masonic Order, and the Veterans' Organization of the Spanish American War. In 1904, he was awarded an honorary degree of law at Kent College, and in 1921, he moved to Los Angeles, California, where he died on March 14, 1923.[23]

Lydston was especially well known as both a Lombrosian criminal anthropologist and a researcher into the body's ductless glands. He is believed to have been just the second surgeon in the world to have successfully transplanted a gland from one person to another, and the only person to have ever transplanted the testicle of a deceased man into his own body, then remove it for research in his lab! As a follower of Lombroso, Lydston strongly believed that criminality had a hereditary basis, and it was within this context that beginning in the late 1880s he studied homosexuality and loosely applied what he understood of Darwin's theory of variation to the origins of sexual perversion,

> Just as we may have variations of physical form, and of mental attributes, in general, so we may have variations and perversions of that intangible entity: sexual affinity... The variations in the methods of sexual gratification—or to attribute it to instinct, of perpetuating the species,—which are presented to the student of natural history, are numerous and striking.[24]

In his mind, the sexual pervert suffered from some sort of natural physical abnormality that was not to be confused with moral perversity, "It is often difficult to draw the line of demarcation between physical and moral perversion. Indeed, the one is so often dependent upon the other that it is doubtful whether it were wise to attempt the distinction in many instances. But this does not affect the cogency of the argument that the sexual pervert is generally a physical aberration—a *lusus naturae*."[25] A major problem for Lydston, however, was his Lamarckian belief that the voluntaristic vice of one bad generation would be inherited by the next, precluding any hope of a viable cure for the offspring. If this situation were to be avoided, one had to prevent the occurrence of vice in the parent generation, otherwise it was too late, and the vice would have turned into a "true constitutional and irradicable vice in the next,"

> It is probable that few bodily attributes are more readily transmitted to posterity than peculiarities of sexual physiology. The offspring of the

abnormally carnal individual is likely to be possessed of the same inordinate sexual appetite that characterizes the parent. The child of vice has within it . . . the germ of vicious impulse, and no purifying influence can save it from following its own inherent inclinations. Men and women who seek variations of the normal method of sexual gratification stamp their nervous systems with a malign influence which in the next generation may present itself as true sexual perversion. Acquired sexual perversion is one generation may be a true constitutional and irradicable vice in the next, and this independent of gross physical aberrations.[26]

Unfortunately, this had happened quite frequently, and in communities all over the United States there existed a "colony of male sexual perverts,"[27] not all of whom necessarily expressed the same types of perversions. Similar to Krafft-Ebing, who he had read, Lydston accepted the distinction between acquired and congenital. With slight modification to Krafft-Ebing's original scheme, Lydston proposed that acquired sexual perversion originated from four general conditions: (1) "Sexual perversion from pregnancy, the menopause, ovarian disease, hysteria, etc."; (2) "Sexual perversion from acquired cerebral disease, with or without recognized insanity"; (3) "Sexual perversion from vice"; and (4) "Sexual perversion from overstimulation of the nerves of sexual sensibility and the receptive sexual centers, incidental to sexual excesses and masturbation." Of congenital "and perhaps hereditary sexual perversion," Lydston developed three typologies: (1) "Sexual perversion without defect of structure of sexual organs"; (2) "Sexual perversion with defect of genital structures, e.g. hermaphroditism"; and (3) "Sexual perversion with obvious defect of cerebral development, e.g. idiocy."[28]

The precise causes of sexual perversion, however, were as elusive for Lydston as they were for Krafft-Ebing, although he did give some credence to Kiernan's theory of reversion to ancestral bisexuality. That, together with natural variations of sexual affinity, might possibly allow for the sexual perversions, of which three general categories existed: (1) an "affinity" for one's own sex; (2) "abnormal methods of gratification"; and (3) bestiality. While Lydston suggested that all three may be either acquired or congenital, it is nevertheless clear from his 1889 articles that he was primarily interested in those sexual perversions in which the individual, usually a male, showed a natural and thus congenital "affinity" for his own sex. To what extent, he wanted to know, was the behavior of this type of person criminal, and if it could be demonstrated that congenital same-sex attraction was normal for those so afflicted, then legal proscriptions might not apply. To the degree that Lydston's ideas moved in this direction, he like Kiernan was part of both the reform and progressive movements that were sweeping America at the time. In some limited instances, perhaps, there were individuals who in spite of themselves were not biologically inclined to behave in a normal manner. For them, the rules of sexual morality were different because their condition was natural, although aberrant. This was a singular departure from the generally conservative approach to sexuality in which the sex drive was considered a gift from God to be used infrequently only for the purposes of reproduction lest too much energy be spent and none left for other activities, such as work or combating neurasthenia.

Theoretical Divergence

Due to the dichotomy between the theories of congenital and acquired same-sex attraction, consensus on the biological roots of homosexuality never existed. The most traditional but least scientifically accepted argument held that same-sex attraction was a sin born of lust, "It is not improbable, however, that some of these [cases of perverted sexual instinct] are rather examples of vicious lust than of pathological perversions."[29] Yet this same author is ambiguous, and within the same article he asserts that while some instances of same-sex behavior are a result of unbridled lust, many, perhaps most, are pathological. It was the job of the physician, therefore, to recognize the distinction and, where possible, pathological perverted sexual instinct should be the province of the physician,

> In conclusion, we believe it to be demonstrated that conditions once considered criminal are really pathological, and come within the province of the physician. We have undertaken, therefore, the disagreeable task of laying some of the facts regarding sexual perversion before our readers. The profession can be trusted to sift the degrading and vicious from what is truly morbid.[30]

Some members of the psychiatric community dissented and considered same-sex attraction a sexual perversion that was strictly a result of a depraved life. Take, for example, the case of Lucy Ann Slater,

> The case of sexual perversion herewith reported, has been under the writer's observation for the past two years and since the development of positive insanity. The early history of her abnormal sexual tendency is incomplete, but from a variety of sources, enough information has been gleaned to afford a brief history of a remarkable life and of a rare form of mental disease.

> Case.—Lucy Ann Slater, alias Rev. Joseph Lobdell was admitted to the Willard Asylum October 12, 1880 . . . Her voice was coarse and her features were masculine. She was dressed in male attire throughout and declared herself to be a man . . . said she was married and had a wife living . . . Her excitement was of an erotic nature and her sexual inclination was perverted. In passing to the ward, she embraced the female attendant in a lewd manner and came near overpowering her before she received assistance. Her conduct on the ward was characterized by the same lascivious conduct, and she made efforts at various times to have sexual intercourse with her associates . . . She gave her correct name at this time and her own history, which was sufficiently corroborated by other evidence to prove that her recollection of early life was not distorted by her later psychosis.[31]

Or of this unnamed individual who was also admitted to an insane asylum,

> He was effeminate from childhood . . . He talked strangely and excitedly, was arrested at his mother's request, and, after being examined, was pronounced insane and sent to the hospital . . . He practices masturbation, but his great propensity is to fondle men, both with his hands and mouth. He has been detected in this loathsome practice a number of times, both in the airing court and at night. This, it appears, was a common practice with him before his admission to the hospital. He is very bold with it, and has ventured to try to make engagements with visitors for such purposes.[32]

In spite of the new information that began to permeate the medical/neurological community, etiologic disagreements remained, and that in turn had an impact upon diagnosis and treatment. For those individuals who accepted the theory that contrary sexual instinct was essentially a biologically natural but abnormal condition, the victim was not necessarily mad, delusional, psychotic, or depraved and but for this condition, one might otherwise be quite normal in appearance in spite of the tendency to be effeminate. If, however, one believed that same-sex attraction was an acquired condition, then insanity was the diagnosis, and placement in a mental hospital the disposition. Thus, if one suffered from a biological perversion of the sexual instinct, bad biology was at fault and under the circumstances one was certainly not responsible for the condition and should be allowed to go about one's business discreetly. If, on the other hand, the condition was acquired as a result of bad habits, then institutionalization was required. According to Dr. Kiernan's report of similar work in his May 1884 essay,

"Sexual Perversion,"

> To remove this condition is out of the question, and Dr. Wise has recommended that these patients be sent to asylums. Krafft-Ebing and [Dr.] Kirn proposed that these patients should be excepted from legal penalties and allowed to follow their inclinations when harmless and not violating public decency.[33]

From the beginning of his research into perverted sexual instinct, Krafft-Ebing had accepted this argument based in part on insights provided by Karl Ulrichs, and in his research published in American journals this position was continuously advanced. For example, in his 1888 essay in the *Alienist and Neurologist* Krafft-Ebing wrote,

> In addition to the scientific interest which this strange freak of nature excites there are connected with it wide-reaching social and legal questions concerning the light in which those thus affected should be regarded in relation to their sexual conduct and actions . . . As we study into the abnormal and diseased conditions from which this malady results, the ideas of horror and criminality connected with it disappear . . . By so doing the investigations of science will be the means of rescuing the honor and reestablishing the social position of many an unfortunate whom unthinking prejudice and ignorance would class among the depraved criminals. It would not be the first time in which science has rendered a service to justice and to society by teaching that what seem to be immoral conditions and actions are but the results of disease.[34]

By 1890, Krafft-Ebing's general arguments with respect to origins, diagnosis, disposition, and responsibility in cases of true congenital contrary sexual instinct were fully accepted within the American medical community, the result of which was a less hostile approach to those so afflicted. "It is certainly less humiliating to us as atoms of the social fabric to be able to attribute the degradation of these poor unfortunates to a physical cause, than to a willful viciousness over which they have, or ought to have, volitional control."[35]

A common theme indirectly related to personal responsibility and disposition was that of the extent and completeness of the instinct's reversal. As George Chauncy Jr. has argued in his article, "From Sexual Inversion to Homosexuality: Medicine and the Changing Conceptualization of Female Deviance," contrary sexual instinct consisted of much more than mere sexual attraction to a member of the same sex. The implication was that the male or the female who suffered from the disease in all probability exhibited a reversal of the sexual role as well, and indeed, sexuality was only one part of the so-called inversion.[36] Here was something more than effeminate men and masculine women. Some physicians believed that people who suffered from the disease were gradually metamorphosed into the opposite sex in a process that might be short or fast and more or less complete.

In 1884, the doctors Shaw and Ferris in their review of the then extant cases noticed that a female victim of the disease was "fond of boys' games" and liked to "dress as a boy." In her dreams, she "appeared to herself as a man," and as she got older, she "had a great desire to be a man." Another victim, this time a male, was known to "blush and tremble" when examined, and expressed a strong desire to act as a women, "He took pleasure in associating with women, dressed as a woman, bought himself all sorts of female ornaments . . . During his stay at the hospital, patient occupied himself with female handiwork—knitted, embroidered, and made ladies hats." Another case described a young thirty-year-old male who felt "himself more of a woman than a man; has a woman's soul, a woman's endurance; would love to kiss, wash, dress, and care for the children, and it would afford him the greatest happiness could he be a mother . . . [he] has a continual desire to act, speak, sing, and walk like a woman; with effort had acquired some male characteristics."[37]

Dr. George Shrady, in his 1884 review of the literature, makes similar observations and even states that "if men . . . they try to dress, or walk like and imitate the habits of women . . . [They] have a mincing gait, and sometimes the hips are broad like those of a women."[38] In 1884, Kiernan also acknowledged a sex inversion with one of his female patients who "liked to play boys' games and dress in male attire."[39] In November, 1886, Leidy and Mills discussed their case of a young man, "effeminate from childhood" who "says his name is Jane and that he is a girl."[40] Krafft-Ebing was also no stranger to the phenomenon, but given that he had initially derived his insights from Ulrichs, the man who had ascribed male same-sex attraction to the consequence of a female brain within a male body and just the reverse for females, this comes as no surprise. Thus, Krafft-Ebing described one of his male patients as "weak limbed and of a nervous organization. He was fond of feminine work and play . . . he had no fondness for boys' games or for hunting and was often laughed at and scolded for his feminine ways," while concurrently in the same article we read of a female victim who appeared to be a male, "At her first appearance the patient attracted attention by her clothing, features, man's hat, short hair, spectacles, gentleman's cravat and a sort of coat of male cut covering her male dress.

She had coarse male features, a rough and rather deep voice, and, with the exception of the bosom and female contour of the pelvis, looked more like a man in woman's clothing than like a woman."[41] Lydston, in his 1889 article on sexual perversion, goes so far as to assert actual physical change, "That mal-development, or arrested development of the sexual organs should be associated with sexual perversion is not at all surprising," and that even if differentiation of sex is "complete from a gross physical standpoint," the "receptive and generative centers of sexual sensibility may fail to become perfectly differentiated," which might result "upon the one hand [in] sexual apathy, and upon the other, an approximation to the female or male type, as the case may be." Even though such change is invisible to the naked eye, it is nevertheless clear it has occurred because of the way victims of contrary sexual instinct behaved, "Such a failure of development and imperfect differentiation of structure would necessarily be too occult for discovery by any physical means at our command. It is, however, but too readily recognized by its results."[42]

Was contrary sexual instinct limited to sexual desire, or was it a symptom of a more or less thorough sexual inversion through which the attributes of the male and female were reversed, to include the formation of rudimentary reproductive organs? Only time and more research would tell, yet it may be argued that because of the nineteenth century's general essentialist assumptions regarding sex and gender, homosexual men and women themselves assumed they were physically and psychically metamorphosing into the opposite sex. Not all those who acknowledged their unusual attractions felt compelled to act in a manner consistent with the opposite sex, however, and some enjoyed acting and cavorting with those who projected a strong and appropriate gender image. As more cases were studied, and as the literature on the subject expanded, only then did researchers begin to differentiate sexual object choice from sexual roles and gender characteristics, and in the process give birth to the more narrow condition of homosexuality irrespective of gender, role differentiation.[43]

In spite of this development, the troublesome side effects of industrialization, urbanization, population growth, and immigration caused many in the medical profession to question their own research into the causes of homosexuality. While for the most part the condition was still conceptualized as congenital in origin, questions arose as to the actual cause of this biological abnormality in the first place. Was the phenomenon a natural variation, a product of hereditary taint, or, heaven forbid, an atavistic symptom of national decline brought about by rapid change that had not allowed the United States to remain faithful to its exceptionalist mission? The unfortunate fact, some neurologists noted, was that modern America had developed at a price, and that price no doubt was moral and physical degeneration that could be passed from one generation to the next. Homosexuality was the most troubling indicator of this situation because it stood the normal order on its head, and the numbers were increasing. Was this a sign of national degeneration as well?

Chapter 9

The Homosexual and the Physician in the 1890s

Sane or Insane?
Is She Cruel Murderess or Irresponsible Lunatic?
Alice Mitchell's Mental Status Now Before the Court.
Her Father Weeps as He Recounts the Family Woes
Her Mother More Than Once Treated for Lunacy
Peculiar Characteristics Developed in Early Youth
A Most Intelligent Jury That
Will Carefully Weigh the Facts
Inquisition of Lunacy in the Celebrated Mitchell Case is Begun
and a Jury is
Impaneled Without Much Trouble or Delay—Evidence of Her Father is
Heard And a Decision Will Probably be Reached Within a Few Days[1]

On January 26, 1892, a banner on the front page of the *New York Times* read, "A Most Shocking Crime/A Memphis Society Girl Cuts A Former Friend's Throat." In the story that followed, the *Times* reported the sensational tragedy of the murder of Freda Ward, 17, by Alice Mitchell, 19, in a bizarre case of love gone wrong. According to the news reports, Alice had "loved Freda desperately, better than anyone else in the world . . . and that long ago they had made a compact that if they should ever be separated they should kill each other." Because Alice had indeed been forbidden to speak with Freda, Alice "knew nothing else to do but to kill her." According to the *Times*, it was evident that Mitchell was "demented,"[2] a claim shared by the defense when it entered a plea of innocent by reason of insanity.

On July 19, Alice was brought before the Shelby County Criminal Court in Memphis, Tennessee, where a jury was asked to determine whether or not she was insane. After opening remarks and testimony from Alice's father about their family life, the defense submitted for the jury's consideration a lengthy "Hypothetical Case" that presented Alice's life and crime in detail in support of their contention that the defendant was insane. Subtle references to the M'Naghten criteria for insane irresponsibility were sprinkled throughout the testimony even though the M'Naghten rule was not specifically mentioned. It will be recalled from the Guiteau trial that the insanity defense could only be applied if the accused was by defect of reason from disease unable to know the nature or the quality of the act committed, or if known, he or she was unable to know that what was committed was wrong. If these conditions were not met, then the defendant was sane and was to be held responsible for the crime,

> ... the jury ought to be told in all cases that every man is to be presumed to be sane, and to possess a sufficient degree of reason to be responsible for his crimes until the contrary be proved to their satisfaction; and that to establish a defense on the ground of insanity it must be clearly proved that, at the time of committing the act, the accused was labouring under such a defect of reason, from disease of the mind, as not to know the nature and quality of the act he was doing, or, if he did know it, that he did not know he was doing what was wrong.[3]

In the "Hypothetical Case," as in Guiteau's, the defense never denied that the defendant had murdered someone. There were a number of witnesses, and Alice herself had admitted to the deed. Instead, evidence was presented that was intended to demonstrate that Alice was legally insane based upon several factors that satisfied the M'Naghten criteria, to include congenital insanity, her masculine behavior, her perverted affections, and an inability to realize that she had committed a crime. Unlike Guiteau, this was not a novel interpretation of M'Naghten where it was argued that the defendant knew right from wrong but was nevertheless unable to control his actions due to congenital insanity. Here was a straightforward situation where the defendant, in spite of congenital insanity, did not know the nature or quality of the act she had committed. The defense was quick to point out that Alice's mother, uncle, great uncle, and several cousins were insane. "She [Mrs. Mitchell, the mother of Alice] gave birth to six children between the first and Alice. With each child her mental trouble appeared in a more or less marked degree. She would be seized with imaginings, for which there were no grounds whatever. These delusive ideas would pass off generally in a few weeks after childbirth ... The parents of Mrs. Mitchell died when she was an infant. One of her brothers was insane for a considerable period, one of her uncles was insane and several of her cousins were insane."[4] From childhood, Alice had furthermore been recognized as a tomboy, had "disliked sewing and needle work," and was

> ... wholly without that fondness for boys that girls usually manifest. She had no intimates or child sweethearts among the boys, and when approaching womanhood, after she was grown, she had no beaux and took no pleasure in the society of young men. She was sometimes rude and always indifferent to young men. She was regarded as mentally wrong by young men toward whom she had thus acted.[5]

Instead of a male beau, Alice had just the opposite, a belle by the name of Freda Ward to whom she proposed marriage in February 1891, and with whom she proposed to live under the pseudonym Alvin J. Ward after they had eloped to St. Louis. However, when this scenario and the closeness of the relationship were discovered by Freda's sister with whom Freda lived, steps were taken by the respective families to keep the two separated. Increasingly distraught by this situation, Alice became determined to kill Freda as per their secret agreement alluded to in the *Times*. On January 25, 1892, Alice managed to carry out her part of the agreement by slashing Freda's throat with a razor she had taken from her father. When apprehended by the police later that same day at home, the defense claimed that although Alice told the chief of police she had "cut" Freda "because she loved her and because Fred did not speak to her," later on she did not realize what she had done, "That night and the next evening she did not seem to realize that she had committed a criminal act."[6]

Over the course of the next several days, testimony from several local expert medical witnesses for both the defense and the prosecution was presented. Each side was interested in presenting evidence to support its position. The defense presented witnesses who supported its contention that Alice was congenitally insane and irresponsible because she didn't recognize the seriousness of her actions when she murdered Freda irrespective of her love for Freda, which, some believed, was of dubious perversity anyway because no sexual relations were legally established. The prosecution presented witnesses who agreed that Alice was congenitally insane, but responsible in spite of her proclivity to perverted love because such an intense relationship naturally begets jealousy and violence.[7] In the end, the jury sided with the defense and concluded that Alice was insane, whereupon she was remanded to the Tennessee State Asylum in Bolivar where she died in 1898.[8]

This case took place during the height of the social purity movement that resulted in the creation of the previously mentioned National Purity Alliance in 1895 from regional and local purity organizations.[9]

Heavily influenced by elite Protestant Christian women reformers from the east coast and Chicago, the goal of the alliance was no less than moral perfection and the creation of a secularized moral society derived from Christian ethics to which individual behaviors conformed. Initially dedicated to the eradication of prostitution, the goals of the reformers expanded over the years to include the eradication of gambling and the double standard in sexual matters; the nature of women's work in society; women's health issues; prison reform; the education of youth; the reduction of sex crimes to include rape and other "unnatural" expressions of the sex instinct; censorship of photos, books, and plays in which obscene material was found; and the closing of brothels and taverns that appealed to the prurient. Indeed, the eradication of virtually any social "pathology" that threatened the perfection of American civilization was emphasized.[10] As the century came to a close, the goals of the purity reformers became commingled with those of the feminists, temperance movement, the Progressive municipal reformers, and others, in response to the problems of modernization and rapid change associated with late nineteenth-century industrialization and urbanization.[11]

As the purity movement grew in the last two decades of the nineteenth century, reformers attempted to enlist the help of the medical community in the hope that physicians would, through their newly found professional expertise, support efforts to identify social problems, and then offer suggestions on how to resolve them. Social hygiene was a critical component of the reformers' agenda, and physicians who supported the general goals of the purity movement helped establish the "medical hygiene movement." A mostly urban phenomenon, the medical hygiene movement identified and researched the physical and social conditions of the city in which crime and vice would most likely develop. A change in these conditions for the better according to the most modern precepts of science informed by Christian ethics, and behavior, too, would be a change for the better. A cure rather than a prison was emphasized (although prison reform was a high-priority issue), thus it was important that in the area of medical hygiene, physicians needed to be clear whether behavior was criminal or not, and if not, why.[12]

Because sex, in the form of prostitution or rape, was an early issue that motivated the purity reformers, the aid of the medical community was enlisted to research the theme of legal responsibility of the sex offender.[13] Some physicians took up the challenge in the aftermath of the Guiteau insanity trial, and in the process they became increasingly interested in the legal responsibility of all sexual perverts, to include those who claimed to be suffering from contrary sexual instinct, or what

Krafft-Ebing dubbed "pure" homosexuality. To a large extent, the debate was about insanity, and indeed, the same James G. Kiernan who had testified for Guiteau in 1881, led the discussion on the issue of "responsibility in sexual perversion" in the 1890s in the wake of Alice Mitchell. Was sexual perversion a form of mental illness, he wanted to know, and were sexual perverts legally responsible for crimes they may have committed? For prosecutors, the answer was no, yet for many purity reformers, a cure was equally important, because they had an interest in not only justice for perpetrators, but in prevention as well.

For the duration of the 1890s this was the backdrop against which the American medical community studied the sexual perversions, only one of which was homosexual behavior. For the most part, researchers were interested in homosexual behavior from the "medico-legal" forensic perspective, and sought to determine if those who committed such acts were sane and thus legally responsible for their "crimes," which in that decade included any same-sex sexual relations. Of those who took an interest in the subject, by far the most frequently cited until the advent of Sigmund Freud were Kiernan and George Frank Lydston, the great Austrian sexologist Krafft-Ebing, and to a lesser extent the Englishman Havelock Ellis. What united these men—especially the Americans Kiernan and Lydston with the Austrian Krafft-Ebing—was a deep concern for the legal rights of those who claimed to be "pure" homosexual. This, of course, had been one of Krafft-Ebing's initial concerns, and an issue of considerable interest to Ulrich two decades before. If it could be scientifically demonstrated that "pure" homosexuality was congenital, then it was neither the product of a depraved mind nor, in all probability, congenital insanity; rather, it was the result of bad heredity against which the individual had no defense, and bad heredity was not in and of itself evidence of insanity or criminal intent. Furthermore, if it could be demonstrated that in the case of the congenital homosexual same-sex attraction and sexuality were natural—albeit perverted manifestations of the normal sexual attraction of man for woman and vice versa—then the American legal system ought to recognize this reality and adjust legal codes accordingly. The real concern was not the inversion per se, but rather the social and environmental conditions that created the perversion in the first instance. Subsequent to this, any claim of legal irresponsibility by reason of insanity brought by those who suffered from any sexual perversion, and homosexuality in particular, had to be individually weighed. The sexual perversions were not in themselves sufficient for a verdict of insanity; it was also necessary that other conditions be present, and what those conditions were depended upon the individual and the nature of the crime. Same-sex activities between consenting homosexuals should not be a matter for the courts but rather of the physician or in some rare instances, only of the parties involved.

To make the case and prove their point, researchers had to systematically delve into the etiology of all the sexual perversions and this required the application of the best and most informed medical minds available. Lydston in particular was up to the task, and together with Kiernan and Krafft-Ebing, they worked to ensure that homosexuality was understood by the American doctor to be an unfortunate congenital condition based upon a degenerative hereditarian predisposition. Although largely forgotten today, Lydston and less so Kiernan were considered by their peers to be the most knowledgeable researchers on homosexuality in the United States at the turn of the twentieth century. In Chaddock's 1892 preface to his translation of *Psychopathia Sexualis*, both doctors were specifically thanked for their contributions to the study of the sexual perversions for which the entire American medical community was grateful, and largely dependent.

For Lydston and Kiernan and for several other American neurologists as well, the issue was fundamentally quite simple: homosexual men and women were not insane. This diagnosis, however, was fraught with yet another concern, and that related to the origins of the predisposition in the first place, an issue that was later taken up by Lydston in the context of a discussion on the relationship between civilization, modernity, and the nervous system. In the meantime, the new approach to homosexuality was not universally accepted by either neurologists or psychiatrists. Many challenged the positions of Lydston and Kiernan, and via medical journals they offered alternative explanations for homosexuality, the most frequent being either insanity by reason of habitual human depravity or congenital insanity by reason of the inheritance of said depravities. Echoes of the argument are still heard among those who take an interest in the issue under the rubrics "nature" or "nurture."

Biological Theories of Homosexuality

In 1892, three important works on sexual perversion appeared, "Responsibility in Sexual Perversion," by James Kiernan;[14] "Sexual Perversion" by G. Frank Lydston; and *Psychopathia Sexualis* by Richard von Krafft-Ebing. By 1895, the writings of the Englishman Havelock Ellis and of the American Charles G. Chaddock also became available, completing the list of authorities from whom the American medical and legal communities drew their insights into the condition of what had been first labeled "pure" homosexual by Krafft-Ebing in 1886, then repeated for the first time in the American literature by Kiernan in his 1892 article on sexual perversion. Other physicians, to be sure, added their insights to the growing list of those concerned with homosexuality, but the main contours of the debate were established by those named previously. As was the situation with the earlier research, several themes evolved during the course of the 1890s most of which were a refinement of the previous decade. They included the legal responsibility of acts committed by sexual perverts; the origins of the sexual perversion; medical diagnosis of sexual perversion; and discussions of appropriate cures for those suffering from perversions of the sexual instinct.

James Kiernan was the first American to tackle the issue of responsibility within the context of causes and origins. On March 7, 1892, Kiernan read a paper on responsibility in sexual perversion before the Chicago Medical Society and in May it was reprinted in the *Chicago Medical Recorder*. The subject of this essay was the correct application of the M'Naghten rule in cases of sexual perversion. Although he suspected that the "need of such a [M'Naghten] test in sexual perversion will seem strange to most American physicians and lawyers in whom there is a tendency to regard sexual perversion as a purely morbid phenomenon," in view of modern science, the time was now appropriate to determine whether or not sexual perversions impaired free will to such an extent as to require a "MacNaughten acquittal." After a brief review of the literature and "sexual perversions" practiced by the Native American burdache within the Zuni, Pueblo, and Plains Indian cultures, Kiernan asserted that these "aberrations" were suggestive of the complexity of the sexual appetite. If this were true, then the question arose as to how this came about, and that led Kiernan to discuss what he called the nature of the sexual propensity, ultimately defined as "protoplasmic hunger" a term he borrowed from other scientific "authorities" who claimed that the sexual appetite originated from the merging and assimilation of one "monad" or amoebae by the other:

> Aberrations of the types described indicate a greater complexity in the sexual appetite than is usually suspected. The nature of the sexual propensity hence becomes of interest. Dallinger and Drysdale have described how fission of the monad was preceded by the absorption of one form by another. One monad fixed on the sarcode of another, and the substance of the lesser or under one passed into the upper one. In about two hours the merest trace of the lower one was left, and in four hours, fission and multiplication of the larger monad began. Leidy insists

that the ameba is a cannibal, whereupon Michels expresses the opinion that each cannibalistic act, if the term be admissible, is a copulative one. Lawson a decade later detailed additional data to sustain this position. Clevenger basing his opinion on these data cited additional evidence to prove that the sexual appetite had its origin in protoplasmic hunger. This position has been supported by later biologists.[15]

In humans, a complex forebrain acted as a "check on the purely vegetative functions" and took precedence over the "primary-ego" of instinctual behaviors and the hunger of the sexual appetite. If the inhibition became weak then a "disordered predominance of the natural instincts or impulses occurs," but if the inhibition was lost completely then the individual was a criminal "who opposes the ethical order of society" and by doing so became a parasite who destroyed his "host." Criminal tendencies were thus "reversions in type indicating the original source of the inhibition."

Kiernan then turned to a discussion of sexual selection, a phenomenon he believed resulted from the evolution of a physical desire to satisfy the protoplasmic hunger. Such selection demonstrated that pleasure was no longer dependent upon simple sexual "conjugation" but had evolved from a desire to satisfy that protoplasmic hunger into "ideas of beauty," attraction, and maternal love. Evolutionary inhibitions, he argued, have prevented the explosion of the natural instinctive behaviors and thus the pleasure originally associated with "conjugation with a certain subject" arose, instead, at the sight of the "subject" in an attempt to please it. The repressed "explosive manifestations of the sexual appetite" produced in turn a more intellectual society than one overtly sexual, and attempts to please the cause of sexual pleasure could by means of association, please "without the presence of the original cause." Thus, according to Kiernan, among the civilized societies of the world, romantic love developed that restrained the primary ego and created the basis for morality. Among "savage" societies, however, the primary ego remained uninhibited and romantic love was impossible. Interestingly enough, in the same essay a similar conclusion was drawn about female "reformers" who, Kiernan asserted, suffered from an atavistic reversion to conditions beneath the birds and mammals to a condition "analogous" to the "female" workers of bee communities who were the "autocrats" of the community,

> ... the labor value of women interfered with the germ of romantic love developed already in the mammals. The equality of the sexes in the division of labor, the ideal of certain female "reformers" of the present era, sank the mother in the fellow-laborer and caused an atavistic reversion to

conditions beneath birds and mammals, analogous to the bee communities, where the males and queen bee carry on reproduction, while the imperfect "female workers" are the autocrats of the community. This is the ideal of the female "reformers": a few degenerate females are with the males to propagate the race then be "removed," while the imperfect female "worker" reconstructs the world on the "bee" ideal.[16]

Just so the sexual pervert who by virtue of the same atavistic mechanisms no longer acted in conformity to the essentialist characteristics appropriate to sex or species. This situation was not a moralists' notion, Kiernan added, because their ultimate goal was the abolition of the sex drive, not its control. In the case of the sexual pervert, however, control of the sex appetite was paramount because its abolition was simply unrealistic. Kiernan then proceeded into a physiological discussion of the sex act based upon Krafft-Ebing's investigations, and concluded that over and above the physics of orgasm, sexual pleasure was in the mind, or what he called the "psychical action in the cerebral cortex." The more the "cortical center" was affected by the "generative organs," the more intense the pleasure. The key organ here was the "brain" that, because it influenced sexual pleasure, had to be healthy if sexual pleasure derived from sexual intercourse culminating in reproduction were to be achieved.

Sometimes, however, an orgasm could be achieved "only" by the perverse action of the cortex's psychical center, as in "mutual masturbation or pederasty" among males. In this instance, the inability to have sexual intercourse with a female culminating in ejaculation arose from "neurasthenia." "Normal desire" was absent, although a psychical factor was still evident from the dreams of perverted images that were not of "females in voluptuous poses" but that were nevertheless followed by nocturnal emissions.[17] The infrequency or lack of orgasms directed toward the female, that "instinctive feeling toward the opposite sex [which] may find expression in a desire for coitus which may become uncontrollable" was obviously not caused by the inability to have an erection, but rather by a problem with the cerebral cortex.

Kiernan's research told him that this abnormal condition was persistent and that it had been acquired early on through an organic "reversion" to the "original bisexuality of the ancestors" due to disease or congenital defect. Some individuals might have been born with the genitals of both sexes, the true hermaphrodite, while others might have exhibited "psychical hermaphroditism" in which a female brain occupied a male body, and vice versa. "It seems certain that a femininely functioning [sic] brain can occupy a male body and vice versa."[18] In a world where the bisexuality of the lowest animals was but a complete reversion to the "ancestral type," Kiernan had no problems accepting the belief that a "femininely functionating [*sic*] brain alone should be developed at times with its psychical consequences" resulting from a central nervous system that had been "atavistically affected." Similar to Krafft-Ebing whose works he had read, Kiernan had adopted Ulrichs' original theory of the male–female brain–body swap, dressed up in the language of science.

The "complexity" and "variety" of these conditions led Kiernan to employ three general classification systems "for clinical and forensic reasons" drawn from his own work, from Lydston, and from Krafft-Ebing. Kiernan's intention was to provide a clinical reference guide with examples of the sexual perversions for consultation by expert witnesses in order to determine legal responsibility in criminal cases. In general, the perversions were categorized as congenital or acquired, and mental or neurological. Same-sex attraction was one of the subcategories that Kiernan expanded upon through case reviews to determine criminal responsibility under the law. With the exception of one case, the remaining instances of "Uranism" were of women. Based upon the theory that real women were naturally less sexual than men, their perversions were considered acquired mental abnormalities consequent to other underlying conditions such as "excess venery" or "insanity" that led to "husband abandonment," "maniacal attack," murder, and Uranism. In the case of the male, legal responsibility for a crime committed was probable since "no other evidence of mental deterioration than being homosexual" was present,[19] leading Kiernan to conclude, "the mere existence of an alleged perversion should never be admitted as proof of irresponsibility. The common law provides for these cases, hence there is no need of legislation. In full accordance with the spirit of the common law, each case should be tried on its own merits, and the exact mental state of the accused determined."[20]

Virtually every physician who followed Kiernan held the same position with respect to legal responsibility, even as they differed slightly regarding causes and origins. Krafft-Ebing, previously discussed, shared Kiernan's position on legal responsibility, and theorized that the origins of congenital homosexuality resided in a hereditarian predisposition. Charles Gilbert Chaddock, the translator of Krafft-Ebing's first American edition of *Psychopathia Sexualia* in 1892, and a neurologist himself, was similarly inclined and at the end of an article entitled, "Sexual Crimes," he concluded,

> Since all forms of perversion may lead to criminal acts, the most important question from a medical-legal standpoint is that which concerns

responsibility. On this point it may be said that the fact that an individual is subject to a perversion of the sexual instinct is not sufficient to establish personal irresponsibility ... in order to show justify a judgment of irresponsibility it is necessary to show that the crime was the result of organic necessity.[21]

As the translator of Krafft-Ebing, Chaddock was an important figure in the transmission of knowledge about sexual perversion to the American medical community. Born in 1861 in Jonesville, Michigan, Chaddock was a second-generation physician who graduated from the University of Michigan College of Medicine and Surgery in 1885, after which he became a physician at the Northern Michigan Asylum in Traverse City. Between 1888 and 1889, he studied in Munich and upon his return to the Michigan asylum, he married. In 1892, he relocated to St. Louis where he became the Professor of Nervous and Mental Diseases at Marion-Sims College, now the Medical Department of St. Louis University. Known for his epicurean tastes, love of culture, translation skills, and European sabbaticals, Chaddock was also a writer of sonnets. Professionally, Chaddock was interested in forensic psychiatry, and was often called upon to testify at trials where insanity was an issue. By the end of the nineteenth century, Chaddock had turned to neurology, specifically the problem of "differentiating between the organic and functional manifestation of nervous diseases, specializing in cerebral pathology." In 1903 he penned a textbook, *Outline of Psychiatry*, and in 1904, he translated Krafft-Ebing's *The Textbook of Insanity* into English and wrote a number of chapters on sexual instinct for another textbook edited by some of his colleagues. For the next ten years, Chaddock continued his clinical research on cerebral pathology, and in 1914, he retired due to his increasing deafness.[22]

As might be expected, Chaddock accepted Krafft-Ebing's theories of the acquired and congenital origins of contrary sexual instinct although he was less sure how one differentiated between the two, "It is still an open question whether we are justified in making a hard and fast line of demarcation between these psychosexual anomalies; certain it is that with our present means of differential diagnosis we are often left in doubt of these categories."[23] In spite of this difficulty, however, Chaddock wholeheartedly accepted the theory of congenital homosexuality and similar to Krafft-Ebing, he ascribed it to "neuropsychical" degeneracy. "Observation shows that for the most part psychosexual anomalies are developed upon a degenerate constitution which may commonly be traced to a neuropathic disposition inherited from ancestors."[24]

Neuropsychical degeneracy was caused, Chaddock believed, by the stresses of "higher civilization" upon the mind and body, and was then passed from one generation to another. In the following generations, this degeneracy was manifested in a number of conditions, one category of which were the sexual perversions. When improper education was combined with a degenerate psyche, as for example when a child was not educated in behaviors consistent with one's anatomical sex, the result was more likely than not to be a perversion of the sex instinct whereby the normal instinct was inverted to produce a person with a contrary sexual instinct. This morbid process was exacerbated by additional "exciting" causes of higher society, specifically "excessive" masturbation, fear of pregnancy, and "venereal infection." Early symptoms of this condition were premature development of sexual desire, weak-mindedness, and moral insanity in addition to neuroses in a child's "progenitors."[25] For the most part, acquired sexual instinct was a more frequent phenomenon, although physicians were told that due to its rarity and intractability, the congenital type was of much more interest to the medical community.

Similar to Chaddock, Havelock Ellis also understood "sexual inversion" to be congenital and acquired in origin. Unlike Chaddock, however, Ellis considered the condition to be almost always congenital, "... I regard acquired inversion as rare, and I should not be surprised to find that a more minute investigation would show that even in these rare cases there is a congenital element."[26] Ellis, a British psychologist and physician who was born in 1859 and died in 1939, is perhaps best known for his seven-volume text, *Studies in the Psychology of Sex* (1897–1928), of which volume two, "Sexual Inversion" completed in 1901, deals with the issue of homosexuality. Previous to this study, Ellis had done much research into homosexuality and published a number of articles during the 1890s in the *Alienist and Neurologist* as an Honorary Fellow of the Chicago Academy of Medicine. In his early writings as well as his later texts, Ellis never claimed to understand the precise origins of the congenital inversion. While he made explicit references to the theories of others, he was personally more interested in helping homosexuals deal with their situation and the opprobrium they received from a hostile society,

> The invert is not only the victim of his own abnormal obsession; he is the victim of social hostility... When I review the cases I have brought forward and the mental history of inverts I have known, I am inclined to say that if we can enable an invert to be healthy, self-restrained and self-respecting we have often done better than to convert him into the mere feeble simulacrum of a normal man.[27]

To his understanding, homosexuality did not imply insanity, with the exception that those so afflicted might be driven insane by their persecutors. "It can scarcely be said that the attitude of society is favorable to the invert's attainment of a fairly sane and well balanced attitude. This is, indeed, one of the great difficulties in his way that causes him to waver between extremes of melancholia and egotistic exaltation."[28] As such, Ellis brought a different tone to the study of homosexuality that was generally not accepted by his American counterparts, including G. Frank Lydston.

In *The Diseases of Society*,[29] a compendium of his writing from the 1890s published in 1904, Lydston tediously described what he labeled the "vice and crime problem" of America in order to expose the "absurdities of our criminal law and penal system." The American penal system, he believed, was archaic and too frequently resorted to absurd punishment for behaviors that were less criminal in nature than pathological consequences of bad environment and heredity. Many so-called criminals were in actuality hereditarian degenerates through no cause of their own, and when apprehended, they were punished by the full weight of anarchic legal system, a tactic that was unfortunately counterproductive. In its stead, Lydston offered a regimen of eugenics, social and medical hygiene. The death penalty and prison had their place, to be sure, but most crime in America stemmed from environmental pressures that resulted in neuropsychical degeneration, which in turn resulted in an impaired ability to know right from wrong, normal from abnormal. If America was to "progress" and remain true to its exceptionalist heritage, then it was necessary that the social obstacles to that proud and unique heritage be permanently removed, and that certainly required the skills of the scientific community, and G. Frank Lydston, criminal anthropologist and neurologist M.D., in particular.

Accordingly to Lydston,

> Society is composed of human integers, upon the physical and psychic health of which its integrity depends. Morbid phenomena affecting the social body exist analogous to those affecting the individual integers. Just as diseases affecting certain areas of the cells ... may vitiate the health not only of the neighboring cells, but of the entire body, so may the mental, moral, and physical diseases of the human body entity [*sic*] react injuriously upon other individuals and also upon the society of which they are apart. In like manner, a constitutional disease may produce secondarily diseases of remote cell areas of the body ... and serious disturbances of the social body may produce disastrous effects in the physical and psychic constitution of individuals, whether taken alone or

as specialized groups or classes. There is, then, a pathology of the social body, comprising most of the evils from which society suffers.[30]

In his book, Lydston attempted explain the "pathological" side effects of an industrial, urban America, and hoped to offer suggestions on how the social pathologies might be countered,

> Crime, prostitution, pauperism, insanity in its sociologic relations, anarchy, political corruption, and adverse economic and industrial conditions and their causes, congeners, and results will be discussed in this volume as the most important phases of social disease. The fact that social diseases are often due to actual physical disease in offenders against society in itself justifies the use of the term, social pathology.[31]

A student of Cesare Lombroso the famed Italian criminal anthropologist, and of George Beard, the famed neurologist who invented neurasthenia, Lydston was a social Darwinist who believed that criminal behavior was the product of bad heredity and neuropathy. He was, as he so often referred to himself, a scientific materialist by which he meant that religion and theology were inappropriate fields for the study of criminology. Science and "cold fact" alone were sufficient to discover the evolutionary laws of criminal behavior, and in the United States, such behavior was first and foremost the product of unfavorable surroundings that had caused a neuropathology that produced crime. All societies had crime, but the more advanced ones were especially prone, particularly the United States and Europe. The environmental factors that placed stress upon the individual were extensive, and included industrialization; urbanization; the "race problem"; lust for wealth; ambition; love of "display"; late hours; lack of rest; excitement; alcohol; heredity; politics; yellow journalism; selfishness; and in parts of the country, the climate.

Each of these conditions in its own way impacted the nervous system and eventually the cerebral cortex, but ultimately the stress placed upon the individual's nerves was too great for the brain to accommodate and nervous exhaustion set in. In certain individuals this resulted in a loss of inhibitions. Primitive instincts that had hitherto been kept in control broke through. Light-skinned Europeans and "Semitic" peoples had the most to suffer because they had the most highly developed civilizations, whereas dark-skinned people, Blacks, Greeks, Italians, Latin Americans, for example, were intrinsically primitive and had never had much control of their instincts. White people, and especially northern Europeans and their American descendants were at greatest risk for victimization because they had more social pressure on their nerves, and were therefore more prone to exhaustion.

Once the pernicious effects of exhaustion had set in, a veritable flood of social ills occurred compounded by the fact that in some "classes" of people, exhaustion was inherited according to the theory of the inheritance of acquired characteristics, and once this process began, then degeneracy became palpably manifest in whole sections of the population—and that on top of the first generation of individuals who had initially degenerated by means of nervous exhaustion in the first place. They are, he wrote, "persons of low grade of development, physically and mentally, with a defective understanding of their true relations to the social system in which they live. Such persons have no true conceptions of that viable thing called morality, and, in the case of the criminal, no respect whatever for the rights of others, save in so far as it may be compelled by fear of punishment."[32] Those with stronger constitutions, primarily highly educated, professional, upper-class white males of the northeast and Chicago escaped the full impact of neuropathic degeneration; but here too, unless the social conditions that caused the neuropathy were eliminated, no one was spared the possibility of disease. Unfortunately, degeneration lurked everywhere.

After one had succumbed to neuropathy, then came the potential for crime, which to Lydston was virtually any behavior that rocked the status quo or that smelled of "vice." Prostitution; "pauperism"; sexual perversion; theft; murder; fraud; feminism; gambling; anarchism; the strike; alcoholism; graft; masturbation; unemployment; laziness; fornication; adultery; egotism; cheating; and miscegenation were all categories labeled crimes that Lydston thought derived in part or completely from neuropathy and that were symptomatic of a degeneracy that might be passed along to one's progeny. Indeed, this was a virtual litany of the evils of the purity reform movement. Although the United States was not as degenerate as the European aristocracy, and in spite of the high numbers of degenerates in its midst, America had not yet reached a full state of evolutionary decline, at least for the time being.[33]

Of the identified criminal categories, Lydston considered sexual "psychopathy" or "aberrations of the erotic impulse" of the greatest importance "in their criminological, social, and medico-legal aspects."[34] Traditionally, he argued, individuals who suffered from sexual perversion or inversion were branded moral perverts but that was incorrect because their condition was not a matter of morality; instead, these were examples of a physical and mental defect, a psychosexual aberration the origins of which were neuropathic, not moral depravity. Victims of these conditions were degenerates, and the law had to recognize that fact, otherwise it risked improper solutions to what was in reality a medical problem. Lydston was quite concerned that due to an absolute increase in the numbers of the perversions, any improper solution would only contribute to their growth, thus it was critical that proper, scientific steps be taken to ensure that this does not occur.

In the case of sexual inversion in which there existed a "sexual perversion without defect of structure of the sexual organs due to aberrant psycho-sexual differentiation," what those steps were was ambiguous. If the condition was acquired, a difficult diagnosis in any case, then one had to determine how it was acquired before steps could be taken. If the condition was congenital, then one had another set of problems to contend with, namely the "naturalness" of it from the perspective of the victim. Lydston's discussion of the congenital theories was borrowed from Krafft-Ebing, Kiernan, and others, and thus he had no difficulty in attributing it to a reversion to some primitive "primordial" bisexuality that had failed to properly differentiate. Aberrant sexual differentiation was caused by either structural or by functional defects without structural abnormality, the latter "dependent upon imperfect differentiation of sexual affinity. As sexual affinity is but a form of hunger . . . sexual perversion might naturally be expected to result." Examples of imperfect differentiation of sexual affinity without physical defect included "pederasts, Urnings, Subjects of bestiality," and "Affinity of the female for her own sex" and constituted a failure of development, not moral depravity, although this last is implied only about Urnings and females. As to the origins of this condition relating to Urnings and females, Lydston could only speculate, but concluded that the presence of the abnormality in women was attributable to a "reversal of type," while Uranism was caused by either "imperfect evolutionary development" or to a "reversal of type as well," the difference between them attributed to a lack of research about the female.[35] Those who suffered from congenital homosexuality were not responsible for their situation nor automatically insane and—unless other underlying pathologies of the mind could be diagnosed or nonconsensual sexual activity was noted—they should be held fully accountable for their actions.

Nonbiological Theories of Homosexuality

The closely related biological theories of Lydston and Kiernan represented one generic argument about the etiology of homosexuality, even though everyone accepted the notion of legal responsibility absent a diagnosis of mental incapacity due to insanity. Charles H. Hughes, Professor of Neurology and Psychiatry at the Barnes Medical College of

St. Louis, William Lee Howard, M.D. of Baltimore, and Morton Prince, M.D., Instructor of Diseases of the Nervous System at the Harvard Medical School developed alternative, nonbiological theories supporting the notion that homosexuality was the result of human depravity. They rejected the congenital theory of sexual perversions as applied to homosexuality, and presented an argument derived from Christianity that vice was the cause of such behavior. In a summary to his article, "Sexual Perversion or Vice? A Pathological and Therapeutic Inquiry," Morton Prince most aptly expressed their position,

> Finally, the fact must not be lost sight of—it is not questioned—that cultivation is capable of generating this aberration and developing it to its most intense degree, even to the feeling of repulsion for the opposite sex and to the acquisition of contrary tastes and habits ... It follows as a necessary corollary that this so-called perversion is not really a perversion, but a perversity,—a vice rather than a disease.[36]

William Howard's diagnosis was similar. Depravity led weak-willed men and women to engage in such excesses of sexual activity that their heightened lust could only be satisfied by means of perverse sexual encounters such as homosexual fellatio—"buccal onanism"—or prostitution.[37] Morton Prince was much more emphatic in his position. As an ardent supporter of the theory of human depravity, Prince was a medical and social hygienist in the purity movement mold who felt that all perversions of the sex instinct to include homosexuality "deleteriously affect social decency and order."[38] He took exception to the prevailing theory that sexual perversions were an "expression of pathological conditions of the nervous system," and suggested that the "depraved" instincts were "cultivated" by those suffering from insanity or "imbecility." The persistence of the perversions might lead a casual observer to believe that they were congenital when in actuality they were a true psychosis that had the "force" of an "imperative feeling," but nothing more.

In a direct challenge to Krafft-Ebing, Prince maintained that the evidence for a congenital theory of contrary sexual instinct was "incomplete and unreliable" and very few of his studies would stand up under further analysis. Cultivation, Prince believed, was a better explanation because it commended itself to "the intelligent and common-sense-mind." Drawing upon the research of the then well-known German psychiatrist Albert von Schrenck-Notzing, Prince criticized Krafft-Ebing's conclusions as too patient-dependent. Any patient might have felt that his or her condition was inborn, but just because one felt that way did not make it a scientific fact.

> ... an examination of the congenital-perversion theory shows that it rests entirely upon the auto-biographies of perverts and certain assumptions ... regarding the normal development of the vita sexualis, and of the tastes, habits, and modes or thought peculiar to each sex ... Even taking an ordinary medical history we should hesitate to accept such testimony as final, and I think we should be even more cautious in our examination of autobiographies which attempt to give an analysis founded on introspection of the feelings, passions, and tastes of degenerate individuals who attempt to explain their first beginnings in early childhood, and attribute each to its proper excitant ... Probably there is no class of people whose statements will less stand the test of a searching cross-examination that the moral pervert.[39]

In essence, Prince thought Krafft-Ebing had relied too much upon patient histories without doing any real independent research into the actual cause of homosexuality. The results of Krafft-Ebing, Kiernan, Lydston, and others had to be modified, therefore, and looked at in a different light, one which Prince supplied. In his view, the constant repetition of "vicious" acts by the weak willed, however that condition may have come about, led to "habit neuroses or psychoses," independent of the will,

> Thus it is conceivable that sexual feelings and actions may by constant excitation (cultivation) become associated together and developed into a sort of quasi-independent neural activity which may thus become practically independent of the will, or in other words, a psychosis ... Such a perversion may acquire all the force or imperative ideas or feelings, as von Schrenck-Notzing thinks. Finally, the important point, clinically, socially, and forensically, is the recognition of the fact that many perverts ... are insane.[40]

Sexual perversion was by this account not the least bit inborn, but rather the sign of a grave mental disturbance. Any other explanation was merely a flight of the imagination, a "fanciful" notion that reminds one of early legends of humans beings who appeared in the form of animals,

> Various theories, many of them fanciful, have been proposed to account for the origin of this (according to this view) anomalous condition. Ulrich, himself a pervert, thought a female mind was enclosed in a male body. This condition he considered due to atavism. This fanciful notion which reminds one of some of the early legends of human beings appearing in the form of animals, is maintained even by later medical writers. This same idea appears in a new form in the hypothesis of Kiernan,

adopted by Lydston, that contrary sexuality is a reversion to the primitive type of the lowest forms of this which are bisexual.[41]

No, Prince continued, contrary sexual instinct was more in accordance with the theory of the French psychologist Alfred Binet who argued that the perversion was acquired through "the force of association of ideas." The origins were to be found in external circumstances rather than from a hereditarian predisposition. External suggestions, pornography for example, or unconscious mimicry that affected the subconscious state of the individual's personality could trigger the perversions. It was not even beyond the realm of possibility that "perfectly healthy individuals" harbored a degree of erotic feeling or ideas for a "person of the same sex" that were kept in check by "social customs, habits of thought, unwritten laws and moral precepts." A person of a "tainted constitution," however, would do "everything in his power to foster, indulge, and cultivate the perverse instinct while in such a soil the feelings themselves acquire a monstrous force." Under these circumstances, Prince concluded that the perversions of the sex instinct were less a real perversion in the Kiernan, Lydston, and Krafft-Ebing sense than a "perversity—a vice rather than a disease."[42]

Could Homosexuality be Cured?

Disagreements regarding the causes of homosexuality naturally gave way to disagreements about whether or not a cure was appropriate, and if so, which was most effective. Ranging broadly from a do-nothing program to castration and a life in an asylum or prison, most physicians wanted to clean up society and offered suggestions about how to go about doing so, frequently on the backs of homosexuals. Havelock was the exception, and although an Englishman with sensibilities stemming from his work in the United Kingdom, his articles were widely circulated throughout the American medical community by means of the *Alienist and Neurologist*. In response to the nagging question put forward by the various purity reformers of the day about what to do with the alleged congenital homosexuals, Ellis was unequivocal: leave them alone! If the condition was acquired, then it was simply a matter of removing those conditions responsible for the acquisition, which for Ellis was the school, the "breeding ground of artificial homosexuality among the general population—at all events in England." The congenital type, however, was a different story in as much as no amount of therapy could change what was inborn, and any attempt to do so only produced depression and neurasthenia in the patient. Perhaps, he thought, an invert might momentarily engage in sexual relations with the opposite sex, but that was only temporary as "the treatment is usually interrupted by continued backsliding to homosexual practices." Under these circumstances, the best therapy was to help the invert adjust to his condition in order to be "healthy" and "self-respecting."[43]

American neurologists were not so forgiving. Some, for example, the doctors F. E. Daniel, E. Stuver, and C. H. Hughes argued from the perspective of social Darwinism, and recommended castration in order to reduce the pervert's sex drive and reduce his ability to ensnare the unsuspecting. Absent castration, all perverts, to include the homosexual, should be subject to "perpetual sequestration from society."[44] Others, such as Morton Prince, recommended hypnosis, while yet another group of physicians were unable to make up their minds and recommended a variety of therapies to include permanent removal to an asylum, castration, sterilization, and hysterectomy in the case of women. James Kiernan simply suggested intense "management" by a doctor monitoring the patient's condition since inversion had no cure, although he implied that perhaps hypnosis or possibly even sequestration might be necessary in some cases. A few doctors such as Mark Milikin of Cincinnati, Ohio, and De Causey of Austin, Texas, recoiled at castration as too barbaric, and suggested instead that a better therapy would be reform while in restriction, however the nature of the reform was left unstated.

No American neurologist or psychiatrist accepted homosexuality as a normal, albeit minority, condition. Each expressed the hope that the condition could be ameliorated, and the most vocal physicians on this issue, people such as Rosse, Hughes, and Lydston, condemned the modern society that produced the homosexual and other perverts in the first place. For them, castration, "sequestration" in prison or asylum were merely short-term solutions to the larger problem of reforming America and returning it to the traditions and standards that had once made the country great.

Irving C. Rosse, Professor of Nervous Diseases at Georgetown, observed that due to "manifest disturbances of a badly-balanced nervous system" caused by "large population centers," "nihilism," and "anarchy," the United States was caught in the vicious grip of "uncleanness forbidden by God and despised by man." "Obscene" and "Saphic" literature; the "unclean realism or Zola and Tolstoi"; the "importation of vice" from Europe; pornography; "indecent" advertising; "corrupt and immoral publications"; "human vampires"; "luxury and unbridled lust"; and "sexual hypochondriasis and perversion of the genesic [reproductive] instinct" were to be found in abundance across the country, but especially in urban centers along the eastern seaboard. The resolution to America's new problems was not to be found with more restrictive legislation, however, but with prevention and education "with the employment of appropriate medical and surgical measures . . . that any intelligent physician can suggest." Medical, social, and "psychic" hygiene rules could be counted upon to restore America to its past greatness. Otherwise, like Rome, the United States was sure to be enveloped in rot and decay,

> Although we may not share the belief of a preacher, who speaks of unbridled lust as the great danger that threatens America today, it may be well to bear in mind the results of Roman impudicity, more cruel than the sword, according to the energetic suppression of Juvenal, and that more recent admonition found in two lines of the Deserted Village:
>
> *"Ill fares the land to hastening ills a prey,*
> *Where wealth accumulation and men decay."*[45]

For C. H. Hughes, the social situation in the United States was very much similar, only he was more explicit in his references to neurasthenia and social Darwinism. Societies evolved from the savage to the civilized in which the "higher mind" was regulated and restrained, giving rise to "health, vigor, and tranquility." But many people in the United States, the most highly developed civilization to date, were suffering from the same sort of lascivious libertinism and perverted sexual vices associated with Roman and Greek antiquity, clearly an "atavic descent" capable of "direct hereditary transmission." The origin of this condition was "neuropsychical instability" due to the "over-strain and over-indulgence" of the modern American. In their lust to liberate themselves from their past and the restraints of tradition, Americans had demanded "retrograde changes" for more physical, political, moral, and mental freedoms that unfortunately unleashed the impulse for moral degradation and relaxed the faculty of self-restraint. Modern America had become a cauldron of unstable passion as each person laid claim to his or her individuality, unchecked by religion or reason, and thus without morality.[46]

Morbid eroticism characterized by a "failure of inhibition" and an "exhalation and perversion of the erotic feelings" was one of numerous conditions that arose out of this cauldron. If this depravity were to be overcome, it was not sufficient that only the morbid conditions be treated; it was also necessary that the underlying social pathology be cured as well, and that required a massive cleanup job across the entire country that would stop the forces of degeneration and put an end to "atavic descent." This could only be accomplished if religion once again became a "regulation of moral conduct"; if ambition signified a growth in "moral worth and grandness of self-control" rather than the desire to "shine and scintillate"; if "prudent restraint" replaced "pursuit of pleasure"; if the purpose of ambition meant position and not "self-equipoise"; and if the aims of many were not limited to "self-gratification of the pleasing propensities." In short, Hughes was prescribing a return to a romantic vision of a pre-urban rural society liberated, as it were, from the rough edges of industrial America. Only then would happiness on a national scale be realized. The state, Hughes believed, was the instrument through which social hygiene and thus happiness could be realized by the elimination of the "moral pestilence." Together with the "Law," medicine would act to "mercifully" protect society and the "maimed victim of a sexually and mentally degenerate organism," but that could happen only if Americans understood that the roots of their current evils were derived from a neuropathy originating in the stresses and strains of an urban, industrial society freed from the constraints of tradition and addicted to the greed of unfettered laissez-faire capitalism.[47]

Homosexuality and Social Decay

G. Frank Lydston developed the most thorough critique of American society as it related to sexual perversions and homosexuality in particular. Other physicians, to be sure, wrote about social decay and reform in America, and some also included short asides about sexual perversions. For example, in *Sexual Debility in Man* (1900) by Dr. F. R. Sturgis, an associate of Lydston, several paragraphs are devoted to the numerous perversions of the sex instinct, but the information is scanty and the reader was referred to other sources for greater insight. Earlier still, individuals such as John Harvey Kellogg in *Plain Facts for Old and Young* (1879), and "A Physician" in *Satan and Society* (1876), fleeting references were made to a close relationship between the temptations of modern America, masturbation, and unnatural love to which "onanism" would lead. Such was the literary stock and trade of the purity reformers. In *Criminology* (1892), the American criminal anthropologist Arthur MacDonald briefly addressed the problem of sodomy and mutual "onanism" but only within the context of juvenile delinquency and its social origins. In 1894, Charles Gilbert Chaddock in his article "Sexual Crimes" made quick reference to the relationship between the sexual perversions and a neuropathic nervous system caused by modern stresses. But it was Lydston in his tome *Diseases of Society*, who most fully articulated a theory that the sexual perversions and homosexuality were critical manifestations of a society that was extremely ill, morally, neurologically, psychologically, politically, economically, and socially.

What is important about Lydston to the history of American homophobia is the larger social Darwinist context within which he conceptualized homosexuality. While this context was clearly popular among the social purity reformers, some Progressives, and many of the educated elites of the day, medical or otherwise, it was Lydston who most thoroughly and comprehensively applied social Darwinist sentiment to the underlying etiology of homosexuality. Accordingly, acquired and congenital homosexuality were "diseases of society" that demanded draconian measures to ultimately eradicate them if the United States were to be healed and returned to a state of health and vigor. First, the United States had to reduce the stresses that plagued it in order that neuropathy cease. Practically speaking, this implied a return to a preindustrial, rural America of the antebellum period in which he romanticized an environment liberated from the smothering effects of smokestacks, the rush of city life, women in the work force, the putative breakdown of the (rural) family, immigrants, and the usual vice attendant upon large urban centers. Simultaneously, the medical community, and neurologists in particular, had to develop therapies that relieved the individual victim of the neuropathic condition. Therapies were to be both preventive and curative. Preventive therapies consisted first and foremost of "marriage control," or the granting of marriage licenses only to those who showed no "signs" of mental or moral deficiency, for it was a well-known "fact" that inappropriate marriages were "the fountain-head of the stream of degeneracy that sweeps through all social systems."[48] Good marriages produced healthy children who grew up to be good citizens. If control over who was able to marry were lacking, then society would open the door to a degenerate population, "The criminal, the insane, the epileptic, the syphilitic, and the drunkard are here authorized by law to begin the procreation of their kind, the number of their progeny being limited entirely by the volition and physical capacity of the individuals immediately concerned."[49] Society had the right to protect itself from degenerates, and thus it was justified in curtailing who could and could not get married. Only those with good hereditary history free from taint should be allowed to procreate in order to produce good offspring that in turn would create a healthy social body, "In brief, I believe that man will one day devote to the breeding of human beings some of the knowledge he has acquired in the breeding of the lower animals. Stirpiculture [stock breeding] will be the salvation of the race, and is the rational antidote for degeneracy and its train of evils—social and individual."[50]

Additional preventives included improving the economic and environmental conditions of the poor through the "gospel of work, health and cleanliness" paid for by the social taxation of the "great philanthropists [sic] in our midst." Good books and periodicals were highly recommended, as was attending Christian workingmen's clubs. Lydston was especially keen about the benefits of rural life, "The free air of heaven, sunshine, trees, birds, flowers, and running brooks are worth as much in moral as in physical development. As further palliative to the immoralities of modern American, communing with nature in "broad acres and forests, remote from the city," and "farming for the employment of juveniles, delinquent and non-delinquent" were prescribed.[51]

The education of children was central to all of Lydston's recommendations for the prevention and cure of crime. Educate the young, he argued, and those who were not born "imbeciles" could be prevented from becoming delinquent. Thus for the generation of infants not born of an hereditary taint, the key was to prevent the transmission of acquired disease to offspring—and that required the sound-of-mind to be isolated from the vices of modern society. Physical and moral training in conjunction with fresh air, and the benefits of a rural environment would help predispose the individual to a good life, free from taint. But this was not in and of itself sufficient for the prevention of degeneracy. The country as a whole had to dedicate itself to a crusade against all that contributed to degeneracy, and that included reforming all the social evils, from political corruption to pornography; masturbation to prostitution, alcoholism, and the perversion of the sex instinct as well as excesses of wealth; slough; labor agitation; "foolish" ambition; political and economic "plutocracy"; "genteel" occupations; poverty; feminism; and the poor sanitary conditions of the city. Lydston's message was clear: either America cleaned itself up, or it could expect additional degeneracy, which in any event already threatened America's perfectionist and exceptionalist promise.[52]

For the habitual criminal, Lydston recommended sterilization, asexualization [castration], isolation, and even death. Castration, he believed, had the desired effect of relieving the criminal of his primitive instinctive desire to lead a life of crime. "The castration of the adult criminal would not result in the development of savage instincts, but if the experience of the ages counts for anything, the operation would be likely to tone down to a marked degree such savagery as atavism had developed in him."[53] Sterilization was another option since it "accomplishes precisely the same results,"[54] and prevented another generation of criminals from seeing the light of day. Another solution was permanent isolation, perhaps in prison or in an asylum designed for just such a degenerate.

In those instances where neuropathy had already resulted in incurable congenital or incurable inherited "taint," isolation and even elimination might be warranted. Incurables had no claim to civil rights and their disposition ought to humanely reflect this fact. "The incurable criminal is regarded as an individual who is absolutely forbidden all rights—save the right to treatment as humane as consistent with perpetual isolation." A healthy society, like a healthy body, naturally eliminated its wasteful products, and by analogy, "A healthy society, like a healthy body, eliminates from itself the morbid and morbific dejecta, whose retention would imperil vitality." In point of fact, the incurable might be so degenerate that justice demanded his very life be forfeited, a person "who, in strict justice, has not even the right to live."[55]

Tucked away quietly in a large chapter on the "Treatment of Sexual Vice and Crime," Lydston categorically states that congenital inverts had to be permanently removed from the social system so that their moral contagion not pollute the rest of society. "The congenital variety is incurable. All incurable victims should be permanently removed from our social system. They are sources of moral contagion and promoters of sexual crime to whom the right to remain in society should be denied."[56] The key to Lydston's prescription is the phrase "removed permanently." At times, he seems to suggest removal to an asylum; at others, prison, euthanasia, or under surveillance. Yet throughout *Diseases*, his reliance upon asexualization, sterilization, and euthanasia contextualize his entire discussion of the disposition of the incurable, the congenital, and the otherwise criminally predispositioned by reason of hereditary "taint." The medicalization of homosexuality had, in Lydston's imagination, created an incurable entity relegated to the status of permanent exile from society, either through some form of incarceration, permanent monitoring, or death. This was hardly the dream of Krafft-Ebing, Kiernan, or of homosexuals themselves.

Chapter 10

An Emerging Homosexual Identity During the Gilded Age

> The number of these sexual perverts in America is astonishing to one unacquainted with this most important branch of neuropathic studies. As I have said, they belong to the intellectual classes, and are found in the pulpit, at the editorial desk and in the studios, as well as before the bar and at the bedside. They exist in both male and female societies and clubs, and by some subtle psychic influence these perverts recognize each other the moment they come in social contact. They are well read in literature appertaining to their condition; they search for everything written relating to sexual perversion; and many of them have devoted a life of silent study and struggle to overcome their terrible affliction. They have but little faith in the general practitioner, and their past treatment justifies their lack of confidence . . . All this suffering is due to the fact that they realize they are looked upon as unclean beasts; that they are socially ostracized, that they are misunderstood, and that those who should aid them, the physicians, are the very ones to cast the huge stones of obloquy and disgust.[1]

Throughout the Gilded Age, homosexuality was neither unseen nor unheard, and that, of course, was exactly the problem for those who were concerned and threatened by it. Indeed, the medical and legal communities made frequent mention of its presence across the country, but primarily within the larger urban centers of St. Louis, Chicago, New York, and Washington, DC. Undeterred by civil or legal sanction, however, homosexuals developed enclaves that catered to their sense of emergent identity as to who they were and what they liked. A product of urbanization and a desire for legitimization and companionship, these enclaves helped to create a sense of community and personal identity. For those who lived in rural America, however, such communities were nonexistent, and the individual was left adrift.

To a very large extent, the development of a homosexual identity was a social construction among and between the disparate parties to the discussion. Basic to this discussion was the debate between homosexual and homosexual; physician and physician; physician and the general public; physician and homosexual; homosexual and the general public. Each party to this process contributed their understanding of what they thought it meant to be homosexual, what caused it, and the personal and social consequences of this condition. Sometimes opinion converged; for example, the tendency of many physicians to accept the assertion ultimately derived from homosexuals themselves, that the condition was inborn. Sometimes opinion differed, especially with respect to therapeutics, consequences, and the appropriateness of a homosexual lifestyle within a marginalized subculture. Homosexuals themselves knew that euthanasia, "conversion," permanent assignment to an asylum, a prison, or other forms of forced isolation were out of the question, although precisely how one should express oneself publicly and privately remained an open question. Indeed, the presence of divergent lifestyles and communities attested to the rejection of the physician-recommended "solutions" to the "homosexual problem."

By the end of the nineteenth century, a core identity had been recognized that was acceptable to all even if it was tentative and no conclusions could be reached about the consequences of that identity. In spite of an enormous diversity regarding etiology, all participants to the debate agreed that congenital homosexuality was real, a virtually exclusive and ineradicable psychosexual attraction for a member of the same sex, often but not always expressed sexually. How one reacted to this realization was, of course, another matter. The fact that one might be attracted to a member of the same sex was no guarantee that one accepted one's "orientation." Nor did it necessarily follow that those who were heterosexual rejected this new orientation—or from time to time did not engage in sex acts patently homosexual in nature, such as paying a male prostitute to perform fellatio. Furthermore as George Chauncy has argued, for some individuals, be they homosexual or not, homosexuality was conceptualized as a complete inversion of the sex role, not limited to the sex object alone. Most physician neurologists—Kiernan, Krafft-Ebing, and Lydston, for example—even recognized that many people were potentially bisexual, and sexual attraction was frequently not directed exclusively to one sex or the other all the time. Indeed, if "normal" or heterosexual sexual attraction were to be attained, they believed it was critical that individuals be educated to that end, otherwise an abnormal or "perverted" sexuality directed to the wrong sex object might develop, particularly among the "weak-willed." Such was Morton Prince's position, which to varying degrees was shared by the medical community at large. Nevertheless, same-sex attraction was foundational to the identity of the modern homosexual even as the social context in which the homosexual was situated changed, and debates continued about the nature of the "pure" homosexual. This was particularly relevant to those who knew themselves to be attracted to a person of the same sex. They were under no illusions about the object of their desires, and although they were often perplexed, confused, even depressed due to their difference, they understood the depth of their attraction. It was, as so many attested, a fact beyond their control.

The issue of human moral depravity did not go away simply because physicians said so, and homosexual acts might still be committed by those who suffered from "moral insanity." But this position did not change the fact that a novel medical diagnosis of congenital homosexuality came to dominate the discourse of late nineteenth-century science and posited the existence of an innate homosexual identity. Since this identity was the result of multiple sources, its precise nature was fluid and, while it always revolved around the core desire of same-sex attraction, its peripheral manifestations practically defied categorization. For all of the papers written about homosexuals and for all of the autobiographies by homosexuals, be they American or European, no consensus existed about how they acted, dressed, had sex, developed relationships, what they looked like, where they lived, played, worked, or met each other. All that was really agreed upon was that congenital homosexuals claimed to feel toward the same sex what "normal" men and women felt for each other. Yet another questioned remained: Was this behavior sufficient in itself to give rise to a distinct identity that would distinguish the homo from the hetero?

The answer must of necessity be ambiguous, especially during this period. Congenital homosexuality was a novel condition with no public or private history, thus no one had a traditional homosexual role model against which the novel condition could be compared. Who we are or who we perceive ourselves to be is the product of our own past as well as of our present and future. A homosexual identity presupposes the presence and reality of a public and private homosexual orientation against which a person can judge ones behavior, and then choose to identify as homosexual or not. If one rejects a homosexual identity in spite of behaviors that might lead an outside observer to the opposite conclusion, is one homosexual? On whose authority was a homosexual identity conferred? The physician? The police? The individual? The public? The question of who precisely was a homosexual and why thus became central to the issue of homosexual identity, a concept that during the Gilded Age was far from settled.

A Story Told in Words and Pictures

In the absence of extensive interaction with those who claimed same-sex attraction, many American neurologists relied upon the firsthand experience of other doctors, frequently that of the Austrian Krafft-Ebing or the Englishman Havelock Ellis. Their insights and case autobiographies were reprinted across the country and provided most doctors with what they believed was sufficient knowledge upon which to base their diagnosis. Not surprisingly, Karl Ulrichs was central to all future discussions of the emergent homosexual identity. It will be recalled that back in the 1860s and 1870s he had written a number of pamphlets in which he defended same-sex attraction as a naturally occurring phenomenon that was not the product of moral depravity. Neither true man nor true woman, the male "Urning" was, according to his assessment, a mixture of man and woman, and indeed, just the opposite was true by analogy of women who were attracted to their own sex. Neither woman nor man, they, too, were a mixture. Why such individuals came to be was an open question, but that they existed and were a product of nature was clear enough. "How and why nature has called such intermixed beings into existence is a riddle not yet solved. On the other hand, that it does act in this way, that it is nature which gives the Urning his sexual love, is now beyond dispute."[2] Ulrichs accepted his own condition, and sought to define and clarify it to outsiders in such a way as to legitimize his own inclinations as natural and therefore neutral, if not good.

Ulrichs' self-proclaimed theory of the naturalness of the Urning was a precursor to the creation of a homosexual identity. Urnings existed, they were different, and their difference was a natural condition that set them apart from the rest of humanity, a position that was generally accepted by Ellis and Krafft-Ebing and confirmed in their research. The congenital or "pure" homosexual was a distinct type of individual who was acutely aware of and sensitive to that separating him or her from everyone else, and that distinction related to the object of sexual attraction. Individuals so inclined developed an understanding of who they were by virtue of this unique difference, as a consequence of which, they sought others so constituted—even if from time to time they might act out their inclinations with others not so constituted. Thus we read an autobiography from a typical Ellis case of true congenital sexual "inversion,"

> My own sexual nature was a mystery to me. I found myself cut off from the understanding of others, felt myself an outcast, and with a highly loving and clinging temperament was intensely miserable. I thought about my male friends—sometimes boys of my own age, sometimes elder

boys, and once even a master—during the day and dreamed about them at night, but was too convinced that I was a hopeless monstrosity ever to make any effectual advances. Later on it was much the same, but gradually, though slowly, I came to find that there were others like myself. I made a few special friends and at last it came to me occasionally to sleep with them and to satisfy my imperious need by mutual embraces and emissions. Before this happened, however, I was once or twice on the brink of despair and madness with repressed passion and torment.[3]

Krafft-Ebing's subjects echoed similar concerns, as one of his male autobiographies makes clear,

> My sexual instinct awakened when I was thirteen, and from the moment of its appearance was directed toward youthful, strong men. At first I was not really certain that this was abnormal, but consciousness of it came when I saw and heard how my companions were characterized sexually . . . Thereafter I made the acquaintance of a young artist, who very soon noticed that I was abnormal, and confessed to me that he was in the same condition. I learned from him that this abnormality was very frequent and this knowledge overcame the trouble I had had in supposing that I was alone in my abnormality.[4]

Both Ellis and Krafft-Ebing discussed female inversion, but gave it less consideration than that of the males. One consequence of this aversion is the paucity of firsthand autobiographical information regarding late nineteenth-century lesbian identity formation as opposed to that of the male. One exception is to be found in Ellis' 1901 edition of *Sexual Inversion* where he included a firsthand account of a woman who defended female inversion, which may be described as one of the earliest expressions of a specifically lesbian identity,

> Inverts should have the courage and independence to be themselves, and to demand an investigation. If one strives to live honorably, and considers the greatest good to the greatest number, it is not a crime nor a disgrace to be an invert . . . All that I desire—and I claim it as my right—is the freedom to exercise this divine gift of loving, which is not a menace to society nor a disgrace to me. Let it once be understood that the average invert is not a moral degenerate nor a mental degenerate, but simply a man or woman who is less highly specialized, less completely differentiated, than other men and women . . . I know what it means to be an invert—who feels himself [sic] set apart from the rest of mankind—to find one human heart who trusts him and understands him, and I know how almost impossible this is, and will be, until the world is made aware of these facts.[5]

Women were frequently diagnosed in the third person. Therefore their sense of who they were was filtered by the physician who often perceived the same-sex sexuality of their female patients as a sign of inversion absent the emergence of a lesbian identity. Under this construction, female inverts were isolated instances of homosexuality between two individuals who suffered from the debilitating effects of a congenital condition. Males, by way of contrast, were not necessarily isolated in as much as they would eventually learn to recognize each other and come to live in communities in urban centers. Whereas the male homosexual was developing an identity that delineated him from nonhomosexual males, the female acted alone without identity, a solitary pervert, but no less congenital for all that. This, of course, was consistent with the Victorian patriarchal ideal that men were in charge of the public sphere while women were in charge of the private. This is not to suggest that individual women were unaware of their difference; they weren't. Krafft-Ebing made this quite clear when he wrote that even should the female invert marry, she was unhappy and depressed as a wife. If happiness were achieved, it was elsewhere, outside the marriage. ". . . her greatest happiness was in correspondence with her former lover. She felt that this was wrong, but she could not give it up; for to do so made her miserable."[6]

Unlike Ulrichs, however, Krafft-Ebing did not embrace homosexuality as a naturally occurring good. Instead, he considered congenital homosexuals the "stepchildren of nature" and although they were not particularly bad for all that, they were nevertheless the poor victims of nature gone amok. This was not the same as Ulrichs' near celebration of his condition, nor did it reflect the acceptance of the German Magnus Hirschfeld, the Englishmen Edward Carpenter and John Addington Symonds, early advocates for homosexual emancipation in Europe, nor of the American poet Walt Whitman.

Magnus Hirschfeld (1868–1935), a homosexual Jewish physician from Berlin, is considered the "grandfather" of gay liberation. In 1897 he established the "Scientific-Humanitarian Committee" for the express purpose of abolishing the antihomosexual statute in the German legal code, paragraph 175. Throughout the course of his life, Hirschfeld was dedicated to removing the social and legal stigmata that were associated with homosexuality, and to helping the Urning develop a positive sense of self in the otherwise nasty social and political environment of late nineteenth-century Germany and Europe.

In 1891, the English physician and advocate of homosexual rights, John Addington Symonds (1840–1893), published *A Problem in Modern Ethics*, in which the British medical community's negative portrayal of homosexuals was condemned. In Symonds' opinion, the modern physician thoroughly misunderstood the nature of homosexuality, and presented the public and the homosexual with "vulgar errors" that needed correction. A male who loved his own sex was not, he argued, a morbid freak of nature or scum of the earth as diagnosed by the doctor or conceptualized by the general public. Those views were totally erroneous. The true sexual invert, by contrast and without antisocial characteristics, was noble. Inspired by Walt Whitman's celebration of comradely love and manly fellowship, Symonds celebrated manly love particularly in its spiritual and emotional manifestations. Freedom, not prison, was the answer, and England would do well to rescind its laws as they pertained to the Urning, and leave him free to go about his business without the threat of humiliation and incarceration.[7]

Edward Carpenter (1844–1929), gay, socialist, admirer of Whitman, and turn-of-the-century activist for women and homosexuals, was also supportive of homosexual rights and the development of a positive gay identity. Rejecting the popular and medical arguments that homosexuality represented a morbid condition, Carpenter insisted that the "Urning type," male or female, was healthy and far from abnormal since "many are fine, healthy specimens of their sex, muscular and well-developed in body, of powerful brain, high physical structure or constitution."[8]

In the main, the writings of these men, especially the English, were generally unknown in the United States outside of a small circle of individuals around Walt Whitman. Hirschfeld was better known in the medical community, but less for his advocacy than his research into the origins of homosexuality, which tended to reflect the ideas of Ulrichs. The difficulty for Americans was that no one spoke out on their behalf for anything remotely approximating a "positive" identity for those who preferred love and sex with their own. With the exception of a very limited number of writers mentioned in chapter 2 (of this book) and Whitman—who, in any event, only indirectly made reference to physical relations between men—the issue of homosexuality was essentially a medical one. The development of a homosexual identity, therefore, took place within the context of the discovery of a new pathology that was vigorously studied so that it might be controlled by the authority of the scientific community in order to stop degeneration in its tracks. After all, it was the physician's duty to assure society that American exceptionalism would not collapse under the weight of crime and corruption.

In the United States, investigators like Kiernan and Lydston accepted the validity of congenital homosexuality as developed by European doctors without much additional input from case studies except that contained in the works of Krafft-Ebing, Ellis, the German Albert Moll, and others from France, Italy, and Russia. Some American neurologists, Chaddock, in particular, interviewed a few men and women, and felt their insights confirmed the conclusions of Krafft-Ebing as well as additional European and American doctors he consulted from time to time, most notably Kiernan and Lydston. Here was an exercise in circularity that allowed for no new insights. It was this paucity of original research and the methodologically flawed reliance on autobiographies, as has been discussed earlier, that led Morton Prince to reject their findings as unscientific. Nevertheless, this did not prevent American physicians from discussing what it meant to be and live as a congenital homosexual. They were not advocates for the invert, and they never accepted the condition as benign.

Outside of a few medical autobiographies and the writings of a handful of authors, the majority of Americans inclined toward same-sex eroticism, be they male or female, were silent. If they did read Carpenter, Symonds, Wilde, Hirschfeld, Whitman, Melville, Taylor, Stoddard, Sturgis, or other late nineteenth-century literati who quietly took up the issue, what insights they might have gained were not shared publicly. The images of same-sex attraction that emerged from these writers varied, but in general it was one of beauty in love or sadness in its denial. The authors accepted themselves for who they were, but found it difficult to allow their characters to act on their love in a world that did not acknowledge its validity. They created identities that were freed from the control of science, but that were nevertheless sensitive to their discovery by a hostile environment. Bayard Taylor's protagonists Joseph and Philip are split apart by Joseph's marriage; Charles Stoddard finds fleeting love on the distant shores of the Pacific islands; Howard Sturgis secretly pines after the school boy Tim from afar; and Whitman's romantic love between men touches the soul but never the body. The writers were in a class of their own, and paid little attention to the physicians or the police.

Others were not so fortunate because they became pawns in the scientific and legal debates that surrounded the discovery of the homosexual. Ironically, what little is currently known about the alleged homosexual was filtered through the eyes of the observer, be it physician, police, or press. For the most part, the outsiders interpreted what information they had from the perspective of their own social, economic, sexual, ethnic, and class biases. In some respects, they functioned not unlike Jeremy Bentham's panopticon, his model prison in which all inmates could be watched and assessed through the lens of a great wall of glass. Yet in spite of these barriers, it is still possible to gain a limited insight into how some saw themselves in comparison to those around them.

Similar to their European counterparts, the physician-identified inverts were found in rural as well as in urban environments, and were considered to be sexual outlaws, uniquely different from the majority. Just how different depended upon the individual and the community in which the individual was situated. Males who lived openly in communities within the large urban centers appeared to have developed countercultures revolving around a sexuality that was publicly frowned upon: male prostitute; "cock-sucker"; mutual masturbator; pederast; cross-dresser; and voyeur; all types of behaviors that would have driven Anthony Comstock or any purity reformer crazy.

We can gain a small insight into the types of sexual behaviors that some of these Americans engaged in by reviewing some of the pornographic literature that still exists today. In *The Rotenberg Collection: Forbidden Erotica*,[9] Mark Rotenberg has compiled more than a thousand underground erotic pictures with the bulk from the 1870s until the early 1920s gathered from the United States and Europe, primarily France. The majority is of men and women engaged in a multitude of sexual acts that were traditionally condemned by the moralist, such as fellatio, cunnilingus, anal intercourse, bestiality, menage-a-trois, and sixty-nine. From a modern point of view, the sexual activity of the nineteenth-century photos shows a remarkable affinity with current pornography and sexual behaviors and attitudes. The images and their popularity tell us something about the appeal and possible extent of condemned Gilded Age sexual practices, Anthony Comstock notwithstanding. In a word, more was going on than simple missionary style sexual intercourse, and none of it was intended for reproductive purposes. For the viewer, it was desire; for the manufacturer, profit; and for the participant, money (out of desperation?), fame, pleasure, and/or all three.

Some of the most interesting photographs are homosexual in nature, male and female. The photos of men show anal intercourse, passive-active; mutual masturbation; fellatio, passive-active; mutual fellatio; and french kissing with and without sex. Of the women, there is mutual masturbation; cunnilingus, active-passive; mutual cunnilingus; mutual masturbation; breast/nipple sucking; and vaginal intercourse with a dildo strapped on to the active female partner. In sum, there is a whole panoply of illicit sexual acts that make for very interesting viewing and that, if one did not know, might have been taken recently. While most of these individuals clearly enjoyed posing *in flagrante delicto* for the camera, the images of same-sex sexuality tell us nothing about the sexual identity or emotional engagement of the participants. Just because a man is sucking the erect penis of another and his erect penis in turn is being sucked by someone else does not necessarily prove that this is the image of two inverts. Likewise with the image of a young man who is engaged in anal intercourse with another young man. What these images do tell the viewer is that these acts took place; they were photographed, and by virtue of their underground sales there was a market among segments of the United States population, enough at any rate that Comstock became involved and made pornography of this sort a national issue. To the outside observer, police, press, or physician, however, the images of homosexual acts were suggestive of an inversion, acquired or congenital no less than the sight of men who seemed to act in the female role with respect to dress or mannerisms and, it was suspected, in the sex act too, which was to believe that they were "passive" during sexual intercourse, and "received" the penis, just like in the pictures.

Out on the Town

Whether derived from a desire to be with others of their "kind" or from a feeling that they had nowhere else to go, the fact remained that the communities were generally safe places for sexual nonconformists who openly expressed their sexuality in ways that could not be done elsewhere, and which might subject them eventually to the long arm of the law. According to Earl Lind (aka Ralph Werther, Jennie June et al.), in New York City between Fourth Avenue and Fourteenth Street there was one such community where sexual nonconformists congregated. Referred to as the Underworld, this area also had a well known and infamous "sex resort" named "Paresis Hall," a sarcastic if not campy use of a medical term that in those days meant insanity. The Hall catered to homosexually oriented drag queens and straight dressing inverts and was accepted as a gathering spot where one could meet others of similar persuasion who referred to themselves as "pansies" and assumed such colorful names as Mollie, Plum, Fairsea, and Prince Pansy. Here was an identity that, on the face of it, suggested the acceptance of the intermediate sex theory advanced by Ulrichs and picked up by many within the medical community who were always on the look out for physical signs of inversion, a "turning into" the opposite sex. No less a figure than Oscar Wilde confirmed this opinion, especially in the aftermath of his visit to the United States and his infamous trial in 1895. For those who identified themselves as an intermediate sex, to become a Mollie or Prince Pansy with rouged lips was most appropriate, as was, according to Katz, their role as "cock-sucker" in the sex act, a role traditionally played by a woman, debauched or not.[10]

Due to its overt and "depraved" clientele, the Hall was subjected to raids by the police as well as to the opprobrium of the public and religious community who referred to it as "Sodom."[11] Lind made the argument that the raids and public outrage were actually ridiculed by the regular patrons who mocked the police and the public's antipathy,

> Plum, the invert is not fit to live with the rest of mankind! He should be shunned as the lepers of biblical times. If generously allowed outside prison walls, the law should at least ordain that the word "Unclean" be branded in his forehead, and should compel his to cry, "Unclean! Unclean!" as he walks the streets, lest his very brushing against decent people contaminate them.[12]

With no particular claim to universality, the lifestyles of the patrons of the Paresis Hall community offered those so inclined one model of behavior they could emulate if it suited their personality and legitimated their needs. This is not to argue that they identified themselves as congenital homosexuals since we do not have their testimonies to that effect. What we do know is that they defied the strict Victorian gender barrier, as some of them were by their own accord known to make themselves sexually available for other men. Whether they considered themselves homosexual is another matter altogether. Physicians, on the other hand, were quick to label them homosexual; the only debate was whether it was due to acquired or congenital factors.

In another instance of outside labeling, the neurologist Chaddock wrote of the black and white inverts who cruised for sex anonymously in public parks in Washington, DC, and of others who were guests at a large ball with statues of nude men around whose penises red bows were tied. In neither case is there any indication that those who participated in these acts identified themselves as homosexual. In all cases, however, a common reference point was the erotic attraction for a person of the same sex, around which the participants developed rituals and symbols that expressed their difference while simultaneously alerting others who might want to celebrate that difference. A red ribbon around a statue's penis at a male drag ball is a strong message for those so inclined. What is important is that everyone recognized the rituals for what they were, elements of an identity upon which they could all agree and that suggested same-sex eroticism. Not that they labeled themselves homosexuals, but rather that there was an unspoken assumption that same-sex attraction was a desired goal. The physician neurologist would label that homosexual, and some people bought into this designator only because they had no other term to describe themselves. Some were even thankful that their condition now had a name even if they were poorly received by the medical community and the public at large. At least they knew what was wrong with them.

In this fashion, the homosexually oriented, the police, the public, and the physician worked together to produce a new identity that was gradually, if begrudgingly, accepted, and whose characteristics were derived from the personal histories of those afflicted as well as by the observed behaviors of those in the urban communities. A behavioral and social history was thus created against which the individual could now judge his or her actions in order to determine whether or not a label of homosexual was warranted. If it was, then one could assert, "I am a homosexual," and a new identity was assumed. But due to the negative social pressures that were pervasive during the Gilded Age, there was little or no incentive to do so, a fact that would retard the full development of a homosexual identity for more than fifty years. Why, for example, would a person who knew him, or herself, to be a congenital invert assume a homosexual identity if it was truly believed that homosexuality represented a form of degeneracy? What benefit might the individual gain from such an identity? On the other hand, if one were a congenital invert and drawn to the metropolis, one might be persuaded to assume as much of a homosexual identity as was necessary in order to be welcomed in to unwrap the ribbon, cruise the street, or quietly find the perfect mate for a Boston marriage. These actions could bring personal benefit that far outweighed any negative effects of a homosexual identity; namely, the ability to form human relationships with others like oneself. Loneliness can be a powerful incentive to act.

In *Love Stories*, Jonathan Katz makes this point. According to a story that appeared in an 1892 edition of the *New York Herald* about a popular bar known as the Slide, effeminate men "whose cheeks were rouged and whose manner suggested the infamy to which they had fallen,"[13] engaged in homosexual acts for money or a perverted sense of enjoyment. Women were present as well, most notably as prostitutes, and similar to their male counterparts, they engaged in "depraved" acts for money or from a perverted sense of enjoyment as well. The not so subtle category of congenital homosexuality was never referred to by the author, and the reader is left with no other conclusion about the behaviors than to conclude that they were the product of a singular depravity that allowed men and women to give in to their unnatural lusts, be they "cock-sucking," or cunnilingus.

Although the article was politically motivated and written to shock the reader, one may nevertheless learn a bit more from it about the formation of a homosexual identity in late nineteenth-century America. From the perspective of the police and the press, same-sex eroticism was both a depravity and a public nuisance that was located in the less desirable parts of the inner city. It had to be monitored because it assaulted public decency, and like any other public crime it had to be strictly controlled. In short, the police and the press did not consider homosexuality as much a congenital condition as a rather unpleasant consequence of urbanization, overcrowding, and the breakdown of traditional morality. Homosexuals had no identity, so to speak, except that of depraved criminal. But this position was, naturally enough, rebuffed by the participants themselves, as the habitués of Paresis Hall and no doubt the Slide would have felt. After all, these places were popular and had a large clientele who in spite of the police, or perhaps because of them, continued to come out and be seen publicly, rouge, periwig, and all.

We may never know exactly how the men and the women of the Slide or other pick-up bars felt about themselves, but it is clear that by virtue of their regular patronizing of a bar that catered to them in all their glory, they rejected conformity in favor of community. Rather than change who they felt they were, they banded together and publicly acknowledged their difference, often with great fanfare. They participated in any number of nonconforming sex and gender behaviors because they wanted to, even if they did not know why. Some may have been happy, and some frequently depressed, but in either case, they chose to enter a community of like-minded that allowed the expression of certain long-established behaviors that were recognized as valid by themselves, as a consequence of which, these behaviors were legitimated. Conversely, they knew that they were hated by the police and that, too, contributed to a sense of identity that said, "Not them." Contrary to what the police thought, the bar patrons really had an identity even if that rebellious identity was still under development, especially in the area of what we now label "homosexual orientation."

A Prisoner for Life

As the only complete memoir by an American male homosexual during the Gilded Age, *The Story of a Life* by Claude Hartland[14] offers a unique insight into identity formation and the difficulties one man confronted when, as a young person from the Midwest, he decided to act upon his inclinations and meet others similarly constituted. It was not an easy process, and in Hartland's case, it resulted in massive confusion and depression even as he felt justified in seeking out same-sex partners for erotic encounters and possibly love. Claude tells us that he first had stirrings that he was different when at around the age of ten he enjoyed dressing in girl's clothing, after which he described himself as effeminate and without any friends who were boys. When he was eleven, we are told that upon seeing and listening to his cousin for the first time, a "tall, well-developed young man," Claude's blood rushed to his face, and "an erection immediately followed and I longed to spring from my bed, clasp [him] in my arms, kiss his lips, and give full expression to this new passion."[15] Thrilled at the thought of sleeping naked with his cousin, this new passion overwhelmed Claude although it made him unhappy because he did not know what it meant except that it was the "demon of unnatural lust." Shortly thereafter, he noticed that he felt the same lustful passions for every "handsome and well-developed man" he came across in spite of a sense of shame and guilt.

Eventually, Hartland learned how to masturbate while fantasizing about handsome young men, but "relief" was only temporary. Beset by strange dreams, nervous guilt, and confusion about his passions, Claude kept his thoughts to himself. At thirteen, he and his family moved into a small city near his rural farm, where he soon found himself "constantly tortured" with an "unnatural desire" by the presence of "so many handsome men" that could only be relieved by "self-abuse." At fifteen, Claude's family once again returned to a rural farm, and the opportunities for an encounter with a handsome man ceased, although his lustful appetite for men did not, and much anguish followed as Claude attempted to rid himself of his continuous sexual obsession with handsome men. He even "converted" to Christianity in order to find redemption in Jesus, and just when he thought he had been saved, the lure of men crept back into his mind and "self-abuse" resumed. Now more lustful than ever, one night when he was seventeen, Claude was forced by circumstances to share a bed with his brother's friend. In less than five minutes, he and this young man went "wild with passion," during which time "the intense animal heat and the friction between our organs soon produced a simultaneous ejaculation, which overstepped my wildest dream of sexual pleasure."[16] Shamed by his intense enjoyment from this brief sexual encounter, Claude vowed to never do it again, although he knew that was impossible. From that moment on, he "flamed with desire for every handsome man" he saw, and shortly thereafter, managed to sleep with his brother's friend again with the predictable consequences. Together, these two young men happily experimented with male–male sexuality, and in the process learned to relish it in spite of Claude's reservations about the propriety of his actions. If Hartland is to believed, their sexual experimentation consisted of mutual petting to the point of orgasm, kissing, and caresses. This was, in his mind, the culmination of male–male sexuality. For the next two years during college, Claude sought sex in this form wherever he could, "not one but scores of such nights with different men,"[17] after which he claimed to regret his actions in spite of his inability to stop because he concluded, "Such intercourse was perfectly natural to me."[18] The "evil" passion persisted despite his desire to be "pure" and "good."

At nineteen, he took a job as an assistant teacher, and almost immediately fell in love with a youth under his care, a love he believed was pure and not made evil by his passion for handsome men. For a short while, Claude was content with his nonsexual attachment to his pupil and was determined that he remain so rather than give in to the "animality" of sex. But such was not to be, and shortly after his young ward "hurriedly left the room" and withdrew himself from Claude's affections forever, Hartland was seized by his passion for men, "and it was stronger than ever—so strong that I could scarcely keep from laying hold of strangers on the street."

Crushed, Claude returned home and set up his own subscription school, had sex with two handsome men, closed up his school, and swore not to give into his passion, including self-abuse. Yet once again, his desire for sex with men became an obsession, "The hot blood tingled in my veins from head to foot, and I hardly knew what I did."[19] Angry and unable to control his desires, Claude began a new teaching position and boarded with a new friend "with whom sexual relations soon began." The intensity and frequency of his sexual activities was so great that he soon became ill, returned home, but still unable to control himself, resumed sexual relations with a friend, which drove Claude into an even deeper state of depression. Vow upon vow was made not to have sex, and each time he broke it—here the handsome stranger, there the local preacher—mental anguish and guilt always followed, which in turn led him to develop "pure" relationships with one or more of his male students. These in turn were followed by nearly manic attacks of "lustful desires" that culminated in a sexual relationship with one of his fifteen-year-old students. That was the last straw, and Claude now sought out the help of physicians, one of whom was a neurologist who recommended "sexual intercourse with women as a relief."[20]

Disgusted by the experience that was nevertheless successful only because he fantasized about men, Claude foreswore women forever. His passion for men quickly returned, and now that he was in a city, he became aware of the large number of individuals "suffering from a disease similar to my own," which relieved him greatly even as he was "grieved to find the victims so numerous."[21] Grievance gave way to acceptance, and for the next several months, Claude cruised the city, picking up men whenever, wherever he could, and for the first time, he seemed to enjoy it as a natural expression of his character.

At twenty-seven, Hartland returned once again to his home, and struck up a relationship with his niece. Upon her unexpected death, he left his home for good and migrated to St. Louis in November 1899, where he vainly sought to overcome his condition. With a great amount of anguish and discipline, he was successful for a brief period under the platonic guidance of a new friend whose expertise was "mental discipline." Eventually, his mentor withdrew, leaving Claude alone to fight his own devils, which he was unable to do. Soon he was cruising the city streets, picking up tricks along the way, and upon one occasion, was physically assaulted and robbed. Frightened by this experience, Claude consulted with an eclectic mix of professional healers, to include a "skilled physician," and a "leading minister," but to no avail. His passions would not go away, and even worse, he was completely unable to find the love that would satisfy his passions, and so, he wrote, never again would he attempt to find happiness or relief with men, "I would never, so long as I lived, make another attempt to find happiness or relief through love. I had done all I could, and my conscience was perfectly clear."[22] From now on, he would cease hope of recovery, but continue to "submit" to treatment as a "prisoner for life in the gloomy dungeon of an abnormal passion."[23] Yet even as Claude expressed resentment about his condition, he never gave up seeking out handsome men. The problem he felt, was perhaps less the attraction to "large," good-looking men than the inability to form a lasting relationship due to the perverse nature of that love.

Looking Backward and Forward

In spite of the sheer numbers of men Hartland met, it is clear that he never felt legitimated as a homosexual either by the physicians from whom he sought help or by those with whom he spent time. Although he was frequently satisfied sexually, he never grew to accept his condition, and ran away from it more often than not. Earl Lind, on the other hand, appears to have celebrated his difference, surrounded by others who were equally content to live their lives as sexual outsiders and challenged all those who might have condemned them, as the name Paresis Hall implied. Walt Whitman was another who celebrated the comradeship of men and was not afraid to do so through the Calamus poems in the *Leaves of Grass*. This work, however, was not overtly erotic, and the reader was free to interpret it accordingly. Yet not everyone read Whitman, and it remains unclear if the inner-city homosexual who attended Paresis Hall or cruised Lafayette Park in Washington, DC, or other similar such locations across the country did so either. The limited evidence available suggests that the homosexual literati were not well-known models of homosexual emancipation for the majority of American men attracted to a member of the same sex. There can be no doubt that there may have been homosexual Whitman admirers across the United States who met secretly in their private drawing rooms to read and discuss. Unfortunately, no records of their discussions or of their organizations have as yet come to light.

Outside of the bar and beyond the world of Claude Hartland and the world of American literature, homosexuals continued to learn about who they were, and in spite of social opprobrium, express themselves in a way that contributed to the development of a homosexual identity. In *Gay New York*, George Chauncy writes in detail about many other locations besides the Slide and Paresis Hall. So infamous were the haunts of New York's homosexual underworld, that middle- and upper middle-class citizens purposely came to view them and their patrons in what was referred to as "slumming." Here, too, the construction of a homosexual identity was not left to the homosexually inclined individual alone.

From poet to bar patron, from the individual to the communities of the inner city, those who were psychosexually attracted to their own sex were gradually awakening to the realization that they were uniquely different from others by virtue of that "ineradicable" attraction. With the help of the physician, the nature of this condition took shape and came to be designated within the medical community as congenital homosexuality, an identity that was not immediately assumed by those so affected. What, then, did it mean to be a homosexual? Can the term be used in any meaningful way when applied to men and women during the Gilded Age? Were there homosexuals before the invention of homosexuality? What role did class, gender, or ethnicity play in the diagnosis and identification of the homosexual? And finally, did those who were designated congenital homosexuals by the neurologist accept this label?

As it has been suggested throughout this chapter, to be a homosexual meant different things to different people. Clearly, some patients, like Claude Hartland, knew that they were attracted to men, and acted upon this attraction even if they did not know that there was a term that identified their condition. Claude identified himself as different, was confused and unhappy about it, and frequently attempted to suppress it or run away. In the end, he could not change a thing, and resigned himself to the life of an outsider, much to his disappointment. Edward Carpenter and Karl Ulrichs, on the other hand, embraced their difference, and self-consciously identified themselves as Urnings through and through. If one reads Whitman closely, one may speculate the same, although he was obviously guarded, and similar to the British authors, presented a rather more spiritual identity with respect to same-sex attraction—a distinction that publicly at least, separates him from Hartland and those who were obsessed with sexual activity.

And what can be said of Alice Mitchell and Freda Ward? They never said they were lesbian, and the attorneys had no reason to believe that they had engaged in "unnatural" intercourse, so were they lesbian? Without their statement or acquiescence to that effect, we will never know, but given the time period, it is doubtful that anything resembling a lesbian identity had had time to develop. The most that may be concluded—because that is what she told the court—is that Alice loved Freda, and that she murdered her because her love object had been taken away. The neurologists and attorneys diagnosed them as probable sexual perverts, yet given the fluidity of that term, their sexual perversion was never acted out physically. Still, the jury found Alice an insane pervert, and shipped her off to an asylum.

And Mollie and Prince Pansy, did they feel themselves to be homosexual? Were their identities as flamboyant female cross-dressers indicative that they self-consciously identified themselves as inverts in the George Chauncy sense, or at least as homosexual, in the Krafft-Ebing sense? Again, the answer must be guarded in the absence of a recorded statement, but it is nevertheless clear that they assumed an identity that reinforced their difference from the tourists who came slumming to see them. But whether or not they sat around, drank tea, and proclaimed, "I am a homosexual," is impossible to say. Their identity was as effeminate cross-dressers who performed traditional female sex acts (cocksucker) on "real" men. Were Mollie's customers homosexual, or were they out for a thrill? In *Forbidden Erotica*, there are a few revealing group photos of men performing and receiving fellatio. These were obviously staged events in which the participants appear to be actors, erections and all. Some of the men were wearing rouge and wore thigh high stockings, and were photographed in both positions. Every male had a smile, and looked as though he was having a great time. A similar picture is of women, engaging in various poses of cunnilingus, smiling, and having a great time. Homosexual acts, yes, but were the actors homosexual? (I am reminded of modern pornographic videos in which two women have sex while a male watches, masturbating.) It is possible the women were lesbian, but it is far more likely that they were simply having sex for the pleasure of someone else, and their behavior was strictly a consumer product. Thus it was with the people in the photographs, and quite possibly with the likes of Mollie and Prince Pansy, or of some of their colleagues.

Perhaps the most that can be realistically stated about a homosexual identity during the Gilded Age is that it was in the process of becoming. No one single person or profession could claim ownership of this process. It came about due to the dialogues among and between the psychiatrist, the neurologist, and those who claimed same-sex attraction. If the neurologist had a view, so too did Whitman, Carpenter, and Ulrichs, as well as Mollie, Claude, Prince Pansy, and Alice. Each interpreted same-sex attraction according to his or her psychological needs and desires. It was up to the medical community, however, to attempt to iron out those differences and squeeze everybody who demonstrated any form of same-sex attraction into the same box. If this could be accomplished, so much the better because then everybody, from physician to poet, patient and public, would have a recognizable entity with which they could deal, a standardized model of sexual perversion. Not everyone agreed, but just enough did and thus a homosexual identity was born that over the course of the twentieth century has been modified to fulfill the needs of those who required that identity.

Another aspect of this process of homosexual identity formation during the Gilded Age was the attitude of the medical profession to sexuality. It will be recalled that they strongly asserted a strict sexual ethic. Sex was confined to marriage; it was to be done in the so-called missionary style for the express purpose of reproduction; and only once in a while was it permitted for pleasure. The body had a limited amount of energy, which was dissipated by ejaculation; thus only a few were allowed if one was not to drain one's vital force and become weak-willed and enfeebled. Masturbation was clearly a threat. Enfeebled men—and women—were prone to insanity, and insanity was not conducive to civilization. An appropriate sexuality, therefore, was necessary not only for the sake of children, but for one's physical and mental health as well as the future of civilization. Everything had to be in harmony if the entire structure were to stand. Neurasthenia challenged the structure, but most people most of the time acted in ways that did not threaten the harmony of the system. Those who acted improperly in sexual affairs risked destroying both themselves and America, and unless their behavior was congenital, they were clearly criminals or insane, best left to the jurisdiction of the court or to the supervision of the asylum. Congenital perverts however, were unable to stop their desires even if they might remain celibate. Neurologists and other physicians were needed to help diagnose this type, and help with the development of appropriate therapies that would reduce the probability that congenital homosexuals would act upon their morbid impulse. Homosexuals who were exposed to this logic had few options except acceptance, rejection, or repression. Acceptance risked a nearly permanent state of mental depression; while rejection frequently resulted in secrecy or participation in communities at the fringes of society, both of which might also lead to depression. The consequences of repression were not dissimilar, with frequent anxiety and depression. Homosexuals not exposed to the physician or the reformer were constrained as well by a society that did not recognize them and were generally repelled by their behaviors, if discovered. If they did develop an identity of homosexual, it was closeted, to be sure.

The consequence of these attitudes on the part of the medical community and homosexual alike was the inability of the homosexually inclined to develop a positive cross-cultural identity that established them as a sexual minority in their own right with civil and social rights equal to those of the heterosexual majority. This process, in fact, was a political development that would only be achieved in the last quarter of the twentieth century, and which in any event, rejected early twentieth-century theories of sexuality based upon Freud, and tentatively confirmed by Alfred Kinsey, that all humans are intrinsically bisexual. The assertion of an exclusive orientation was the creation of gay activists who argued that civil rights could not be denied an entire class of people based on their inherent sexual orientation, and to do so was not only unjust, but unconstitutional as well. This position expressed an essentialism with respect to orientation that harkened back to late nineteenth-century essentialism, an ideology that had caused so much mischief in the first case, and disregarded the critical dialogue between patient and doctor that had informed the initial discussions of the Gilded Age. The difference was that supporters of nineteenth-century sexual essentialism assumed their position was an empirically valid observation based upon the history and tradition of gender roles founded upon sexual dimorphism. Modern gay activists, on the other hand, knew fully well that gender roles were social constructions that had more to do with power, control, and tradition than with binding essentialist universalities. The decision to establish an essentialist homo/hetero dichotomy with which one could identify was a useful tool in the gay movement's push for social acceptance and legal rights. It was a political move that had very little to do with biology or psychiatry, but much to do with the issues of class, gender, and race that were so prevalent during the peace and civil rights movements of the 1960s and 1970s.

Chapter 11
The Limits of Congenital Homosexuality

> The last decade has demonstrated that sexual perversion is much more frequent in America than the general practitioner realizes, and that its victims do not belong to the vicious classes but to those of good health—socially and mentally—and to those who have had educational advantages; many belonging to the professions.[1]

Gilded Age homosexuals were men or women who came in all shapes and sizes, but not from every ethnicity or class, or so it would seem from the doctors who studied them. To be sure, the neurological literature described a few African Americans and Native Americans who seemed to be homosexual, and there were the habitués of the inner city who provided entertainment and a potential sexual outlet for members of the better classes as they slummed their way across a forbidden demimonde. Yet these images only serve to obscure, because in point of fact, most of the specific cases of congenital homosexuality that came from Europe and the United States concerned middle- or upper-class Caucasian males and females. Claude Hartland, Alice Mitchell, and Freda Ward are but three examples that only scratch the surface of those included in this category.

A brief review of the literature will demonstrate this interesting situation. Beginning in Germany, all cases of contrary sexual instinct investigated by Westphal, Krafft-Ebing, and others were of male and female Caucasians (as might be expected given the population pool). Men were more prevalent than women, especially in Krafft-Ebing's studies, although his 1892 English edition of *Psychopathia Sexualis* included some females. Of the approximately thirty autobiographies and secondhand reports contained within the section "Homo-Sexual," two-thirds were of men and the rest of women, two of whom were identified as "maids." Virtually all the males claimed to be of middle- or upper-class background, with occupations ranging from merchant owner to "official" and most frequently, physician. Lower-class inverts were represented, to be sure, but the majority of men stated that they had been educated at a university or a gymnasium, and none of them reported being poor. Similar, too, had been the observations of Karl Ulrichs, who in his series of pamphlets known collectively as *Research on The Riddle of "Man-Manly" Love* (*Forschungen über das Räthsel der mann-männlichen Liebe*), stated categorically:

> In Germany there are Urnings who are judges, state attorneys, police officials, doctors, lawyers, members of the military and clergy, professors, members of parliament, counts, princes, prisoners of war from Koniggratz and victors alike: honorable people in every sense whose estimable character alone offers a surety that what nature demands from them could not be vice or crime.[2]

It was much the same with the autobiographies of Havelock Ellis. For example, in his 1896 studies on male and female inversion, all of the men and women were Caucasian. Most males gave as their occupation businessman, physician, gentleman, "professional," or "official"; only one was described as a manual laborer. In the study of women, information is less available because unlike the men who were quoted, females were accessible only through the voice of Ellis who did not tell the reader anything about their social and occupational status. In his 1915 *Studies in the Psychology of Sex*, vol. II, "Sexual Inversion," however, Ellis included more information about the women as well as the men. Whereas the information on men did not substantially alter their occupational characteristics, the reader is a bit more enlightened about the women. In the subsection, "Sexual Inversion of Women," one learns that the women were all "professional" (educator, businesswoman, artist, professor), and while these cases dated from between 1896 and the publication of the 1915 text, none were from a working-class background. In the following subsection, "The Nature of Sexual Inversions," Ellis summarized his caseloads thus:

> All my cases, 80 in number, are British and American, 20 living in the United States and the rest being British. Ancestry, from the point of view of race, was not made a matter of special investigation. It appears, however, that at least 44 are English or mainly English; at least 10 are Scotch or of Scotch extraction; 2 are Irish and 4 others largely Irish; 4 have German fathers or mothers; another is of German descent on both sides, while 2 others are of remote German extraction; 2 are partly, and 1 entirely, French; 2 have a Portuguese strain, and at least 2 are more or less Jewish.[3]

As for occupation, Ellis was unequivocal that although they were represented in all lines of work, it was in the professions where they were found most frequently, "There are 12 physicians, 9 men of letters, at least 7 are engaged in commercial life, 6 are artists, architects or composers, 4 are or have been actors." With respect to aptitudes, there were clearly "certain avocations to which inverts seem especially called," and among them were literature, medicine, the belles lettres of poetry, prose, history, and the arts, such as theater, music, painting, and sculpture. Indeed, due to their nervous character, "[the] . . . congenitally inverted may, I believe, be looked upon as a class of individuals exhibiting nervous characters which, to some extent, approximate them to persons of artistic genius."[4]

In the United States, the situation was similar to that in Germany and England, and caseloads represented both men and women, with a greater emphasis on men. The demographics of class, ethnicity, and occupation were a little more complex, but not overwhelmingly so. Most males who were reported upon or who left autobiographies were Caucasian, educated, employed, self-sufficient, well nourished, healthy, and intelligent. Some were described as cultured, "of high social status," wealthy, respectable, artistic, and imaginative. There were a few Caucasian males who were described as uneducated, and some were laborers, such as "coomber of wool." One man was an Hispanic "domestic," and another was a "Creole" servant who cross-dressed and kept a "picture of himself and a male friend but no female friend in his room."[5]

The case studies of women were more varied, and usually filtered through the lens of the attending physician. In most instances, they were young Caucasian females with scant information about profession or class affiliation, but when it was mentioned, the occupation was housekeeper, maid, student, servant, manual laborer ("labor that occupied my hands"),[6] "maiden lady," prostitute, and lady. One of Kiernan's patients was "married to secure a position in society,"[7] while other females invert were described by their doctor as "young ladies, the sweetest and fairest of our race,"[8] although Lucy Ann Slater was labeled a "backwoodswoman." There is a body of literature on Native American women who cross-dressed, but it is not from the clinics of the Gilded Age neurologist who studied homosexuality. A small number of secondhand cases dealt with African American men and women.

At issue is the question of who the neurologist physician actually treated as opposed to what he read, saw from afar, or who in fact was homosexual. Virtually all the American neurologists admitted that they had read or heard of communities across the United States where sexual perverts congregated. That was not a secret, nor was the fact that within these communities blacks, whites, and any number of ethnicities such as Italian or Russian Jew, comingled. Yet doctors did not set up practice in these areas. They relied for their knowledge about them from outside sources, classic examples of which were the 1899 New York City Mazet Committee,[9] tasked with the responsibility to investigate the "vicious" underworld of that city, and police reports of the period.[10] Dr. Hughes' postscript to his 1893 essay on Erotopathia is a case in point.[11] He apparently did not have African Americans as his patients, nor did the other neurologists we have encountered. Instead, they referred to the same police and Vice Committee reports and assumed them to be valid statements of how some perverts behaved and lived, black or white, male or female. It was also not unusual for a physician to quote another physician who claimed to have heard a story from a friend or another doctor—anecdotal evidence at best. The inner city was a locus of vice and corruption where depraved "debauchés" chose to live by virtue of their acquired degradations, or so the contention went.

The doctors knew, however, that the vicious denizens of the inner city were of a sort qualitatively different from the congenital inverts they treated. Neurologists believed this assertion because underlying all their medical discourse was a consensus that "pure" homosexuality was, as Krafft-Ebing had so aptly stated a decade before, the degenerative product of an hereditarian predisposition caused by a neuropathy due to the stresses and strains of modern life. In short, congenital homosexuality was a disease of middle- and upper-class white Euro-Americans caught in the vice grip of a rapidly changing world that played havoc on one's nerves. The condition represented a reversion to an extremely primitive state in human evolution, one perhaps below savagery. On the other hand, the poor and lower-class whites who engaged in homosexual behavior were members of the criminal class, as Lombroso and Lydston had called them, and the unfortunate biproduct of earlier reversions due to any number of primary "initiating" causes—syphilis, alcohol, self-abuse, excess sexual intercourse—that had been passed along from one generation to the next. Nonwhites were by definition less evolved than whites, and it was to be expected that the savage and semi-savage had a greater potential for immorality than the white. The "real" homosexual was generally of good stock but for this unusual condition, and represented an actual degeneration rather than the cumulative effects of the inheritance of "taint" from past generations.

Inherently racist and chauvinist, this theory was predicated upon the belief that white, Anglo-European Americans of predominantly Northern European heritage sat at the apex of human evolution by virtue of their culture, civilization, morality, sexual ethics, sense of beauty, romantic love, manners, health, wealth, and religion. White America no less than white England, Germany, and Scandinavia were the empirical manifestations of evolution at its best, and all other civilizations and cultures paled in comparison, unable to catch up, as it were, because Northern European whites had evolved beyond the rest of the peoples of the world. In the opening sentence of chapter 3 of the 1892 English edition of *Psychopathia Sexualis* ("General Pathology"), Krafft-Ebing set the tone for interpreting homosexuality within social Darwinist perimeters when he asserted, "Abnormality of the sexual functions proves to be especially frequent in civilized races."[12]

By no means an explicit racist or social Darwinist, Krafft-Ebing nevertheless accepted some of their basic assumptions that evolution was a "straight line" process that began with a one-celled organism and continued directly up a ladder, through the plant world, the animal world, and culminated with humankind. Within humankind, the line continued from savage to civilized, and came to an end with the middle- and upper-class Anglo/Northern white European. By these standards and those of other European and American opinion makers, no other people of the world could claim to be as highly evolved. At the bottom of the evolutionary scale were Black Africans and other indigenous peoples who, try as they might, could never overcome those in front of them on this ladder. All civilizations, however, passed through phases as they evolved higher, indigenous people no less than the civilized, yet they could never jump ahead of those in front. As the economically successful white European neared perfection and the completion of the evolutionary climb, all those behind them remained fixed at the level they had attained throughout the duration of this process. By definition, they were the savage, the semicivilized, and poor, uncultured whites, depending on where they stood on the ladder.

Every society and each people acted and behaved in ways consistent with their particular level of evolutionary development. As the most evolved, the white West in general valued peace; the savage, war. The West accepted monotheistic Christianity; the savage, polytheism. The West valued monogamy and male/female sexual intercourse expressly for the production of children within the bounds of marriage; the savage valued multiple partners and sexual excess expressly for the purpose of gratification without benefit of marriage or children. The cultured, white European Christian placed a premium on the ideals of beauty and love; the savage, semi civilized and poor white knew nothing of these concepts. Notwithstanding the fact that the savage–civilized dichotomy was concocted from the perspective of the middle- and upper-class European, social Darwinists self-servingly accepted it as legitimate, especially as it allowed the West to justify its control over nonwestern parts of the world during this period of late nineteenth-century neo-imperialism and colonialism. The West was to be a role model that could help elevate the morals and manners of the savage and barbarian, if not to the peak of Western perfection, then certainly to a level where peace, Christianity, and monogamy might serve as examples of the capabilities of a truly perfect people. Krafft-Ebing was immersed in this ideology, particularly as it related to sexual mores:

> It seems of high psychological interest to trace the developmental phases through which, in the course of the evolution of human culture to the morality and civilization of today, the sexual life has passed. On primitive ground the satisfaction of the sexual appetite of man seems like that of the animal. Openness in the sexual act is not shunned; man and woman are not ashamed to go naked. Today we see savages in this condition; as, for example, the Australians, the Polynesians, and the Malays of the Philippines. The female is the common property of the males, the temporary booty of the strongest, who strive for the possession of the most beautiful of the opposite sex, thus carrying out instinctively a kind of sexual selection.[13]

Psychopathia Sexualis was his attempt to understand the deviant sexual practices of the civilized West within the context of the logic of social Darwinism. The savage was not his concern. If the West was actually as highly evolved as it was supposed to be in moral, social, and other arenas, then how was it that there was so much sexual immorality to be observed? A number of explanations were offered. In spite of Christianity that gave "the most powerful impulse to the moral elevation of the sexual relations by raising woman to social equality with man and elevating the bond of love between man and woman to a religio-moral institution," the increased demands placed upon the nervous system by modern society resulted in moral decadence, effeminacy, and sensuality. Highly civilized urban cities alone created the conditions under which a neuropathology developed that ostensibly allowed the most successful within society to revert, or degenerate to an earlier phase of evolution associated with the savage, the semi civilized, and the depraved.

Fundamentally, Krafft-Ebing thought congenital homosexuality was a reversion to a specific period of evolutionary history through which the civilized and morally upright had already progressed. This was a condition that mimicked a pre-Christian period of sensuousness and immorality, and in this sense, homosexuals were evolutionary throwbacks, an "atavism" in the biological terminology of the day. He was not alone in his beliefs. The American neurologists Kiernan, Lydston, Chaddock, and to a lesser extent Hughes, accepted Krafft-Ebing's conceptualization of homosexuality as a reversion, and embellished it. Sometimes the Americans were of the opinion that homosexuality was a reversion to a prehuman state in so far as a few asserted that savages did not know the sexual perversions; others suggested that homosexuality was in fact a reversion to a condition of savagery, an implication made very clear from William Hammond's essay on the "Disease of the Scythians" and from those who had observed the Native American burdach. Lydston in particular built his entire theory of congenital homosexuality on this point predicated upon his study of criminal anthropology, the quintessential social Darwinist theory on the origins of the criminal classes modeled after the theories of the Italian Casare Lombroso.

Because Lydston was so widely read among the neurological community and because he was so frequently quoted for his insights into homosexuality, it is worth spending a few moments looking closely at how he conceptualized those he labeled congenital homosexuals within his general theory of criminal anthropology. In essence, Lydston was a social Darwinist who accepted the argument that evolution was a real, straight line, teleological process that culminated in the moral, physical, and mental perfection of the civilized Indo-European and "Semitic" races:

> Evolutionary law is evidenced all along the line of the physical, intellectual, moral, and social development of man through the long vista of years that lies behind us, through which the human species has evolved from its most primitive type to what is alleged to be the acme of perfection, as seen in the Indo-European and Semitic races of today.[14]

Each category—intellectual, physical, moral—became more developed and more perfect as the process of evolution unfolded, not blindly, but deterministically forward until perfection had been achieved. Accordingly, past societies were less developed physically, morally, and intellectually, thus necessarily more savage; races other than Indo-European and "Semitic" were less perfect, which is to say, imperfect, both of which were to be expected if Lydston's proposition were true. Modern Indo-European societies, such as the United States, in spite of their perfection, had within them pockets of imperfection, or crime, as Lydston preferred to call it. But imperfection could not evolve from perfection because that was an illogical conclusion inconsistent with the teleology of evolution. Yet imperfections nevertheless existed and had to be accounted for. Either the evolutionary drive for perfection was true or false, and since it was true, a mechanism or mechanisms could be discovered that accounted for their existence. According to Lydston, the answers were found in the processes of the inheritance of acquired characteristics and degeneration, both extremely popular theories held by late nineteenth-century social Darwinists.

Lydston was especially fond of degeneracy as it related to crime, "Degeneracy ... is the fundamental cause of the majority of the multiform antisocial acts included under the captions of vice and crime."[15] Here was a process of evolution that explained how an entity at the peak of perfection could literally devolve morally, physically, and mentally to a previous state of "primitive impulses." One simply moved backwards along the same line that had brought one forward, and in the process, old inhibitions were released:

> It is fair to say that the human being is an animal primarily possessing instinctive tendencies to vice and crime, but who is subjected under civilized conditions to certain inhibitory influences that have accumulated through the ages, and which prevent the average man from becoming vicious or criminal. When these inhibitions or restraints are removed, criminal acts result ... Crime and vice are in general simply a harking back to primitive impulses.[16]

Primitive impulses were found among the savages, those who Lydston believed were less morally evolved than the civilized, "The adult savage, even of the most primitive type, has a conscience, such as it is,— a conscience sufficient unto his limited needs. Theoretically he is naturally immoral ..."[17] Thus when one degenerated, one reverted morally to an evolutionary state of development inconsistent with civilized society, "When atavism develops the moral attributes of the savage in white degenerates, the latter simply assume the same inharmonious relations to civilized society as is occupied by the savage of today."[18] But clearly not all instances of vice were true cases of degeneration because degeneration was found only in specific classes within the United States, those successful types who were subjected to the stress and strains of a competitive modern society. Among the poor and unwashed, vice also existed, but that was a sign of depravity due to the inheritance of acquired characteristics:

> Habit, persisted in through succeeding generations, may result not only in physical aberrations attended by psychic abnormality, but in a faulty power of reasoning which, although not characterized by variations of physical conformation, may yet be transmitted through many generations.[19]

or by one's position in the hierarchy of race:

> The natural shiftlessness of the negro, when left to himself, is simply a reversion to the primitive type illustrated by the native African, who is content with a breech-clout, a plentiful supply of grease for his glossy hide, and multitudinous wives to minister to his various appetites. There is but a short span between the primitive African and his American descendants.[20]

Those who were evolutionarily imperfect could not be degenerate because they had not reached that high stage of evolution where degeneration was possible. If they did things that were perceived as vicious or depraved, that was due to the intrinsic savage nature of their evolutionary niche. Only the perfect could degenerate because their status on the hierarchy of evolutionary perfectibility put them at risk for nervous exhaustion,

> I have said that the higher the race of man, the greater inhibitions, "under normal conditions." Advance in civilization is, however, not necessarily coeval with progress in ethical standards. After a certain point is reached, the luxury [sic], appetite exhaustion due to satiety, and unhygienic life of civilization bring brain and body degeneracy in their train, and type reversions are more frequent. History shows that extinction of entire social systems may result.[21]

If one were not lower on the evolutionary scale of life but sexually depraved nevertheless, it was due to the aberrant behaviors of a past generation that had been inherited by the current generation in the form of a weak will that stripped away the inhibitions that the more evolved and naturally successful kept in check. The weak-willed committed perversities and were not victims of a degenerative perversion like congenital homosexuals whose sexual behavior perverted the natural ends for which it was intended. Practically speaking, the depraved might have felt as though their actions were a true perversion, but the neurologist knew that the real cause was their inherited inability to resist vice. More often than not, the naturally enfeebled ancestors of the currently depraved lived in the economically depressed centers of the city, where long ago they settled because of their biological inferiority. Had it been otherwise, they would have become successful professionals of the middle and upper classes.

Theoretically, only a certain class of white Americans of Northern European stock could degenerate by this standard, and all crime in America except that committed by people of color or those determined by the physician to be suffering from the taint of inheritance was due to degeneration. "The assumption that the criminal, in particular, is a product of evolution, is in absolute harmony with the evolutionary theory in general."[22] Congenital homosexuals were but one example of this theory, and were not members of the class of "less" evolved or hereditarily tainted, even though they might behave the same. If the tainted or less evolved were involved in same-sex eroticism it was because that was what the savages and weak-willed did. The congenital homosexual, however, was a "true" degenerate who suffered from a biological reversion to a state of savagery equal to the "less" evolved and acted as though depraved, but in fact was not. It may have been true that individuals in both camps could not help themselves overcome their unfortunate situations, yet for the "less evolved," vicious classes, deviance was expected, whereas in the "acme," it was not. The immediate problem, however, was that too many who were evolutionary perfect had degenerated,

> There are in every large community colonies of male sexual perverts and inverts, who are usually known to each other, and who usually congregate together. They often operate in accordance with some definite and concerted plan in quest of subjects wherewith to gratify their abnormal sexual impulses. They are frequently characterized by effeminacy of voice, dress, and manner. In a general way, their physique is apt to be inferior—a defective physical make-up being quite general among them, although exceptions to this rule are numerous. Sexual perversions, and more particularly inversion,—i.e. homosexuality, or sexual predilection for the same sex,—is more frequent in the male . . . Many female inverts are met with, however. For example, there are numerous instances of women of perfect physique, moving in good society, who have a fondness for women and are never sexually attracted to men. There are numerous cases in which the female is sexually by women, yet has a perverted desire for the opposite sex. In general, inversion is less likely that perversion to be the result of depravity.[23]

Most Americans did not understand this behavior and found it puzzling, but "If considered in the light of reversion of type, however, the subject is much less perplexing."[24] With proper instruction from the physician, the public would learn about these things, especially young men in school and in college,

> Upon the physician devolves the major part of the duty instructing the public in the delicate matters germane to sexual vice and crime . . . Physicians should be encouraged to write and disseminate among the public dignified and discreet treatises on various sexual and venereal topics. The more advanced pupils in our boys' schools and colleges should be taught, not only physiology, but elementary principles, at least, of venereal pathology.[25]

For the neurologist, here is where the possibility of congenital homosexuality existed. Congenital homosexuals were not inebriates, paupers, gamblers, prostitutes, unemployed, insane, ignorant, illiterate, people of color, or in general, members of the dangerous classes. They were, almost to a person, white men and women honorably engaged with life, be they student, a female servant, or male physician. And while more females than males were from the working class, that would not be unusual in a society that limited the career opportunities of women. What is clear is that the patients were upwardly mobile Anglo-American men and women who represented by age and occupation the promise and best hope of American society, not the worst: those savages within the country among whom such behavior was reluctantly acknowledged, the dark skinned and those who had already "reverted."

Most American neurologists understood congenital homosexuality much the same way as Lydston, namely, a white man's disease found within civilized society. Kiernan, of course, was in total agreement with both Krafft-Ebing and Lydston on this point, and although he did not develop an elaborate theory to that effect, he picked up where others had left off. For example, Kiernan assumed the existence of degeneration when he penned his 1892, "Responsibility in Sexual Perversion," and as background for his observations, he noted that the sexual perversions, of which same-sex eroticism figured prominently, was abhorred among the "Celto-Teutonic" races but more or less accepted among those he deemed to be lower, evolutionarily speaking,

> One phase of sexual perversion, consequent on sea-faring, was early designated by an Anglo-Saxon term but branded by an epithet which indicated a person entirely worthless. This designation, which expresses the abhorrence of the Celto-Teutonic races which formed the Anglo-Saxon, explains the healthy tendency of that race to regard sexual perversion as an abnormal phenomenon. This abhorrence is not so marked among Continental European and Asiatic peoples. Indeed, as the Hippocratic oath denotes, seduction of a boy was equally, but not more heinous, than seduction of a maid. In this tolerance a religious phase of sexual perversion played a part among the Aryan, Shemite, and Cushite races alike. In America such religious practices are found among the relatively civilized Pueblo Indians.[26]

Kiernan went on to discuss the origins of sexual perversion by reference to a "reversion in (ancestral) type" from the individual whose conscience upheld the civilized social order, to one who existed in a "parasitic" phase of life, thereby destroying civilization that demanded the altruistic bonds of conscious and ethics. Somewhat later in his argument, he reinforced his position when he restated the by now common medical belief that same-sex eroticism was caused by an organic reversion to that stage of human development marked by the incomplete sexual differentiation of humankind's original bisexuality,

> The persistence of this psychological element (same sex eroticism) indicates that it must have been acquired early, since the original bisexuality of the ancestors of the race shown in the rudimentary female organs of the male could not fail to occasion functional if not organic reversions within mental or physical manifestations were interfered with by disease or congenital defect... The lowest animals are bisexual and the various types of hermaphroditism are more or less complete reversions to the ancestral type.[27]

The physicians C. H. Hughes, Charles Chaddock, F. E. Daniel, and E. Stuver conceptualized same-sex eroticism much the same way. Hughes argued that evolution produced a complementarity of the male and female that in the cultured and civilized races resulted in a refined and delicate love that was distinct for each sex and remained so even before puberty and after the "decline in virility" in men or "climacteric" in women,

> When we ascend from the lower animals up to man, and still further from the lowest human substratum of savage and semi-civilized man to the higher type of civilized and cultured manhood, we observe so refined and delicate a blending of passion and love that the two seem really separate and separable from each other, and in fact are so in the earlier and later years of human life, i.e., before puberty and after the decline of virility in man or the passage of the climacteric in women.[28]

Hughes' understanding of sex-appropriate love was in direct contrast to the same-sex eroticism that was the subject of a part of his essay that described homosexual love as a "neurotic degeneracy." This condition resulted in behaviors consistent with the "human substratum of savage" that from the civilized point of view were abnormal, in that "normal love cherishes the loved one. Abnormal passion, solely selfish in desire and aspiration, considers not the welfare of its object so much as the wishes of self, but for the accomplishment of its end, wound body and mind, and destroys both, if necessary."[29] Homosexuals, Hughes thought, were "selfish."

In "Sexual Crimes" Chaddock was no less adamant that same-sex eroticism was a sign of degeneration. "Neuropsychical degeneration," he claimed, was an important factor in sexual perversion, because "Observation shows that for the most part psychosexual anomalies are developed upon a degenerate constitution." Consistent with Krafft-Ebing, Chaddock accepted as true the assertion that sexual inversion demonstrated functional and anatomical signs of degeneration, both of which were themselves the sign of a neuropathic constitution. In most cases, however, the anatomical signs were harder to find than were the functional signs of degeneration, which in any event were self-evident in cases of sexual inversion.

Daniel and Stuver were both concerned with therapy, and argued that sexual perverts, including those who demonstrated same-sex tendencies, ought to be castrated so that their degenerative condition would end with them. They were ostensibly less concerned with the origins of homosexuality than were Lydston or Krafft-Ebing, but were nevertheless troubled by the sheer increase of sexual perverts. Stuver was particularly upset that degeneration in the form of sexual perversion and inversion was rampant within the United States, and if those tendencies became dominant, then the United States was at risk for collapse, "That there are tendencies to degeneration, and some very strong ones, too, in our present advanced civilization, no one competent to form an intelligent opinion will, I believe, deny. Whether these tendencies will become dominant and lead to our downfall, the future alone can reveal."[30] Though less concerned with the collapse of civilization, Daniel fully accepted the analysis of Krafft-Ebing, Kiernan, and Lydston, and recognized that moral and physical degeneration were real forces that could warp even the most robust and healthy, especially if they should engage in masturbation, which in turn could lead to perversion and inversion.[31]

The American congenital homosexual was thus an individual similar to Ellis and Krafft-Ebing who came for the most part from the Anglo-European middle and upper classes of the urban metropolis. Homosexual depravity existed alongside, to be sure, but that was the consequence of racial inferiority or of the inheritance of an acquired characteristic tendency to masturbation, excess "venery," alcohol, pornography, bad education, or what have you—and had nothing to do with the congenital type. Congenital degeneration was an unfortunate condition that was ultimately caused by modern civilization itself because it placed an excessive amount of strain on the nervous system, causing the individual to degenerate into a biological freak. Congenital homosexuality was therefore a condition limited to the fittest in America and because it was not their choice, they were not to be held responsible for their disease even as the disease was resoundingly condemned by the neurologists who studied and treated it. This new disease of the middle class did not go away, however, and remained to confound all those who confronted it, victim no less than doctor.

Chapter 12
Conclusion

> All history and science teach us that neither individuals nor nations can remain stationary; they must either advance to a higher development and a nobler civilization or, by a retrograde process, degenerate, decay, and disappear.
> Our wonderful progress and remarkable material achievement as a nation, have, I fear, made us unduly optimistic, and either closed our eyes to, or rendered us careless of the many demoralizing tendencies that are sapping the vitality of our people and will, unless overcome, endanger the integrity and greatness of our nation.
> That there are tendencies to degeneration, and some very strong ones, too, in our present advanced civilization, no one competent to form an intelligent opinion, will, I believe, deny. Whether these tendencies will become dominant and lead to our downfall, the future alone can tell.[1]

The creation of a homosexual identity owes much to the Gilded Age neurologist, who in his quest for authority pulled same-sex eroticism from the depths of moral depravity and handed it over to the clarity of modern science. No other event was as important to the future of gays and lesbians as was this because for the first time, those who were psychosexually inclined to their own sex were infused with a special nature that set them apart from the rest of humankind. Concerned about the legal status of men and women who claimed that they were not responsible for their "perverted" condition, European and American physicians were determined to find out if these claims were true. If so, then the responses from the legal, religious, medical, and psychiatric communities had to be adjusted to recognize this fact. Punishment for certain condemned behaviors had to be altered or abolished; the nature of depravity had to be reconsidered; new insights into the human psyche needed to be explored; and the social conditions examined in which this perplexing condition developed.

Until the psychoanalytic theories of Freud became ascendant, congenital homosexuality was conceived as a biologically degenerate condition by a majority within the American neurological community, and the reasons are not difficult to ascertain. As dedicated social Darwinists, those neurologists like Kiernan and Lydston who chose to specialize in the sexual perversions conceptualized all life within the context of an evolutionary hierarchy moving toward perfection, no matter how ambiguous that concept was. Not unlike St. Thomas Aquinas who, it will be recalled, believed the universe was moving toward the perfection of God, American social Darwinists also accepted the premise that life on Earth mirrored the same process, at least as it pertained to the white middle- and upper-classes of the United States. The Gilded Age was perhaps the period during which this belief system was most pronounced, especially among the Old Stock Caucasian elites. For them, the cardinal issue was the ability to project enough power to ensure social and economic stability. According to this popular theory, individuals rested at a certain point on a hierarchy of race and civilization by virtue of the survival of the fittest, and such inequality as existed due to wealth, opportunity, race, or gender was natural and therefore quite normal. Any change in status on the hierarchy of life sent major shock waves throughout the system and threatened the integrity of the entire structure. To guard against this unwelcome possibility, any challenges to the hierarchy were condemned as abnormal and contrary to nature.

Profoundly conservative by nature, social Darwinists recoiled at the notion of any change that appeared to rock the status quo, particularly if that impinged upon the prerogatives of those at the top. It was accepted precisely because it provided a quasi-scientific rationale for maintaining the existing race, class, gender, and economic hierarchy. Self-serving, to be sure, social Darwinism was also easy to understand and provided pat answers to the inexplicable, in this instance, homosexuality. Darwin stated that the flipside of evolution was degeneration, and neurologists thought they had discovered a prime example of this phenomenon in homosexuality. The authority of science was harnessed to prove this point, and homosexuals were conceived as nothing but biological freaks of nature, a condition caused by the impact of the stress and strains of modernization upon the nervous system. Yet in spite of this tidy analysis, a deep fear crept into their thoughts.

Whereas the behavior of the depraved was explained by the inheritance of a weak will due to the inheritance of acquired characteristics of generations past, homosexuality was a disease found among America's current best "stock." As the century came to a close, the number of those who seemed to be diseased with congenital homosexuality increased exponentially, and that set off alarm bells. Depravity was a condition of the lower classes that might be eradicated by sterilization, segregation, and laws that restricted marriage to those free of hereditary taint. Homosexuality, on the other hand, was an incurable degenerative condition found among the very same members of the good stock who were credited with being the most fit to lead the exceptionalist push to perfection in the first place. What could be done to halt this disturbing reversal of evolution?

Neurologists believed they could offer insights into this perplexing situation, and were quick to share it with the public. Since they had concluded homosexuality was incurable and its etiology environmental—stress and strain—prevention was the only long-term option possible. For this to be realized, society had to eliminate the original stresses that pressed upon the nervous system and produced congenital homosexuality. At this juncture, however, a problem arose. Since high civilization and stress went hand in hand, to eliminate the latter implied eliminating the former, and that put the United States at risk. What had made America unique among nations past and present was that the inevitable stress of civilization had not led to degeneration but rather to perfectibility, a condition made possible by its exceptionalist heritage, at least up until the current period of the Gilded Age. If this was a correct assessment, as neurologists believed it was, then what was it about Gilded Age stress that set it apart from the stress of earlier periods? Something new had affected society that had been absent in earlier periods. Was industrial modernization the culprit, and if so, would it not be appropriate to reassess it against the rise of the sexual perversions, particularly congenital homosexuality?

Neurologists thought so, and took it upon themselves to expound upon modernization, less as doctors than as holy men in search of the truth. America, they argued, had to remove the debilitating sources of modern stress that culminated in biological degeneration if the nation were to remain exempt from the law of historical decline. The medical theories of homosexuality they enumerated were thus designed to respond to concerns about modernization from the perspective of those physicians who accepted exceptionalism. Predicated upon faith in God's covenant derived from seventeenth-century colonial Puritans, modified by the Enlightenment's emphasis on perfectibility and reason as applied to the spectacular development of the American Republic during the nineteenth century, exceptionalism provided the white elites—including physicians—a frame of reference against which they could compare America to the rest of the world. They believed the United States was a special place and its culture and civilization were exempt from history, allowing the nation to evolve along a teleological path toward perfectibility and increasing freedom. But the physicians knew that there was something deeply wrong with this scenario as applied to society during the Gilded Age. The historical pull of exceptionalism was challenged by a dark force that threatened to derail America's destiny.

The name of that dark force was degeneration, and it was caused by modernization itself, all the more disconcerting because that process seemed natural and inevitable. But was this actually a correct assessment, and were there alternatives to Gilded Age modernization that precluded degeneration but still allowed the exceptionalist process to take its course?

The answer was yes, and fundamentally Jeffersonian: Americans had to reject urban, in favor of rural, modernization. In short, the neurologists advocated a return to the values of a preindustrial America that were informed by the "instructed conscience" of the antebellum period. The modern city was the site of unbridled economic development, of competition, of industrialization, of strikes, of greed, and of the dangerous classes. It was a crowded and unhealthy environment where people rushed about in a frenzy and engaged in any number of unmentionable vices. Nerves were constantly frayed, and neurasthenia had reached near epidemic proportions. The urban centers represented an unwanted path to decline that mirrored that of Old World Europe and of empires past. The environment of rural America, by way of contrast, was healthy, pure, and conducive to wholesomeness precisely because life was not as frenetic, and the nervous system was not strained to the point of disease. If cities bred immorality, sin, depravity—and now degeneracy—the country inspired morality, vigor, and health. Even if one could not in actuality return to the country, and most neurologists accepted that reality, city folk might still halt the evils of industrial modernization by living more in accord with the values of the instructed conscience, that is, temperance, thrift, honesty, and integrity. Should this be accomplished, then the United States did not risk losing its exceptionalist heritage, and the nation would survive intact, but only after it had cordoned off those who were depraved or degenerate so that they would not infect the remaining healthy stock.

Romantic and idealist to the core, the Gilded Age neurologist ironically bemoaned what he felt were the deleterious effects of a competitive, capitalist, and materialist society upon the individual. The dangerous classes were the most obvious example of the evil that could befall a civilization if it strayed too far from its roots. Initially small in number, their presence grew in successive generations by virtue of the inheritance of acquired characteristics so that by the 1890s, society was awash with the insane and weak-willed who committed any number of immoralities because it suited their depraved fancies. More disturbing yet were the congenital homosexuals who by their very presence confounded a popular essentialism that each type had a particular essence that was unique to that type. The cat, dog, man, woman, or knife had an essence that made it what it was, and nothing else. Men and women had mutually exclusive essences that forced them to behave in manners consistent with their sex, an example of which was sexual selection. Men chose women, and women chose men. This was a normal and rational behavior that had stood both the test of time and Darwin's evolutionary insights into the origin of the species. Anything other than this was biologically detrimental to survival, thus irrational from a Darwinian perspective.

Homosexuals turned popular essentialism, no less than exceptionalism, on its head. For the physician and homosexual alike, this new found "degenerative" essentialism confounded the imagination. Ulrichs claimed that the homosexual had an essence that consisted of a female mind in a male body, and vice versa. Unable to insert this new essence into the tableau of accepted essences for men and women, congenital homosexuality was naturally condemned as freakish, a mistake of nature. Yet rather than question the legitimacy of either essentialism or exceptionalism, each was conceptualized as absolutes against which the novel pathology of congenital homosexuality was compared. There was simply no way under these conditions that homosexuality would have been considered normal or accepted as legitimate.

This was the legacy that the Gilded Age neurologist bequeathed to the twentieth century, and one from which the homosexual would suffer for the next one hundred years. Here was a devastating diagnosis that condemned homosexuals, often with terrible consequences. They were relegated to the status of a pathogen that defied a cure and whose presence, like that of the proverbial sick canary, anticipated catastrophe. As pathologized people, homosexuals were condemned to live their lives under the stigma of disease. Marginalization and ostracization were endemic as homosexual men and women were harassed and hounded by the general public, lawyers, and doctors alike, sometimes to the point of suicide or death by murder. Not even Freud could help, since he, too, considered homosexuality a disease, although less a degenerative condition than one of arrested development of the psyche. Homophobia, although a word not then in use, found its roots in this matrix of disease, degeneration, and national decline. Homosexuals represented the antithesis of everything that the public considered healthy and normal in America. If it was the nation's destiny to circumvent the historical laws of growth and decline, homosexuals were a sorry reminder of what would happen if the country strayed too far from its exceptionalist promise. The long-term consequences of this mentality dictated that homosexuality would never be accepted as normal, and as long as society considered homosexuality a sign of disease or depravity, this would always be the case.

Yet despite the havoc created by the late nineteenth-century neurologist, it is quite evident that homosexuals attempted to carve out their own space, especially within the taverns, dance halls, and salons of the inner cities. With little or no insight into their condition, homosexuals often turned to each other and experimented with what might work to give their lives meaning in an otherwise hostile society. Whether a Whitman, Princess Pansy, or Alice Mitchell, they all strove to make sense out of their same-sex attraction within the context of their lives; that was all they had and all they could do. For members of the middle class, perhaps an occasional visit to the neurologist was a reassuring exercise, especially when one was told that congenital homosexuality was a naturally occurring degeneration rather than a depraved moral lapse. For others, particularly those from the "dangerous classes," the doctor was more of an impediment than a source of relief. Jenny Lind was of this mind, and rejected medical theories as ignorant and ill-informed mirrors of the interests of the well to do and the powerful. We can see Lind's mentality played out within Paresis Hall among its denizens who mocked neurologists and the outside world. At no time were homosexuals taken on their own terms, except perhaps, in the initial discovery of its allegedly congenital origins. Beyond this, however, each side to the discussion assigned values to homosexuality that were almost mutually exclusive. If the physician had an ulterior agenda, that of saving the exceptionalist promise, then the homosexual's was less grandiose, limited to finding happiness in a society that was deeply hostile and frequently violent.

For the most part, homosexuals lived silent lives, particularly those who came from the middle and upper classes. No doubt many of the men and women who had been labeled as depraved and who cavorted in the less than genteel environment of the inner-city tavern or nightclub were by the standard of the day "congenital," even if that diagnosis was reserved for the privileged. Although homosexuality cut across class, gender, and race, its official presence as a "degenerative condition" was limited to those who were economically and socially well-off, and this is reflected in the cases of the neurologists as contrasted with their description of the "perversities" of the inner cities. For the middle and upper class who suffered from congenital homosexuality, theirs was a disease of civilization, a mark of success gone amok. Whereas the neurologists rejected the claim that what was natural must by necessity be normal, many who suffered took just the opposite position and argued that their condition, because it was natural, was implicitly normal, especially as there were no other debilitating conditions that would prevent one from participating fully in society. This, of course, was the reason why the congenital invert was discovered among the otherwise most "fit." They were not depraved; they were often cultured and people of "genius." Degeneration relieved them of any of the opprobrium of depravity, and that in turn allowed them to avoid the issue of responsibility that was so prevalent among the weak-willed. To be medically diagnosed as congenital and therefore not responsible for the condition helped the middle-class homosexual maintain his distinction from the lower order of humans and thereby keep his dignity intact. That the depraved and the congenital homosexual might have behaved the same was beside the point. One was diseased through no fault of his own, whereas the other was so by virtue of "taint." Except for their rejection by society, congenital homosexuals felt themselves to be as good as anyone else, with much to contribute to America's future. Some were confused, as was Claude Hartman, but they were unconvinced that they were the evolutionary degenerate as described in the medical literature, and they could point to a few doctors to make the point. For example:

> The first studies of the inversion gave rise to the assumption that it was a sign of innate nervous degeneration.
> The term, degeneration, is open to the objections which may be urged against the promiscuous use of this particular term, It has, in fact, become customary to designate all morbid manifestations not of traumatic or infectious origin as degenerative... It would seem more appropriate not to speak of degeneration: (1) where there are not many marked deviations from the normal; (2) where the capacity for working and living do not in general appear markedly impaired.
> That inverts are not degenerates in this qualified sense can be seen from the following facts:
> 1. The inversion is found in people who otherwise show no marked deviation from the normal.
> 2. It is found also in people whose mental capacities are not disturbed, who on the contrary are distinguished by especially high intellectual development and ethical culture.

3. If one disregards the patients of one's won practice and strives to comprehend a wider field of experience, he will encounter facts in two directions, which will prevent him from considering inversion as sign of degeneration.[2]

This position was a minority one, yet it spoke to the concerns of many who had been diagnosed by the neurologist in the last quarter of the nineteenth century. Unfortunately for future generations of homosexuals, the aspirations of the physician to help the homosexual turned into a prescription for homophobia. In spite of their good intentions to remove homosexuality from the asylum and confessional, it nevertheless remained captive to social hostility when it became a pathology that could not be cured. It was this sentiment that fueled twentieth-century homophobia, and not just a revulsion of same-sex eroticism. Indeed, were it only a question of doing what one should not, that could have been resolved through the traditional Jeffersonian emphasis on education. But this was not an issue that education could resolve. Jefferson was wrong, and so were the Enlightenment and the theology of the Puritans. Only Darwinism supplied the answers, and thus to Darwin they turned, even if they misapplied it. Biology could not be unlearned and it represented a much more sinister force in society than bad habits, which could always be unlearned with a little bit of discipline and public pressure; if not, off to jail or an asylum. Biology, however, was not so flexible and had to be dealt with differently, through elimination of the diseased elements, be that by eugenics, social engineering, or forced isolation. Middle- and upper-class congenital homosexuals knew this, and rather than face these dismal prospects, retreated into a world of silence where they would remain for the next seventy years.

Notes

Introduction

1. Jonathan Ned Katz, *Gay American History: Lesbians and Gay Men in the United States*, (New York: Meridian, 1992).
2. See, for example, George Chauncy Jr., "From Sexual Inversion to Homosexuality: Medicine and the Changing Conceptualization of Female Deviance," *Salmagundi*, 58–59 (1982–1983), pp. 114–146.
3. The most complete early discussion of this remains that of Richard von Krafft-Ebing's *Psychopathia Sexualis*, (Philadelphia, PA: The Medical Bulletin Printing House, 1892).
4. Ernst Mayer, *The Growth of Biological Thought: Diversity, Evolution and Inheritance*, (Cambridge, MA: The Belknap Press of Harvard University Press, 1982), pp. 45–47.
5. *Growth of Biological Thought*, p. 50.
6. For good discussions on the issue, see Bert James Loewenberg, "Darwinism Comes to America, 1859–1900, *The Mississippi Valley Historical Review*", 27, no. 3 (December 1941), pp. 339–368.
7. Carl N. Degler, *In Search of Human Nature: The Decline and Revival of Darwinism in American Social Thought*, (New York: Oxford University Press, 1991), chapter 5, passim.
8. Dorothy Ross, *The Origins of American Social Science*, (New York: Cambridge University Press, 1982), pp. XIV–XVI.
9. Barry D. Adam, *The Rise of a Gay and Lesbian Movement*, (New York: Twyne Publishers, 1995), revised edition, pp. 20–22.
10. Perhaps the most infamous of these situations was the Alice Mitchell-Freda Ward case of 1892. See "Sane or Insane: Is She Cruel Murderess of Irresponsible Lunatic," *The Memphis Commercial*, 5 (July 19, 1892), p. 1.
11. See, for example, Katz, *Gay American History*; John D'Emilo and Estell B. Freedman, *Intimate Matters: A History of Sexuality in America*, (New York: Harper & Row, 1988); Bert Hanson, "American Physicians' 'Discovery' of Homosexuals, 1880–1900: A New Diagnosis in a Changing Society," in *Framing Disease: Studies in Cultural History*, ed. Charles E. Rosenberg and Janet Golden, (New Brunswick, NJ: Rutgers University Press, 1992), pp. 104–133; David F. Greenberg, *The Construction of Homosexuality*, (Chicago: University of Chicago Press, 1988); George Chauncy Jr., *Gay New York: Gender, Urban Culture and the Making of a Gay Male World*

1890–1940, (New York: Basic Books, 1994); and "From Sexual Inversion to Homosexuality; Medicine and the Changing Conceptualization of Female Deviance," *Salmagundi*, 58–59 (1981–1982), pp. 114–145; Jennifer R. Terry, *An American Obsession: Science, Medicine, and Homosexuality in Modern America*, (Chicago: University of Chicago Press, 1999).

Chapter 1   The Origins of a National Ideology
up to the Civil War

1. Genesis 19: 4–22. *The New American Bible*, (Nashville, TN: Thomas Nelson Inc., 1971), pp. 18–19.
2. Jonathan Edwards, "The Justice of God in the Damnation of Sinners," *The American Intellectual Tradition: vol. I 1630 – 1865*, ed. David A. Hollinger and Charles Capper, 2nd ed., (New York: Oxford University Press, 1993), p. 68.
3. Genesis 3: 14–17, *New American Bible*, pp. 4–5.
4. Edwards, "Justice of God," p. 70.
5. John Winthrop, "A Model of Christian Charity," in *The Harper American Literature*, vol. 1 (New York, NY: HarperCollins, 1994), pp. 168–169.
6. Polybius, "The Histories of Polybius," trans. W. R. Paton, in *Versions of History from Antiquity to the Enlightenment*, ed. Donald R. Kelley, (New Haven, CN: Yale University Press, 1991), pp. 44–45.
7. Louis Le Roy, "Vicissitudes or Variety of Things in the Universe," in *Versions of History*, p. 271.
8. J. G. A. Pocock, *The Machiavellian Moment: Florentine Political Thought and the Atlantic Republican Tradition*, (Princeton, NJ: Princeton University Press, 1975), pp. 84–85.
9. Ibid., pp. 36–37.
10. Samuel Willard, "A Compleat Body of Divinity," in *The American Intellectual Tradition*, vol. I, 1630 – 1865, ed. David A. Hollinger and Charles Capper, 2nd ed., (New York, NY: Oxford University Press, 1993), p. 18.
11. For a good discussion of this topic, see Jack P. Greene, *The Intellectual Construction of America: Exceptionalism and Identity from 1492 to 1800*, (Chapel Hill, NC: University of North Carolina Press, 1993).
12. Benjamin Fanklin, "To Joseph Priestly," in *The American Enlightenment*, ed. Adrienne Koch, (New York: George Braziller, 1965), p. 91.
13. John Trenchard and Thomas Gordon, "Liberty Proved to be the Inalienable Right of all Men," in *Cato's Letters: Or Essays on Liberty, Civil and Religious, and other Important Subjects*, (Indianapolis, IN: Liberty Fund, 1995), vol. I, ed. Ronald Hamowy, pp. 406–407.
14. John Allen, "An Oration upon the Beauties of Liberty," in *Political Sermons of the American Founding Era, 1730–1805*, ed. Ellis Sandoz, (Indianapolis, IN: Liberty Fund, 1991), p. 313.
15. Benjamin Franklin, The Autobiography of Benjamin Franklin, (Atlanta, GA: Communications and Studies Inc., 1923), pp. 212–213.
16. Abraham Williams, "An Election Sermon," in *American Political Writing during the Founding Era, 1760–1805*, vol. 1, ed. Charles S. Hyneman and Donald S. Lutz, (Indianapolis, IN: Liberty Fund, 1983), pp. 7–8.

17. John Adams, "To Mercy Warren," in *The American Enlightenment*, p. 182.
18. Ibid., p. 183.
19. Thomas Jefferson, "Report of the Commissioners for the University of Virginia," in *Writings*, (New York: Library of America, 1984), p. 460.
20. Jefferson, "To Peter Carr," in *Writings*, pp. 901–902.
21. For a good discussion of rioting and public disorders in American history, see Paul A. Gilje, *Rioting in America*, (Bloomington, IN: Indiana University Press, 1996).
22. D. H. Meyer, *The Instructed Conscience: The Shaping of the American National Ethic*, (Philadelphia, PA: University of Pennsylvania Press, 1972), p. 3.
23. Ibid., p. 3.
24. Ibid., p. 63.
25. Alexis de Tocqueville, *Democracy in America*, trans. George Lawrence, (New York, NY: HarperCollins, 2000), p. 430.
26. Meyer, *Instructed Conscience*, p. 89.
27. Ibid., p. 110.
28. Sylvester Graham, *A Lecture to Young Men*, (Providence, RI: Weeden and Cory, 1834), p. 35, reprinted by Arno Press, New York, 1974.
29. Ibid., pp. 49–50.
30. Ibid., p. 43.
31. Ibid., p. 8.
32. Ibid., p. 42.
33. Jefferson, "Notes on the State of Virginia," *Writings*, p. 270.
34. Sara M. Evans, *Born to Liberty: A History of Women in America*, (New York, NY: The Free Press, 1989), p. 55.
35. Alasdair MacIntyre, "Essence and Existence," in *The Encyclopedia of Philosophy*, vol. 3, (New York, NY: Macmillan Publishing Co. & The Free Press, 1967), p. 59.
36. Aristotle, "Politics," in *The Basic Works of Aristotle*, ed. Richard McKeon, (New York, NY: Random House, 1941), p. 1133.
37. MacIntyre, "Essence and Existence," p. 60.
38. Genesis I: 20–28, *New American Bible*, p. 3.
39. Romans I: 22–28, *New American Bible*, p. 1243.
40. St. Thomas Aquinas, *Summa Theologica*, literally translated by Fathers of the English Dominican Province, vol. 2, pt. 11–11, question 154, (New York, NY: Benziger Brothers, 1947), pp. 1825.
41. Ibid., p. 1826.
42. See Olivia Blanchette, *The Perfection of the Universe According to Aquinas: A Teleological Cosmology*, (University Park, PA: Pennsylvania State University Press, 1992).
43. MacIntyre, "Essence and Existence," p. 59.
44. *Essay on Human Understanding*, as quoted in "Essence and Existence," p. 59.
45. Alexis de Tocqueville, *Democracy in America*, in *Documents of American Prejudice*, ed. S. T. Joshi, (New York, NY: Basic Books, 1999), pp. 13–14.
46. Tocqueville, *Democracy in America*, pp. 600–601.
47. Anders Stephanson, *Manifest Destiny: American Expansion and the Empire of Right*, (New York, NY: Hill and Wang, 1995), pp. 39–40.

48. John O'Sullivan as quoted in *Manifest Destiny*, p. 40.
49. Ibid., p. 52.
50. "Certain Dangerous Tendencies in American Life," *The Atlantic Monthly: A Magazine of Literature, Science, Art, and Politics*, XLII (October 1878), pp. 386–367.

Chapter 2 The Rise of an Urban Middle-Class in the Post–Civil War Era

1. Some scholars carry the Gilded Age forward to 1920. See Robert H. Wiebe, *The Search for Order: 1877–1920*, (New York: Hill and Wang, 1967), passim.
2. Mark Twain and Charles Dudley Warner, *The Gilded Age: A Tale of Today*, (New York, NY: Meridian, 1994).
3. Ibid., p. 12.
4. *Historical Statistics of the United States: Colonial Times to 1970*, vol. I, Bicentennial Edition, (Washington, DC: U.S. Department of Commerce, Bureau of the Census, 1975), pp. 11–12.
5. Ibid., p. 12.
6. Ibid., p. 15.
7. Ibid., p. 55.
8. Ibid., p. 105.
9. Jonathan Hughes, *American Economic History*, 3rd ed., (New York, NY: HarperCollins, 1990), pp. 310–314.
10. *Historical Statistics*, vol. I, pp. 105–111.
11. Ibid., pp. 105–106.
12. Ibid., p. 112.
13. Ibid., p. 111.
14. Northeast is defined in the *Historical Statistics*, vol. I, p. 5 as Maine, New Hampshire, Vermont, Massachusetts, Rhode Island, Connecticut, New York, New Jersey, and Pennsylvania. North Central is defined as Ohio, Indiana, Illinois, Michigan, Wisconsin, Minnesota, Iowa, Missouri, North and South Dakota, Nebraska, and Kansas.
15. Paul Boyer, *Urban Masses and Moral Order in America, 1820–1920*, (Cambridge, MA: Harvard University Press, 1978), pp. 123–127.
16. *Historical Statistics*, vol. I, pp. 11–12.
17. Boyer, *Urban Masses*, pp. 123–124.
18. *Historical Statistics*, vol. I, pp. 22–23.
19. Ibid., p. 117.
20. Ibid., p. 224.
21. Ibid., vol. II, p. 958.
22. Hughes, *American Economic History*, pp. 310–332, passim.
23. Ibid., p. 134.
24. Stuart M. Blumin, *The Emergence of the Middle Class: Social Experience in the American City, 1760–1900*, (Cambridge, MA: Cambridge University Press, 1989), pp. 1–16.
25. Ibid., pp. 60–65.
26. Ibid., pp. 67–106, passim.

27. Alexis de Tocqueville, *Democracy in America*, ed. J. P. Mayer, trans. George Lawrence, (New York, NY: Perennial, 1988), part 11, p. 551.
28. See Thomas J. Schlereth, *Victorian America: Transformation in Everyday Life, 1876–1915*, (New York, NY: HarperCollins, 1991).
29. See Robert C. Bannister, *Social Darwinism: Science and Myth in Anglo-American Social Thought*, (Philadelphia: Temple University Press, 1979).
30. J. H. Van Evrie, "White Supremacy and Negro Subordination," in *Documents of American Prejudice: An Anthology of Writings on Race from Thomas Jefferson to David Duke*, (New York: Basic Books, 1999), p. 291.
31. Ibid., p. 292.
32. Frederick L. Hoffman, "Race Traits, and the Tendencies of the American Negro," 1896, in *Documents of American Prejudice*, p. 305.
33. John W. Burgess, "The Ideal of the American Commonwealth," in *Documents of American Prejudice*, p. 116.
34. Matthew Frye Jacobson, *Barbarian Virtues: The United States Encounters Foreign Peoples at Home and Abroad, 1876–1917*, (New York, NY: Hill and Wang, 2000), p. 151.
35. George A. Custer, "My Life on the Plains; Or Personal Experiences with Indians," in *Documents of American Prejudice*, p. 254.
36. Telemachus Thomas Timayenis, "The Original Mr. Jacobs," in *Documents of American Prejudice*, p. 371.
37. Henry George, "The Chinese in California," in *Documents of American Prejudice*, p. 431.
38. Herbert Howe Bancroft, "Pastoral California," in *Documents of American Prejudice*, p. 472.
39. Francis A. Walker, "Restriction of Immigration," in *Documents of American Prejudice*, p. 510.
40. Eugene Talbot, 1898, as quoted in *Creating Born Criminals* by Nicole Hahn Rafter, (Urbana, IL: University of Illinois Press, 1997), p. 120.
41. Carl N. Degler, *In Search of Human*, pp. 26–27.
42. Darwin, *Origin of Species and The Descent of Man*, (New York, NY: Modern Library, n.d.), p. 873.
43. Ibid., p. 908.
44. Stephen Jay Gould, *The Mismeasure of Man*, (New York: W. W. Norton & Company, 1981), p. 20.
45. Ibid., p. 26.
46. As quoted in ibid., p. 21.
47. Evans, *Born of Liberty*, pp. 119–143, passim.
48. Glenna Matthews, *The Rise of Public Woman: Woman's Owner and Woman's Place in the United States, 1630–1970*, (New York, NY: Oxford University Press, 1992), pp. 147–171, passim.
49. David I. Macleod, *Building Character in the American Boy: Boy Scouts, YMCA, and their Forerunners 1879–1920*, (Madison, WI: University of Wisconsin Press, 1983), pp. 3–95, passim.
50. Judy Hilkey, *Character is Capital: Success Manuals and Manhood in Gilded Age America*, (Chapel Hill, NC: University of North Carolina Press, 1977), pp. 131–141.

51. T. L. Haines, *Wealth and Worth*, (Chicago, IL: Brandt and Bruce, 1884).
52. Ibid., p. 203.
53. Ibid., pp. 26–27.
54. Ibid., pp. 24–25.
55. Theodore Roosevelt, "The Strenuous Life," a speech given before the Hamilton Club of Chicago, April 10, 1899, in *Theodore Roosevelt: An American Mind, Selected Writings*, (New York, NY: Penguin Books, 1994), p. 184.
56. Jacobson, *Barbarian Virtues*, p. 3.
57. James Bryce, *The American Commonwealth*, vol. 1, (Chicago, IL: Charles H. Sergel & Co., 1891), p. 615.
58. Ibid., p. 618.
59. Andrew Carnegie, "Wealth," in *A Documentary History of the United States*, ed. Richard D. Heffner, (New York: Mentor Books, 1991), p. 173.
60. Ibid., pp. 174–175.
61. "The Populist Party Platform," in *Documentary History*, pp. 197–198.
62. Degler, *Human Nature*, pp. 112–115.

Chapter 3   Nineteenth-Century Gay America

1. Walt Whitman, "When I Peruse the Conquer'd Fame," in *Leaves of Grass*, (New York: Barnes and Noble Books, 1993), p. 108.
2. Richard Godbeer, *Sexual Revolution in Early America*, (Baltimore, MD: The Johns Hopkins Press, 2002), pp. 64–65.
3. William Bradford, "Of Plymouth Plantation," in *Gay American History*, ed. Jonathan Katz, (New York, NY: Meridian, 1992), p. 21.
4. See Katz, *History*, pp. 16–23, passim.
5. Thomas Jefferson, "A Bill for Proportioning Crimes and Punishments," in *Writings*, pp. 355–356.
6. Ibid., p. 356.
7. Louis Dwight, "The Sin Of Sodom is the Vice of Prisoners..." in Katz, *History*, p. 27.
8. Alvar Nunez Cabeza de Vaca, "I Saw a Devilish Thing," in Katz, *History*, p. 285.
9. Pedro Font, "Sodomites, Dedicated to Nefarious Practices," in Katz, *History*, p. 291.
10. Edwin James and T. Say in Katz, *History*, p. 299.
11. Quoted from "'Writhing Bedfellows' in Antebellum South Carolina," in *Hidden From History: Reclaiming the Gay and Lesbian Past*, ed. Martin Duberman, Martha Vincus, and George Chauncy Jr., (New York: Meridian, 1989), p. 155.
12. D. Michael Quinn, *Same-Sex Dynamics among Nineteenth-Century Americans: A Mormon Example*, (Urbana and Chicago: University of Illinois Press, 1996), pp. 266–267: This is an excellent source on how the Mormons reacted to same-sex eroticism.
13. Jonathan Ned Katz, *Love Stories: Sex between Men before Homosexuality*, (Chicago, IL: University of Chicago Press, 2001), pp. 62–64.

14. Katz, *Gay/Lesbian Almanac: A New Documentary*, (New York: Harper & Row, 1983), pp. 85–86.
15. Ibid., p. 92.
16. Katz, *History*, pp. 302–309.
17. Lillian Faderman, *Surpassing the Love of Men: Romantic Friendship and Love between Women from the Renaissance to the Present*, (New York: Quill, 1981), p. 160.
18. San Francisco Lesbian and Gay History Project, "'She Even Chewed Tobacco': A Pictorial Narrative of Passing Women in America," in *Hidden from History*, pp. 183–194, passim.
19. Faderman, *Surpassing the Love*, pp. 291–293.
20. Faderman, *Odd Girls and Twilight Lovers: A History of Lesbian Life in Twentieth-Century America*, (New York: Penguin Books, 1992), p. 46.
21. See, for example, Jonathan Ned Katz, *Love Stories: Sex between Men before Homosexuality*.
22. Herman Melville, "A Squeeze of the Hand," in *Moby Dick or the Whale*, (London: The Folio Society, 1974), pp. 380–381.
23. Whitman, "City of Orgies," in *Leaves*, p. 105.
24. Bayard Taylor, "Joseph and His Friend: A Story from Pennsylvania," in *Pages Passed from Hand to Hand: The Hidden Tradition of Homosexual Literature in English from 1748 to 1914*, edited with an Introduction by Mark Mitchell and David Leavitt, (Boston: Houghton Mifflen Co., 1997), p. 63.
25. Mary Wilkins Freeman, "Two Women," *Harper's Bazaar*, as quoted in *Nineteenth Century American Women Writers: An Anthology*, ed. Karen L. Kilcup, (Cambridge, MA: Blackwell Publishers, 1997), p. 417.
26. Earl Lind, quoted in Katz, *Gay American History*, pp. 366–368.
27. Chauncy, *Gay New York*, pp. 33–43, passim.
28. Claude Hartland, *The Story of a Life: For the Consideration of the Medical Fraternity*, (St. Louis, 1901) reprinted by Grey Fox Press, San Francisco, 1985, pp. 76–77.
29. Josiah Flynt, "Homosexuality among Tramps," in *Studies in the Psychology of Sex, Vol. II, Sexual Inversion*, ed. Havelock Ellis, (Philadelphia: F. A. Davis Company, 1917), appendix A, p. 360.
30. Mary Warner Blanchard, *Oscar Wilde's America: Counterculture in the Gilded Age*, (New Haven, CN: Yale University Press, 1998).
31. See, for example, Merlin Holland, *The Wilde Album*, (New York: Henry Holt & Co., 1997), pp. 96–99.
32. F. Holland Day, *Suffering the Ideal*, with an essay by James Crump, (Santa Fe, NM: Twin Palms, 1995).
33. Ibid., p. 8.
34. Colin A. Scott, "Sex and Art," *The American Journal of Psychology*, VII, no. 2 (January 1896), p. 216.
35. Irving C. Rosse, "Perversion of the Genesic Instinct," quoted in Katz, *Gay American History*, p. 42.
36. C. H. Hughes, "Postscript to Paper on Erotopathia: An Organization of Colored Erotopaths," in *Alienist and Neurologist*, XIV, no. 4 (October 1893), pp. 731–732.

Chapter 4   A Period of Turmoil and Change

1. "Certain Dangerous Tendencies in American Life," *Atlantic Monthly* (October 1878), p. 401.
2. See Wiebe, *The Search for Order.*
3. Noll, *A History of Christianity*, pp. 305–306.
4. For a more thorough discussion of the relationship between the Purity Reformers and the Progressive movement, see David Pivar, *Purity Crusade, Sexual Morality, and Social Control, 1868–1900*, (Westport, CN: Greenwood Press Inc., 1973).
5. Jon H. Roberts, *Darwinism and the Divine in America: Protestant Intellectuals and Organic Evolution, 1859–1900*, (Madison: University of Wisconsin Press, 1988), pp. 33–37.
6. Mayr, *Growth of Biological Thought*, pp. 517–518.
7. James Turner, *Without God, Without Creed: The Origins of Unbelief in America*, (Baltimore, MD: John Hopkins University Press, 1985), pp. 183–186.
8. Lyman Beecher, as quoted in Turner, *Without God, Without Creed*, p. 242.
9. Dorothy Ross, *The Origins of American Social Science*, p. XV.
10. Ibid., pp. 60–61.
11. Ibid., p. 61.
12. Ibid., pp. 61–62.
13. Ibid., p. 62.
14. Ibid., p. 85.

Chapter 5   Nineteenth-Century American Medicine

1. John S. Haller Jr. and Robin M. Haller, *The Physician and Sexuality in Victorian America*, (Carbondale, IL: Southern University Press, 1974), p. 273.
2. John Duffy, *From Humors to Medical Science: A History of American Medicine*, (Urbana and Chicago: University of Illinois Press, 1993), p. 168.
3. William G. Rothstein, *American Physicians in the 19th Century: From Sects to Science*, (Baltimore, MD: Johns Hopkins University Press, 1985), pp. 200–260, passim.
4. Ibid., p. 287.
5. Ibid., pp. 282–292.
6. *Heritage of American Education*, ed. Richard E. Gross, (Boston, MA: Allyn and Bacon, Inc., 1962), pp. 266–267.
7. George P. Schmidt, *The Liberal Arts College: A Chapter in American Cultural History*, (New Brunswick, NJ: Rutgers University Press, 1957), p. 161.
8. Abraham Flexner, *Medical Education in the United States and Canada: A Report to the Carnegie Foundation for the Advancement of Teaching*, (Bethesda, MD: Carnegie Foundation for the Advancement of Teaching, 1910). Flexner specifically identifies New York University, Syracuse, Northwestern University, Jefferson Medical College in Philadelphia, Tulane University in New Orleans, St. Louis University, and the University of Texas, p. 79.

9. Ibid., p. 80.
10. Ibid., p. 81.
11. Thomas Neville Bonner, "The German Model of Training Physicians in the United States, 1870–1914: How Closely was it Followed?" *Bulletin of the History of Medicine*, 64 (1990), pp. 28–34.
12. Thomas Neville Bonner, *American Doctors and German Universities: A Chapter in International Intellectual Relations, 1870–1914*, (Lincoln, NE: University of Nebraska Press, 1963), pp. 53–36.
13. Ibid., pp. 3–22, passim.
14. Ibid., p. 23.
15. Ibid., pp. 30–39.
16. Ibid., pp. 58–63.
17. John S. Billings, "Literature and Institutions," as quoted in Rothstein, *American Physicians*, p. 205.
18. Paul Starr, *The Social Transformation of American Medicine: The Rise of a Sovereign Profession and the Making of a Vast Industry*, (New York: Basic Books, 1982), pp. 109–110.
19. Ibid., p. 124.
20. Rothstein, *American Physicians*, pp. 203–206.
21. F. G. Gosling, *Before Freud: Neurasthenics and the American Medical Community, 1870–1910*, (Chicago: University of Illinois Press, 1987), pp. 9–11.
22. Ibid., pp. 13–14.
23. Ibid., pp. 101–102.
24. Ibid., p. 97.
25. George M. Beard, *Sexual Neurasthenia: Its Hygiene, Causes, Symptoms and Treatment*, (New York: E. B. Treat & Co., 1898); reprint, New York: Arno Press, 1972, p. 14.
26. Ibid., p. 15.
27. Ibid., pp. 102–103.
28. Ibid., p. 103.
29. Haller, *Physicians and Sexuality*, p. 191.
30. Ibid., p. 191.
31. Rothstein, *American Physicians*, pp. 207–208.
32. G. M. B. Maughs, "Medical Ultraisms," *Transactions of the Missouri State Medical Association*, 23rd session (1880), p. 21, as quoted in Rothstein, *American Physicians*, pp. 210–211.
33. Rothstein, *American Physicians*, pp. 212–215.
34. Starr, *Social Transformation*, p. 142.

Chapter 6   The Debate Between Alienism and Neurology

1. Edward Shorter, *A History of Psychiatry from the Era of the Asylum to the Age of Prozac*, (New York: John Wiley & Sons, Inc., 1997), p. 65.
2. Ibid., pp. 4–10.
3. Ibid., p. 26.
4. Ibid., p. 15.

5. Ibid., p. 45.
6. Allen W. Hagenbach, "Masturbation as a Cause of Insanity," *Journal of Nervous and Mental Diseases*, VI (October 1879), p. 603.
7. Ibid., p. 606.
8. Ibid., p. 612.
9. Shorter, *History of Psychiatry*, p. 70.
10. Ibid., p. 71.
11. Ibid., p. 93.
12. Quoted in Shorter, *History of Psychiatry*, p. 94.
13. See J. B. Lamarck, *Zoological Philosophy: An Exposition with Regard to the Natural History of Animals*, reprint, (Chicago: University of Chicago Press, 1984).
14. Rafter, *Creating Born Criminals*, pp. 38–39.
15. Ibid., p. 110.
16. G. Frank Lydston, *The Diseases of Society: The Vice and Crime Problem*, (Philadelphia: J. B. Lippencott Company, 1904), p. 36.
17. Rafter, *Creating Born Criminals*, p. 117.
18. Ibid., pp. 116–122.
19. Ibid., p. 127.
20. Lydston, *Diseases of Society*, p. 50.
21. Shorter, *History of Psychiatry*, p. 119.
22. Ibid., p. 116.
23. Russell N. DeJong, *A History of American Neurology*, (New York: Raven Press, 1982), p. 41
24. Ibid., pp. 2–3.
25. Ibid., pp. 5–11.
26. As quoted in *History of American Neurology*, p. 20.
27. Ibid., p. 21.
28. Ibid., pp. 23–25.
29. Edward C. Spitzka, "Reform in the Scientific Study of Psychiatry," *Nervous and Mental Disease*, V, no. 2 (April 1878), pp. 206–207.
30. DeJong, *History of American Neurology*, p. 43.
31. Ibid., p. 94.
32. Charles E. Rosenberg, *The Trial of the Assassin Guiteau: Psychiatry and the Law in the Gilded Age*, (Chicago: University of Chicago Press, 1968), pp. 72–74.
33. DeJong, *History of American Neurology*, p. 95.
34. Spitzka, "Reform," pp. 217–218.
35. Ibid., p. 222.
36. Ibid., p. 225.
37. Ibid., p. 224.
38. Ibid., pp. 204–205.
39. Bonnie Ellen Blustein, "New York Neurologists and the Specialization of American Medicine," *Bulletin of the History of Medicine*, 53 (1979), pp. 179–182.
40. Rosenberg, *The Trial of the Assassin Guiteau*, p. 54
41. Kiernan, James G., *The Book of Chicagoans*, (Chicago, IL: A. N. Marquis, 1926), p. 331.

42. Rosenberg, *The Trial of the Assassin Guiteau*, p. 145.
43. Ibid., pp. 147–150.
44. Ibid., p. 152.
45. As quoted in Rosenberg, *The Trial of the Assassin Guiteau*, p. 155.
46. Ibid., p. 158.
47. Ibid., pp. 162–163.
48. Ibid., p. 167.
49. Blustein, "New York Neurologists," p. 42.
50. Ibid., pp. 53–58.

Chapter 7   The German Discovery of the Homosexual

1. Richard von Krafft-Ebing, *Psychopathia Sexualis with Especial Reference to the Antipathetic Sexual Instinct: A Medico-Forensic Study*, (Philadelphia, PA: The F. A. Davis Company, 1892), p. 410.
2. Vern L. Bullough, "The Physician and Research into Human Sexual Behavior in Nineteenth-Century Germany," *Bulletin of the History of Medicine*, 63 (1989), p. 256.
3. Karl Heinrichs Ulrichs, *The Riddle of "Man-Manly" Love*, trans. Michael A. Lombardi-Nash with a foreword by Vern L. Bullough, (Buffalo, NY: Prometheus Books, 1994), vol. 1, p. 34. Ulrich coined the word "Dioning." It means "heterosexual."
4. Ullrichs, *Riddle*, pp. 35–36.
5. Ibid., p. 38.
6. As quoted in Bullough, "Physician and Research," p. 256.
7. Manfred Herzer, "Kertbeny and the Nameless Love," *Journal of Homosexuality*, 12, no. 1 (Fall 1985), p. 1.
8. Shorter, *Psychiatry*, p. 96.
9. Krafft-Ebing, *Psychopathia Sexualis*, p. iv.
10. Solomon Diamond, "Gestation of the Instinct Concept," *Journal of the History of the Behavioral Sciences*, VII (October 1971), pp. 324–334, passim.
11. Krafft-Ebing, *Psychopathia Sexualis*, p. 1.
12. Ibid., p. 5.
13. Ibid., p. 13.
14. Ibid., p. 187.
15. Ibid., p. 188.
16. Ibid., pp. 190–216, passim.
17. Ibid., p. 225.
18. Ibid., pp. 222–223.
19. Ibid., p. 226.
20. Ibid., p. 187.

Chapter 8   American Physicians Discover the Homosexual

1. "Aberrations of the Sexual Instinct," *Quarterly Journal of Psychological Medicine and Medical Jurisprudence* (1867), p. 66.
2. Ibid., pp. 67–89, passim.

3. E. C. Spitzka, "Gynomania: To the Editor of the Medical Record," *The Medical Record*, 19, no. 13 (March 28, 1881), p. 359.
4. Dr. H., "Gynomania," *The Medical Record*, 19, no. 12 (March 19, 1881), p. 336.
5. Spitzka, "Gynomania," p. 359.
6. Spitzka, "A Historical Case of Sexual Perversion," *Chicago Medical Review*, 4, no. 4 (August 20, 1881), p. 379.
7. "Progress in Neurology," *American Journal, of Neurology and Psychiatry*, 1, no. 2 (1882), p. 323.
8. Theodore Deecke, "Primaere and Originaere Verruecktheit: An Historical Sketch with Critical Remarks," *American Journal of Insanity* (April 1885), pp. 430–431.
9. "Progress in Neurology," *American Journal of Neurology and Psychiatry*, p. 325.
10. G. Alfred Blumer, "Case of Perverted Sexual Instinct," *The American Journal of Insanity*, 34 (July 1882), p. 23.
11. William A. Hammond, "The Disease of the Scythians (Morbus Feminarum) and certain Analogous Conditions," *American Journal of Neurology and Psychiatry*, 1, no. 3 (August 1882), pp. 339–341.
12. A review of *Perverted Sexual Feelings* by Richard von Krafft Ebing, *The Alienist and Neurologist*, 3, no. 4 (October 1882), p. 675.
13. C. Shaw and G. N. Ferris, "Perverted Sexual Instinct," *Journal of Nervous and Mental Disease*, X, no. 2 (April 1883), pp. 186–204, passim.
14. Professor Griesinger, quoted in Shaw and Ferris, "perverted Sexual Instinct," p. 186.
15. Ibid., pp. 202–203.
16. All these articles and more are bound in two volumes, which I dubbed *The Kiernan Articles*, vols. I & II, and housed in the Center for Research Libraries (CRL), Chicago, IL.
17. Jas. G. Kiernan, "Lecture XXVI—Sexual Perversion," *Detroit Lancet*, VII, no. 11 (May 1884), p. 481.
18. Jas. G. Kiernan, "Sexual Perversion and The Whitechapel Murders," *The Medical Standard*, IV, no. 5 (November 1888), p. 129.
19. George F. Shrady, "Perverted Sexual Instinct," *The Medical Record* (July 19, 1884), pp. 70–71.
20. Katz, *Gay/Lesbian Almanac*, p. 199.
21. Review of paper presentation given by Clevenger, *Western Medical Reporter*, X, no. 11 (November 1888), p. 208.
22. G. Frank Lydston, "Sexual Perversion, Satyriasis and Nymphomania," *Medical and Surgical Reporter*, LXI, no. 1697 (September 7 and 14, 1889).
23. Lydston, George Frank, *The National Cyclopedia*, (New York: J. T. White, 1930), pp. 123–124.
24. Lydston, "Sexual Perversion" (September 7, 1889), p. 255.
25. Ibid., p. 254.
26. Ibid., p. 255.
27. Ibid., p. 254.
28. Ibid., p. 254.
29. Shrady, "Perverted Sexual Instinct," p. 70.

30. Ibid., p. 71.
31. P. M. Wise, "Case of Sexual Perversion," *Alienist and Neurologist*, 4 (January 1883), p. 87.
32. Philip Leidy and Charles K. Mills, "Case III:—Sexual Perversion," *Journal of Nervous and Mental Disease*, 13, no. 11 (November 1886), pp. 714–713.
33. Kiernan, "Sexual Perversion," p. 484.
34. Prof. Von Krafft-Ebing, "Perversion of the Sexual Instinct—Report of Cases," *Alienist and Neurologist*, 9, no. 4 (October 1888), pp. 565–566.
35. Lydston, "Sexual Perversion" (September 7, 1889), p. 253.
36. Chauncy, "From Sexual Inversion to Homosexuality," p. 119.
37. Shaw and Ferris, "Perverted Sexual Instinct," pp. 187–188.
38. Shrady, "Perverted Sexual Instinct," p. 70.
39. Kiernan, "Sexual Perversion," p. 483.
40. Leidy and Mills, "Case III," pp. 712–713.
41. Krafft-Ebing, "Perversion," pp. 573 and 580.
42. Lydston, "Sexual Perversion," p. 256.
43. Chauncy, "From Sexual Inversion to Homosexuality," p. 214.

Chapter 9   The Homosexual and the Physician in the 1890s

1. "Sane or Insane," *The Memphis Commercial*, 5 (Tuesday Morning, July 19, 1892), p. 1.
2. As quoted in Katz, *Gay/Lesbian Almanac*, p. 223.
3. Rosenberg, *Guiteau*, p. 55.
4. "Sane or Insane," p. 1.
5. Ibid., p. 1.
6. Ibid., p. 1.
7. *N. Y. Times*, etc., in Katz, *Gay/Lesbian Almanac*, pp. 223–226.
8. Lisa Duggan, "The Trials of Alice Mitchell: Sensationalism, Sexology, and the Lesbian Subject in Turn-of-the-Century America," *Signs: Journal of Women in Culture and Society*, 18, no. 4 (Summer 1993), p. 800.
9. Pivar, *Purity Crusade*, p. 186.
10. Ibid., pp. 149–160, passim.
11. Ibid., pp. 255–277, passim.
12. Ibid., p. 258, and chapter 5, passim.
13. Ibid., p. 155.
14. Jas. G. Kiernan, "Responsibility in Sexual Perversion," *The Chicago Medical Recorder* (May 1892).
15. Ibid., p. 188.
16. Ibid., p. 192.
17. Ibid., p. 194.
18. Ibid., p. 194.
19. Ibid., p. 207.
20. Ibid., p. 210.
21. Charles Gilbert Chaddock, "Sexual Crimes," in *A System of Legal Medicine*, ed. Allan McLane Hamilton, M.D. (New York: E. B. Treat, 1894), p. 272.

22. James L. O'Leary and Walter L. Moore, "Charles Gilbert Chaddock: His Life and Contributions," *Journal of the History of Medicine* (July 1953), pp. 301–317.
23. Chaddock, *Crimes*, p. 551.
24. Ibid., p. 555.
25. Ibid., pp. 551–555, 570.
26. Havelock Ellis, "Sexual Inversion in Men," *Alienist and Neurologist*, 17, no. 2 (April 1896), p. 118.
26. Havelock Ellis, "A Note on the Treatment of Sexual Inversion," *Alienist and Neurologist*, 17, no. 3 (July 1896), p. 261.
28. Ibid., p. 262.
29. G. Frank Lydston, *The Diseases of Society (The Vice and Crime Problem)*, (Philadelphia: J. B. Lippencott Company, 1904).
30. Ibid., p. 13.
31. Ibid., p. 13.
32. Ibid., p. 37.
33. Ibid., pp. 13–37, passim.
34. Ibid., p. 374.
35. G. Frank Lydston, "Aberrant Sexual Differentiation," in *Addresses and Essays*, (Louisville, KY: Renz & Henry, 1892), pp. 44–46.
36. Morton Prince, "Sexual Perversion or Vice? A Pathological and Therapeutic Inquiry," *The Journal of Nervous and Mental Disease*, XXV, no. 4 (April 1898), p. 253.
37. William Lee Howard, "Sexual Perversions," *Alienist and Neurologist*, XVII, no. 1 (January 1896), pp. 3–6.
38. Morton Prince, "Sexual Psychoses," in *A System of Practical Medicine by American Authors*, ed. Alfred Lee Loomis, M.D. and William Gilman Thompson, M.D., vol. IV, (New York: Lea Brothers & Co., 1898), p. 881.
39. Ibid., p. 894.
40. Ibid., pp. 885–886.
41. Ibid., p. 893.
42. Ibid., pp. 896–987.
43. Ellis, "A Note," p. 261.
44. See, for example, Charles H. Hughes, "Erotopathia—Morbid Eroticism," *Alienist and Neurologist*, vol. 14, no. 4 (October 1893), p. 563.
45. Rosse, "Sexual Hypochrondriasis," p. 811.
46. Hughes, *Morbid Eroticism*, p. 540.
47. Ibid., p. 540.
48. Lydston, *Diseases*, p. 557.
49. Ibid., p. 558.
50. Ibid., p. 559.
51. Ibid., p. 573.
52. Ibid., pp. 560–589, passim.
53. Ibid., p. 563.
54. Ibid., p. 564.
55. Ibid., p. 566.
56. Ibid., p. 421.

Chapter 10   An Emerging Homosexual Identity During the Gilded Age

1. Howard, "Sexual Perversion in America," p. 11.
2. Karl Heinrich Ulrichs, "Araxes," in *We are Everywhere: A Historical Source of Gay and Lesbian Politics*, ed. Mark Blasius and Shane Phelan, (New York: Routledge, 1997), p. 64.
3. Ellis, "Sexual Inversion in Men," p. 124.
4. Krafft-Ebing, *Psychopathia Sexualis*, p. 271.
5. As quoted in Katz, *Gay American History*, p. 374.
6. Krafft-Ebing, *Psychopathia Sexualis*, p. 277.
7. See John Addington Symonds, *Male Love: A Problem in Greek Ethics and other Writings*, foreword by Robert Peters, ed. John Lauitsen, (New York: Pagan Press, 1983).
8. Edward Carpenter, "The Intermediate Sex," in *We are Everywhere*, p. 118.
9. Mark Rotenberg, *The Rotenberg Collection: Forbidden Erotica*, (Köln: Taschen, 2000).
10. Katz, *Love Stories*, p. 293.
11. Earl Lind, "Evening at Paresis Hall," in Katz, *Gay American History*, pp. 367–370.
12. Ibid., p. 371.
13. Katz, *Love Stories*, p. 290.
14. Claude Hartland, *The Story of a Life: For the Consideration of the Medical Fraternity*, (St. Louis, MO: 1901), reprint San Francisco: Grey Fox Press, 1985 with a foreword by C. A. Tripp.
15. Ibid., p. 18.
16. Ibid., p. 35.
17. Ibid., p. 40.
18. Ibid., p. 41.
19. Ibid., p. 53.
20. Ibid., p. 67.
21. Ibid., p. 68.
22. Ibid., p. 88.
23. Ibid., p. 89.

Chapter 11   The Limits of Congenital Homosexuality

1. Howard, "Sexual Perversion in America," p. 9.
2. Ulrichs, *Riddle*, vol. II, p. 606.
3. Ellis, *Psychology of Sex*, p. 264.
4. Ibid., pp. 295–296.
5. Hughes, "Erotopathia," p. 577.
6. Katz, *Gay/Lesbian Almanac*, p. 201.
7. Kiernan, "Responsibility in Sexual Perversion," p. 209.
8. Katz, *Gay/Lesbian Almanac*, p. 184.
9. Ibid., p. 297.
10. Chauncy, *Gay New York*, pp. 72–74.
11. Vide Hughes' quote, chapter 3, p. 9

12. Krafft-Ebing, *Psychopathia Sexualis*, p. 34.
13. Ibid., p. 2.
14. Lydston, *Diseases*, p. 19.
15. Ibid., p. 86.
16. Ibid., p. 27.
17. Ibid., p. 44.
18. Ibid., p. 45.
19. Ibid., p. 91.
20. Ibid., p. 122.
21. Ibid., p. 54.
22. Ibid., p. 19.
23. Ibid., p. 375.
24. Ibid., p. 378.
25. Ibid., p. 404.
26. Kiernan, "Responsibility in Sexual Perversion," p. 185.
27. Ibid., p. 194.
28. Hughes, "Erotopathia," p. 534.
29. Ibid., p. 535.
30. Stuver, "Would Asexualization...", p. 229.
31. Daniel, "Should Insane Criminals or Sexual Perverts be Allowed to Procreate," p. 277.

Chapter 12   Conclusion

1. E. Stuver and D. Rawlins, "Would Asexualization of Chronic Criminals, Sexual Perverts and Hereditary Defectives Benefit Society and Elevate the Human Race?" *The Texas Medical Journal*, XII, no. 5 (November 1896), pp. 228–229.
2. Sigmund Freud, "Three Contributions to the Theory of Sex" in *The Basic Writings of Sigmund Freud*, trans. and ed. with an introduction by Dr. A. A. Brill, (New York: The Modern Library, 1938), p. 555.

Bibliography

"Aberrations of the Sexual Instinct." *Quarterly Journal of Psychological Medicine and Medical Jurisprudence* (1867).
Adam, Barry D. *The Rise of a Gay and Lesbian Movement*. New York: Twyne Publishers, 1995.
The American Enlightenment. New York: George Braziller, 1965.
The American Intellectual Tradition, Vol. I 1630–1865. New York: Oxford University Press, 1993.
"American Physicians' 'Discovery' of Homosexuals, 1880–1900: A New Diagnosis in a Changing Society" by Bert Hanson. *Framing Disease: Studies in Cultural History*. New Brunswick, NJ: Rutgers University Press, 1992.
American Political Writing During the Founding Era, 1760–1805. Vol. I. Indianapolis, IN: Liberty Fund, 1983.
Aquinas, St. Thomas. *Summa Theologica*. Vol. II, pt. 11-11. New York: Benziger Brothers, 1947.
Bannister, Robert C. *Social Darwinism: Science and Myth in Anglo-American Social Thought*. Philadelphia: Temple University Press, 1979.
The Basic Works of Aristotle. New York: Random House, 1941.
The Basic Writings of Sigmund Freud. New York: The Modern Library, 1938.
Beard, George M. *Sexual Neurasthenia: Its Hygiene, Causes, Symptoms and Treatment*. New York: E. B. Treat & Co., 1898; reprint, New York Arno Press, 1972.
Blanchard, Mary Warner. *Oscar Wilde's America: Counterculture in the Gilded Age*. New Haven: Yale University Press, 1998.
Blanchette, Olivia. *The Perfection of the Universe According to Aquinas: A Teleological Cosmology*. University Park, PA: Pennsylvania State University Press, 1992.
Blumin, Stuart M. *The Emergence of the Middle Class: Social Experience in the American City, 1760–1900*. Cambridge, MA: Cambridge University Press, 1989.
Bonner, Thomas Neville. *American Doctors and German Universities: A Chapter in International Intellectual Relations, 1870–1914*. Lincoln, NE: University of Nebraska Press, 1963.
The Book of Chicagoans. Chicago: A. N. Marquis, 1926.

Boyer, Paul. *Urban Masses and Moral Order in America, 1820–1920*. Cambridge, MA: Harvard University Press, 1978.

Bryce, James. *The American Commonwealth*. Vol. I. Chicago: Charles H. Sergel & Co., 1891.

"Case III:—Sexual Perversion" by Philip Leidy and Charles K. Mills. *Journal of Nervous and Mental Disease*, vol. 13, no. 11 (November 1886).

"Case of Perverted Sexual Instinct" by G. Alfred Blumer. *The American Journal of Insanity*, vol. 34 (July 1882).

"Case of Sexual Perversion" by P. M. Wise. *Alienist and Neurologist*, vol. 4 (January 1883).

Cato's Letters: Or Essays on Liberty, Civil and Religious and other Important Subjects. Vol. 1. Indianapolis, IN: Liberty Fund, 1995.

"Certain Dangerous Tendencies in American Life." *The Atlantic Monthly: A Magazine of Literature, Science, Art, and Politics*, vol. XLII (October 1878).

Chaddock, Charles Gilbert. *A System of Legal Medicine*. New York: E. B. Treat, 1894.

"Charles Gilbert Chaddock: His Life and Contributions" by James L. O'Leary and Walter L. Moore. *Journal of the History of Medicine* (July 1953).

Chauncy, George Jr. *Gay New York: Gender, Urban Culture and the Making of a Gay Male World 1890–1940*. New York: Basic Books, 1994.

Darwin, Charles. *Origin of Species and the Descent of Man*. New York: Modern Library, n.d.

"Darwinism Comes to America, 1859–1900" by Bert James Loewenberg. *The Mississippi Valley Historical Review*, vol. 27, no. 3 (December 5, 1941).

Day, F. Hollander. *Suffering the Ideal*. Santa Fe, NM: Twin Palms, 1995.

Degler, Carl N. *In Search of Human Nature: The Decline and Revival of Darwinism in American Social Thought*. New York: Oxford University Press, 1991.

DeJong, Russell N. *A History of American Neurology*. New York: Raven Press, 1982.

D'Emilo and Freedman, Estell B. *Intimate Matters: A History of Sexuality in America*. New York: Harper & Row, 1988.

"The Disease of the Scythians (Morbus Feminarum) and certain Analogous Conditions" by William A. Hammond. *American Journal of Neurology and Psychiatry*, vol. I, no. 3 (August 1882).

Documents of American Prejudice: An Anthology of Writings on Race from Thomas Jefferson to David Duke. New York: Basic Books, 1999.

Duffy, John. *From Humors to Medical Science: A History of American Medicine*. Urbana and Chicago: University of Illinois Press, 1993.

Ellis, Havelock. *Studies in the Psychology of Sex*. Vol. II. Philadelphia: F. A. Davis Company, 1917.

"Erotopathia—Morbid Eroticism" by Charles H. Hughes. *Alienist and Neurologist*, vol. 14, no. 4 (October 1893).

"Essence and Existence" by Alasdair MacIntyre. *The Encyclopedia of Philosophy.* Vol. 3. New York: Macmillan Publishing Co. and The Free Press, 1967.

Evans, Sara M. *Born to Liberty: A History of Women in America.* New York: The Free Press, 1989.

Faderman, Lillian. *Odd Girls and Twilight Lovers: A History of Lesbian Life in Twentieth-Century America.* New York: Penguin Books, 1992.

———. *Surpassing the Love of Men: Romantic Friendship and Love between Women from the Renaissance to the Present.* New York: Quill, 1981.

Flexner, Abraham. *Medical Education in the United States and Canada: A Report to the Carnegie Foundation for the Advancement of Teaching.* Carnegie Foundation for the Advancement of Teaching, 1910.

Franklin, Benjamin. *The Autobiography of Benjamin Franklin.* Atlanta, GA: Communications and Studies, Inc., 1923.

"From Sexual Inversion to Homosexuality: Medicine and the Changing Conceptualization of Female Deviance" by George Chauncy Jr. *Salmagundi*, vol. 58–59 (1982–1983).

"The German Model of Training Physicians in the United States, 1870–1914: How Closely was it Followed?" by Thomas Neville Bonner. *Bulletin of the History of Medicine*, vol. 64 (1990).

"Gestation of the Instinct Concept" by Solomon Diamond. *Journal of the History of the Behavioral Sciences*, vol. VII (October 1971).

Gilje, Paul A. *Rioting in America.* Bloomington, IN: Indiana University Press, 1996.

Godbeer, Richard. *Sexual Revolution in Early America.* Baltimore, MD: The Johns Hopkins Press, 2000.

Gosling F. G. *Before Freud: Neurasthenia and the American Medical Community, 1870–1910.* Chicago: University of Illinois Press, 1987.

Gould, Stephen Jay. *The Mismeasure of Man.* New York: W. W. Norton, 1981.

Graham, Sylvester. *A Lecture to Young Men.* Providence, RI: Weeden and Cory, 1834.

Green, Jack P. *The Intellectual Construction of America: Exceptionalism and Identity from 1492 to 1800.* Chapel Hill, NC: University of North Carolina Press, 1993.

Greenberg, David A. *The Construction of Homosexuality.* Chicago: University of Chicago Press, 1988.

"Gynomania" by Dr. H. *The Medical Record*, vol. 19, no. 12 (March 19, 1881).

"Gynomania: To the Editor of the Medical Record" by E. C. Spitzka. *The Medical Record*, vol. 19, no. 13 (March 28, 1881).

Haines, T. L. *Wealth and Worth.* Chicago: Brandt and Bruce, 1884.

Haller, John S. Jr. and Robin M. *The Physician and Sexuality in Victorian America.* Carbondale, IL: Southern University Press, 1974.

Hartland, Claude. *The Story of a Life: For the Consideration of the Medical Fraternity.* St. Louis, 1901. Reprint, San Francisco, CA: Grey Fox Press, 1985.

Heritage of American Education. Boston: Allyn and Bacon, 1962.
Hidden From History: Reclaiming the Gay and Lesbian Past. New York: Meridian, 1989.
Hilkey, Judy. *Character is Capital: Success Manuals and Manhood in Gilded Age America.* Chapel Hill, NC: University of North Carolina Press, 1977.
"A Historical Case of Sexual Perversion" by E. C. Spitzka. *Chicago Medical Record*, vol. 4, no. 4 (August 20, 1881).
Historical Statistics of the United States: Colonial Times to 1970. Vol. I. Washington, DC: U.S. Department of Commerce, Bureau of the Census, 1975.
Hughes, Jonathan. *American Economic History.* New York: HarperCollins, 1990.
Jacobson, Matthew Frye. *Barbarian Virtues: The United States Encounters Foreign Peoples at Home and Abroad, 1876–1917.* New York: Hill and Wang, 2000.
Jefferson, Thomas. *Writings.* New York: Library of America, 1984.
Katz, Jonathan Ned. *Gay American History: Lesbians and Gay Men in the United States.* New York: Meridian, 1992.
———. *Gay/Lesbian Almanac: A New Documentary.* New York: Harper & Row, 1983.
———. *Love Stories: Sex between Men before Homosexuality.* Chicago: University of Chicago Press, 2001.
"Kertbeny and the Nameless Love" by Manfred Herzer. *Journal of Homosexuality*, vol. 12, no. 1 (Fall 1985).
The Kiernan Articles, Center for Research Libraries, Chicago, IL.
Krafft-Ebing, Richard von. *Psychopathia Sexualis with Especial Reference to the Antipathetic Sexual Instinct: A Medico-Forensic Study.* Philadelphia: The Medical Bulletin Printing House, 1892.
Lamarck, J. B. *Zoological Philosophy: An Exposition with Regard to the Natural History of Animals.* Chicago: University of Chicago Press, 1984.
"Lecture XXVI—Sexual Perversion" by James G. Kiernan. *Detroit Lancet*, vol. VII, no. 11 (May 1884).
Lydston, Frank G. *Addresses and Essays.* Louisville, KY: Renz & Henry, 1892.
———. *The Diseases of Society: The Vice and Crime Problem.* Philadelphia: J. B. Lippencott Company, 1904.
Macleod, David I. *Building Character in the American Boy: Boy Scouts, YMCA, and Their Forerunners, 1879–1920.* Madison, WI: University of Wisconsin Press, 1983.
"Masturbation as a Cause of Insanity" by Allen W. Hagenbach. *Journal of Nervous and Mental Diseases*, vol. VI (October 1879).
Matthews, Glenna. *The Rise of Public Woman: Woman's Owner and Woman's Place in the United States, 1630–1970.* New York: Oxford University Press, 1992.
Mayer, Ernst. *The Growth of Biological Thought: Diversity, Evolution and Inheritance.* Cambridge, MA: The Belknap Press of Harvard University Press, 1982.

Melville, Herman. *Moby Dick or the Whale*. London: The Folio Society, 1974.
"A Model of Christian Charity" by John Winthrop. *The Harper American Literature*. Vol. I. New York: HarperCollins, 1994.
Meyer, D. H. *The Instructed Conscience: The Shaping of the American National Ethic*. Philadelphia: University of Pennsylvania Press, 1972.
The National Cyclopedia. New York: J. T. White, 1930.
The New American Bible. Nashville, TN: Thomas Nelson, Inc., 1971.
"New York Neurologists and the Specialization of American Medicine" by Bonnie Ellen Blustein. *Bulletin of the History of Medicine*, vol. 53 (1979).
Nineteenth Century American Women Writers: An Anthology. Cambridge, MA: Blackwell Publishers, 1977.
Noll, Mark A. *A History of Christianity in the United States and Canada*. Grand Rapids, MI: William B. Eerdmans Publishing Company, 1992.
"A Note on the Treatment of Sexual Inversion" by Havelock Ellis. *Alienist and Neurologist*, vol. 17, no. 3 (July 1896).
Pages Passed from Hand to Hand: The Hidden Tradition of Homosexual Literature in England from 1748 to 1914. Boston: Houghton Mifflin, Co., 1997.
"Perversion of the Sexual Instinct—Report of Cases" by Richard von Krafft-Ebing. *Alienist and Neurologist*, vol. 9, no. 4 (October 1888).
"Perverted Sexual Instinct" by C. Shaw and G. N. Ferris. *Journal of Nervous and Mental Disease*, vol. X, no. 2 (April 1883).
"Perverted Sexual Instinct" by George F. Shrady. *The Medical Record* (July 19, 1884).
"The Physician and Research into Human Sexual Behavior in Nineteenth-Century Germany" by Vern L. Bullough. *Bulletin of the History of Medicine*, vol. 63 (1989).
Pivar, David. *Purity Crusade, Sexual Morality, and Social Control, 1868–1900*. Westport, CN: Greenwood Press, 1973.
Pocock, J. G. A. *The Machiavellian Moment: Florentine Political Thought and the Atlantic Republican Tradition*. Princeton, NJ: Princeton University Press, 1975.
Political Sermons of the American Founding Era, 1730–1805. Indianapolis, IN: Liberty Fund, 1991.
"Postscript to Paper on Erotopathia: An Organization of Colored Erotopaths" by C. H. Hughes. *Alienist and Neurologist*, vol. XIV, no. 4 (October 1893).
"Primaere and Originaere Verruecktheit: An Historical Sketch with Critical Remarks" by Theodore Deecke. *American Journal of Insanity* (April 1885).
Prince, Morton. *A System of Practical Medicine by American Authors*. New York: Lea Brothers & Co., 1898.
Quinn, D. Michael. *Same-Sex Dynamics Among Nineteenth-Century Americans: A Mormon Example*. Urbana and Chicago: University of Illinois Press, 1996.
Rafter, Nicole Hahn. *Creating Born Criminals*. Urbana, IL: University of Illinois Press, 1997.

"Reform in the Scientific Study of Psychiatry" by Edward C. Spitzka. *Nervous and Mental Disease*, vol. V, no. 2 (April 1878).

"Responsibility in Sexual Perversion" by James G. Kiernan. *The Chicago Medical Recorder* (May 1892).

Roberts, Jon H. *Darwinism and the Divine in America: Protestant Intellectuals and Organic Evolution, 1859–1900*. Madison, WI: University of Wisconsin Press, 1988.

Rosenberg, Charles E. *The Trial of the Assassin Guiteau: Psychiatry and the Law in the Gilded Age*. Chicago: University of Chicago Press, 1968.

Ross, Dorothy. *The Origins of American Social Science*. New York: Cambridge University Press, 1982.

Rotenberg, Mark. *The Rotenberg Collection: Forbidden Erotica*. Köln: Taschen, 2000.

Rothstein, William G. *American Physicians in the 19th Century: From Sects to Science*. Baltimore, MD: Johns Hopkins University Press, 1985.

"Sane or Insane: Is She Cruel Mistress or Irresponsible Lunatic." *The Memphis Commercial*, vol. 5 (July 5, 1892).

Schlereth, Thomas J. *Victorian America: Transformation in Everyday Life, 1876–1915*. New York: HarperCollins, 1991.

Schmidt, George P. *The Liberal Arts College: A Chapter in American Cultural History*. New Brunswick, NJ: Rutgers University Press, 1957.

"Sexual Inversion in Men" by Havelock Ellis. *Alienist and Neurologist*, vol. 17, no. 2 (April 1896).

"Sexual Perversion and the Whitechapel Murders" by James G. Kiernan. *The Medical Standard*, vol. IV, no. 5 (November 1888).

"Sexual Perversion or Vice? A Pathological and Therapeutic Inquiry" by Morton Prince. *The Journal of Nervous and Mental Disease*, vol. XXV, no. 4 (April 1898).

"Sexual Perversions" by William Lee Howard. *Alienist and Neurologist*, vol. XVII, no. 1 (January 1896).

"Sexual Perversion, Satyriasis and Nymphomania" by G. Frank Lydston. *Medical and Surgical Reporter*, vol. LXI, no. 1697 (September 1889).

Shorter, Edward. *A History of Psychiatry from the Era of the Asylum to the Age of Prozac*. New York: John & Wiley & Sons, Inc., 1997.

"Sex and Art" by Colin A. Scott. *The American Journal of Psychology*, vol. VII, no. 2 (January 1896).

Starr, Paul. *The Social Transformation of American Medicine: The Rise of a Sovereign Profession and the Making of a Vast Industry*. New York: Basic Books, 1982.

Stephanson, Anders. *Manifest Destiny: American Expansion and the Empire of Right*. New York: Hill and Wang, 1995.

Symonds, John Addington. *Male Love: A Problem in Greek Ethics and Other Writings*. New York: Pagan Press, 1983.

Terry, Jennifer R. *An American Obsession: Science, Medicine, and Homosexuality in Modern America*. Chicago: University of Chicago Press, 1999.

Theodore Roosevelt: An American Mind. New York: Penguin Books, 1994.

Tocqueville, Alexis de. *Democracy in America*. New York: HarperCollins, 2000.

"The Trials of Alice Mitchell: Sensationalism, Sexology, and the Lesbian Subject in Turn-of-the-Century America" by Lisa Duggan. *Signs: Journal of Women in Culture and Society*, vol. 18, no. 4 (Summer 1993).

Turner, James. *Without God, Without Creed: The Origins of Unbelief in America*. Baltimore, MD: Johns Hopkins Press, 1985.

Twain, Mark and Warner, Dudley Warner. *The Gilded Age: A Tale of Today*. New York: Meridian, 1994.

Ulrichs, Karl Heinrich. *The Riddle of "Man-Manly" Love*. Buffalo, NY: Prometheus Books, 1994.

Versions of History from Antiquity to the Enlightenment. New Haven, CN: Yale University Press, 1991.

We Are Everywhere: A Historical Source of Gay and Lesbian Politics. New York: Routledge, 1997.

"Wealth" by Andrew Carnegie. *A Documentary History of the United States*. New York: Mentor Books, 1991.

Whitman, Walt. *Leaves of Grass*. New York: Barnes and Noble Books, 1993.

Wiebe, Robert H. *The Search for Order: 1877–1920*. New York: Hill and Wang, 1967.

"Would Asexualization of Chronic Criminals, Sexual Perverts and Hereditary Defectives Benefit Society and Elevate the Human Race" by E. Stuver and D. Rawlins. *The Texas Medical Journal*, vol. XLL, no. 5 (November 1896).

Index

Aberrant sexual differentiation, 146
Aberrations of the erotic impulse, 145
Adams, John, 18, 19
Addams, Jane, 62
Agassiz, Louis, and rejection of Darwinian evolution, 63
Alienism, 7, 83
Alienism and psychiatry, debate between, 83–99
Americados, 51
American civilization, feminization of, 45
American Economic Association, 62
American Medical Association, 72, 81
American Medico-Psychological Association, 90
American Neurological Association, 76, 91, 116, 117
American Purity Alliance, 62
American Social Science Association, 67
America's promise, as a reflection of a romantic vision, 46
Androgynism, 111
Anthony, Susan B., 43
Aquinas, St. Thomas, 3, 24, 28, 105, 194
Aristotle, 3, 23, 24, 27
Assumptions, essentialist, 128
Atavic descent, 151
Atavism, 185, 186
Augustine, Saint, 3, 27

Bacon's Rebellion, 19
Barbarian Virtues, 45
Beard, George M., 76, 78, 89, 95, 121, 144
Bestiality, 50
Bible, 1, 11
Binet, Alfred, 149
Biology, scientific, 39
Bismarck, Otto von, 102
Blumer, G. Adler, 115
Bourgeois elite, 38
Bradford, Governor William, 49
British North America, 12
Bryce, James, 46
Buggery, 49, 50
Burdashe, Native American, 137

Calamus, 54
Carnegie, Andrew, 46
Carpenter, Edward, 162, 163, 164, 174
Chaddock, Charles Gilbert, 136, 140, 141, 142, 152, 164, 167, 185, 190, 191
Chain of being, 24
Character, 10
    good, 38, 44, 45, 48, 75, 99
Characteristics, essential, 23
    inborn, 42
Chauncy, George, Jr., 9, 126, 158, 173, 174
Class formation, 33
Cold War, 1

Colleges, proprietary, 75
   resistance to Jews, women, and
     people of color, 75
Common-sense realism, 20, 67, 75
Comstock, Anthony, 62, 165, 166
Comstock Law, 62
Conträre Sexualempfindung, 101, 112
Cornbury, Lord, 113
Corruption, political, 33
Cosmos, Newtonian, 10
Criminal anthropology, 87, 88
Cult of domesticity, 43, 45, 77

Dangerous classes, 8, 61
Darwin, Charles, 3, 4, 5, 63, 67, 87, 105, 194
   theory of arrested development, 120
   theory of natural selection, 28
   theory of variation, 122
Darwinism, 5, 63, 200
Day, F. Hollander, 57
de Anza, Juan Bautista, 51
Declaration of Independence, 17
Degeneracy, 9, 87, 110, 145, 186
   neuropsychical, 141, 190
   neurotic, 190
Degenerates, 107
   hereditarian, 143
   moral, 110
Degeneration, 5, 53, 85, 88, 99, 106, 109, 129, 163, 182, 194, 195, 196, 199
   anatomical signs of, 191
   and decay, 48
   and national decline, 198
   and taint of inheritance, 188
   biological, 195
   congenital, 191
   functional, 117
   functional sign of, 108, 109
   national, 129
   naturally occurring, 198

   neuropathic, 145
   neuropsychical, 143
Degeneration theory, 86, 87, 88, 98
Dejecta, morbid and morbific, 155
Demasculinization, 45
D'Emilio, John, 9
Democracy in America, 20
Democracy, mass, 37
Determinism, biological, 42, 43
de Vaca, Cabezza, 51
Dewey, John, 48
Differences, biological, 41
   essential, 41
Diseases of society, 153
Diseases of Society, 143
Diversity, ethnic, 33
Divine Grace, 15
Divine providence, 31
Dugdale, Richard L., 87

Economic competition, 46
   laissez-faire, 47
Education, moral, 22, 44
Edwards, Jonathan, 12
Elite, biological, 38
Ellis, Havelock, 56, 135, 142, 149, 160, 164, 180, 181, 191
Ely, Richard, 62
Empiricism, common sense, 3, 10
Enlightenment, 13, 15, 16, 20, 71, 83, 200
   and perfectibility, 195
   post-, 19
   Scottish, 20
Equality, 45
   inconsistencies in, 47
Essence, 8
   African-American, 39
   "Anglo-Saxon," 41
   Aryan, 40
   Asia
   Chinese, 40–41
   concept of, 27

created, 24
criminal, 40–41, 88
dimorphic, 4
immigrants, 40–41
"Indian," 41
"Indian America," 40
Jews, 40–41,
Latinos, 40–41
"Latin races," 41
"Mongolians," 40–41
"Negroes," 40–41
nominal, 28
Northern European, 40
of an object, 23
rightfully expressed, 25
Teutons, 40
women's nurturing, 43
Essentialism, 4, 5, 30, 45, 48, 63, 64, 65, 99, 112, 176
American, 26
common sense, 10
degenerative, 197
popular, 23, 27, 28, 29, 63, 197
scientific, 38, 42, 43
sexual, 10, 176
stamp of scientific legitimacy, 39
viability of, 28
Essentialist ideal, 5
Euthanasia, 155, 158
Exceptionalism, 5, 7, 30, 38, 48, 99, 195, 196, 197
American, 10, 22, 67, 75, 163
Exceptionalist course of American history, 66
Experiment, Puritan, 12

Faderman, Lillian, 52
Fall, the, 24, 25
Fairies of New York, 57
Female, essence of, 26
inversion, 161
Flexner, Abraham, 73
Flight from psychiatry, 89

Florence, 15
Florentine Republic, 14
Flynt, Josiah, 56
Font, Pedro, 51
Forefathers, Puritan, 20
Forms and ideals,
Platonic, 4
transcendent, 23
Founding Fathers, 16, 17
Franklin, Benjamin, 16, 17
Freedman, Estelle, 9
Freeman, Mary Wilkins, 54

Garfield, James, 58
President, 61, 92, 95, 97
George, Henry, 62
Gender roles, male and female, 43
Gentry, antebellum, 38
German scholarship, 72
Gladden, Washington, 62
Gordon, Thomas, 16
Gould, Stephen Jay, 42
Graham, Sylvester, 21
Great Awakening, Second, 30
Greenberg, David, 9
Gross national product, 36
Growth, urban, 33
Guiteau, Charles, 58, 92, 95, 96, 97, 115, 119, 135
Guiteau trial, 96, 132

Haines, T. L., 44, 45
Hall, G. Stanley, 45
Hammon, Mary, and Sara Norman, 52
Hammond, James H., 52
Hammond, William Alexander, 90, 95, 116, 185
Hanson, Bert, 9
Harper's Ferry, 54
Hartland, Claude, 56, 169–172, 173, 174, 175, 179
Harvard, 72, 73

Hereditary "taint," 108, 128, 155, 195
Hermaphrodites, psycho-sexual, 108
Higher education, American, 67
Hirschfeld, Magnus, 162, 163, 164
Homoerotic communities, 55
  and New York, 55
  and San Francisco, 56
  and St. Louis, 56
  and Washington, D.C., 58
Homophobia, 1, 2, 9, 197, 200
Homophobic, 3
Homosexual identity, core, 158
  emerging, 157–177
  innate, 159
homosexual problem, 158
Howard, William Lee, 147
Hughes, Charles H., 58, 146, 150, 151, 152, 185, 190
Hull House, 62

Identity, homosexual, 53, 157–177
  lesbian, 161, 174
Immigrant, new, 36
Immigration, 33, 128
  Eastern Europe, 34–35
  lure of, 46
  Northern Europe, 35
Incurable victims, permanently removed for our social system, 155
Indigenous populations, 51
Industrialization, 5, 7, 33, 36, 38, 63, 71, 129, 144, 196
Insanity defense, 95–98
  and M'Naghten rule, 95
  see also 132
Instincts, depraved, 147
Inversion, sexual, 5, 6, 8
Inverts, female, 162
  in New York, 57
  sexual, 4, 6, 7

James, Edwin, 51
Jefferson, Thomas, 16, 18, 19, 22, 50, 67, 200
Johns Hopkins, 73, 74, 86
Johnson, Elizabeth, and "unseemly" practices, 52
Johnson, President, 61

Katz, Jonathan Ned, 2, 9, 52, 167, 168
Kellogg, John Harvey, 152
Kertbeny, Karl Maria, 103, 107
Kiernan, James G., 95, 96, 98, 119, 120, 121, 123, 125, 127, 133, 135, 136, 137, 138, 139, 140, 146, 147, 149, 150, 155, 158, 163, 181, 185, 189, 194
Kingdom of Man, 65
Kinsey, Alfred, 108, 176
Krafft-Ebing, Richard von, 49, 103–110, 112–118, 123, 126, 127, 135, 136, 137, 139, 140, 141, 146, 147, 148, 149, 155, 158, 160, 161, 162, 164, 174, 179, 182, 183, 184, 185, 189, 191

Labor force, 36–37
  Blue-collar, 36–37
  farm workers, 36–37
  gainful, 37
  nonfarm workers, 36
  nonmanual workers, 36–37
  white-collar, 36–37
  women, 36
Lafayette Square, 57, 58
Lamarck, Jean Baptiste, 86
Lascivious libertinism, 151
Laws of Nature, 16, 17, 18
Lesbianism, 53
Le Roy, Louis, 14
Liberalism, 10
  popular democratic, 30

Liberty, extension of, 31
Lincoln, President, 61, 90, 117
Lind, Earl, 55, 165, 166, 172, 198
  aka JennieJune, 55, 166
Linneaus (von Linne, Karl), 28
Literati, nineteenth-century, 164
Locke, John, 16, 27, 28
Lombroso, Caesare, 87, 121, 122, 144, 182, 185
Lydston, G. Frank, 87, 88, 121, 122, 123, 128, 133, 136, 140, 143, 147, 149, 150, 152, 153, 154, 155, 158, 163, 164, 182, 185, 186, 189, 191, 194
  and vice, 145
  as social Darwinist, 144
  discussion of the congenital theories, 146

MacDonald, Arthur, 152
Male, essence of, 26
Manifest Destiny, 31, 68
Mead, George Herbert, 48
Medical education, 72
Medical hygiene, 120
Medical hygiene movement, 134
Medical specialization, 80, 81
Melville, Herman, 53, 55, 164
Mexican American War, 31
Meyer, Adolf, 85
Middle Ages, 24
Mismeasure of Man, 42
Missionaries, Spanish, French, British and American, 51–52
Mitchell, Alice, 53, 131, 132, 133, 174, 175, 179, 198
Mitchell, Silas Weir, 76, 90, 95
M'Naghten, 132, 137
Modernization, 7, 8, 38, 60, 63, 194, 195, 196
Moody, Dwight L., 62
Moral insanity, 159
Moral philosophy, 19

Moral sciences, 19
Moral sense, 18
Morality, natural, 65
Morbid eroticism, 151
Morel, Benedict-Augustin, 86, 103
  and degeneration theory, 86, 103
Morgan, Lewis, Henry, 64
Mormons, and same-sex eroticism, 52
Moderato, 116
Myrdal, Gunnar, 42

National ideology, 23
  American, 11
  conservative, 30
National rejuvenation, 79
Native Americans, and same-sex activity, 50
Native American women, and passing, 52
Natural born criminal, 87
Natural selection, 4, 28, 38, 65
Neurasthenia, 7, 76–79, 89, 108, 109, 118, 139, 150, 176, 196
  and sexual exhaustion, 78
  and stress of civilization, 78
  degenerative effects of, 100
  see also Sexual Neurasthenia
Neurasthenics, female, 77
Neurology, British, 89
  French school, 89
  German School, 89
  in the United States, 89–94
  professionalization of, 98–100
  rise of, 89–95
Neuropathic, "taint," 109, 115
Neuropsychical instability, 151
New economy, 37
New educational methods, 72
New World, 15, 49, 64
Nihilism, 71
Noyes, John Humphrey, 111

Old World, 12, 17
Onanism, 51, 152
Origin of Species, The, 4
Originäre Verrücktheit, 114

Paederasty, 115
Paradigm, heterosexual, 10
Paragraph 175,
Paresis Hall, 55, 56, 165, 166, 169, 173, 198
Patriarchy, 23
Pederasts, 146, 165
Perfectibility, 16, 68
   teleological, 64
Perfection, moral, 25
Perversion, theory of, 114
Perversions, as congenital or acquired, 140
Perversity, moral, 122
Physician-identified inverts, 165
Plato, 3, 23
Pocock, J.G.A., 14
Polybius, 14
Population thinking, 4
Populist Party, 1892 platform, 47
Primitive impulses, 186
Prince, Morton, 147, 148, 149, 150, 158
Progressive movement, 62
Propagandistic assertions, of native-born white males, 46
Prussian penal code, 102, 103
Psychiatry, 83, 84, 85, 89, 91, 94
Psychological testing, on people of color and women, 42
Psychopathia Sexualis, 104, 140, 179, 183, 184
Psychosis, degenerative, 113
Puritan imagination, 16
Puritans, 11, 13, 195, 200

Races, "higher and lower," 41–42
Rauschenbush, Walter, 62

Reason, faculty of, 24
   right, 26, 27, 66
Reform, educational, 72
   and leading medical colleges, 72
Regeneration, national, 7
Reimarus, H. S., 105
Renaissance, 14, 27
Republican principles, 16
Republicanism, ethnically based, 30
Research clinic, 74
Rights, inalienable, 16
Rockefeller, John D., 36, 67
Romantic relationships, and women, 52
Roosevelt, Theodore, 45
Rosse, Irving, 58, 150
Rush, Benjamin, 89
   as father of American psychiatry, 83

Saints, 12, 13
Same-sex attraction, literature and the arts as expression of, 53–55
Sankey, Ira B., 62
Scholars, Christian, 24
Science, authority of, 66–69
Scientific expert, age of, 81
Scientific-Humanitarian Committee, 162
Sectarian quackery, 68
Seneca Falls, 23
Separate spheres, 45, 77
Sexual behavior, acquired, 107
   congenital, 107
Sexual feelings, corrupted, 84, 85, 99
Sexual instinct, 104–110
   perversion of, 105
Sexual neurasthenia, 78
   and congenital sexual perversion, 78
   and masturbation, 78
   and sexual perversion, 78
Sexual perversion, acquired, 107, 123
   congenital, 123

Sexual promiscuity, 44
Sexual selection, 41, 42
Shay's Rebellion, 19
Shrady, George, F., 121, 127
Sidney, Algernon, 16
Slater, Lucy Ann, 124–125, 181
  alias Rev. Joseph Lobdell, 125
Slavery, 31
Slumming, 56
Social Darwinism, 38, 39, 63, 150, 151, 184, 194
  and women and people of color, 39
Social Decay, and homosexuality, 152–155
Social Gospel Movement, 62
Social Purity Alliance, 62
Social purity movement, 133
Social reformers, women and people of color, 48
Society, moral, 31
Society for the Prevention of Vice, 62
Sodom, 26
Sodom and Gomorrah, 11
Sodomites, 51
Sodomy, 2, 49, 50, 51, 52
South End House, 62
Specialization, 75
  medical, 79–81
Specialties, clinical, 74
Spencer, Herbert, 38, 64, 76
Spitzka, Edward, 91, 95, 96, 97, 98, 99, 112, 113, 114, 115
Stanton, Elizabeth Cady, 43
Stepchildren of nature, 162
Sumner, William Graham, 68
Survival of the fittest, 38
Symonds, John Addington, 162

Taylor, Bayard, 53, 54, 164
Teleology, cosmic, 4
Telos, 4
Terry, Jennifer, 9

Theories of homosexuality,
  biological, 136–146
  non-biological, 146–149
Theories of inheritance,
  neo-Lamarckian, 87
Tocqueville, Alexis de, 29, 38, 46
Total population
  African-American, 35
  foreign-born, 35
  native-born white, 35
Tramps, American, 56
Tree of Knowledge, 12
Trenchard, John, 16
Twain, Mark, 33

Ulrichs, Karl Heinrich, 49, 101, 102, 103, 107, 108, 109, 126, 127, 148, 160, 162, 166, 174, 175, 180, 197
Unnatural filthiness, 49
Uranism, 146
  of women, 140
Urbanization, 5, 7, 33, 36, 38, 128, 144, 157
Urnings, 101, 102, 108, 115, 146, 160, 162, 163
Utopia, 12

Variability, 4
Virtue, 17, 18, 19, 22
Virtues, barbarian, 40, 45, 79
  bourgeois, 21
  gender specific, 44
  inherent, 43

Ward, Freda, 53, 131, 133, 174, 179
Ward, Lester, 68
Warner, Charles Dudley, 33
Westphal, Karl, 101, 112, 113, 114, 118, 179
Whigs, 16, 17, 31

Whitman, Walt, 49, 53, 55, 57, 162, 164, 173, 174, 175, 198
   and celebration of comradely love, 163
   and homoeroticism, 53–54
Wilde, Oscar, 56, 57, 164, 166
Willard, Frances, 43, 62
Willard, Samuel, 15
Winthrop, Jonathan, 13, 15, 67
Withers, Thomas J., 52
Women's Christian Temperance Union, 43, 62
Women's work, 43
Work and Wealth, 44